Perfect Too

Felicity Cloake is a journalist and food writer from London. She's food columnist for the *New Statesman*, and she writes the weekly columns 'How to Make the Perfect . . .' and 'Readers' Recipe Swap' in the *Guardian*. She also writes, on occasion, for *delicious* magazine, the *Daily Mail* and the *Daily Telegraph*. She was named Food Journalist of the Year and won the New Media of the Year Award at the 2011 Guild of Food Writers Awards. She is the author of *Perfect* and *Perfect Host*.

Perfect Too

92 More Essential Recipes for Every Cook's Repertoire

Felicity Cloake

FIG TREE
an imprint of
PENGUIN BOOKS

For Richard, my long-suffering Tester in Chief

FIG TREE

Published by the Penguin Group
Penguin Books Ltd, 80 Strand, London WC2R 0RL, England
Penguin Group (USA) Inc., 375 Hudson Street, New York, New York 10014, USA
Penguin Group (Canada), 90 Eglinton Avenue East, Suite 700, Toronto, Ontario, Canada M4P 2Y3
(a division of Pearson Penguin Canada Inc.)
Penguin Ireland, 25 St Stephen's Green, Dublin 2, Ireland (a division of Penguin Books Ltd)
Penguin Group (Australia), 707 Collins Street, Melbourne, Victoria 3008, Australia
(a division of Pearson Australia Group Pty Ltd)
Penguin Books India Pvt Ltd, 11 Community Centre, Panchsheel Park, New Delhi – 110 017, India
Penguin Group (NZ), 67 Apollo Drive, Rosedale, Auckland 0632, New Zealand
(a division of Pearson New Zealand Ltd)
Penguin Books (South Africa) (Pty) Ltd, Block D, Rosebank Office Park, 181 Jan Smuts Avenue, Parktown North,
Gauteng 2193, South Africa

Penguin Books Ltd, Registered Offices: 80 Strand, London WC2R 0RL, England

www.penguin.com

First published 2014
001

Text copyright © Felicity Cloake, 2014
Illustrations copyright © Gill Heeley

Set in 12/14.75pt Mrs Eaves
Typeset by Palimpsest Book Production Ltd, Falkirk, Stirlingshire
Printed in Great Britain by Clays Ltd, St Ives plc

A CIP catalogue record for this book is available from the British Library

ISBN: 978–0–241–00312–1

www.greenpenguin.co.uk

Contents

Introduction

*I*f you're reading this simply to find out who on earth is arrogant enough to call a book *Perfect Too*, then please, allow me to explain. Within these pages is collected the culinary wisdom of many of the world's finest chefs and most trusted food writers: the likes of Gordon Ramsay, Elizabeth David and good old Delia Smith.

Me, I'd class myself an enthusiastic home cook; my role here is only to tell you what Michel Roux Jr has to say about gratin dauphinoise, or how Madhur Jaffrey likes her dal — and more importantly, having tried their recipes out, whether these things have any bearing on how you make those dishes. A curator of their expertise, if you will. So really, it's not arrogance. Or, at least, not on my part anyway.

This is in fact the second volume of *Perfect* (see what we did there?), starring the very best recipes to have appeared in my Thursday *Guardian* column since I began work on the first one, back in the winter of 2010.

(Actually I've probably done enough since then to fill a third and fourth book too, but the luxury of choice means these are only the dishes that have elbowed their way into my everyday culinary repertoire — although I enjoyed making borscht, for example, I haven't felt moved to knock up another batch since, whereas spaghetti carbonara and perfect porridge have become regular fixtures. Some recipes are just like that.)

For those of you unfamiliar with the column, or indeed, the first book, the idea behind *Perfect* is to test out as many different versions of a particular dish as possible, in order to discover, once and for all, what really works. Often, as I've found over the years, seemingly trustworthy recipes can vary wildly, and it's confusing to be confronted with a debate when all you want is dinner — which is where I come in. You may not have time to try out six different ways of making macarons, or meatballs, in a day, but I do — and trust me, after three years of doing this, I'm pretty damn critical.

For example, some sages say a summer pudding can only be made with white sliced bread, 'the more plastic the better', while others think it's the surest route to sogginess. Who's right? (Turn to page 270 to find out.) Some people use flaky pastry for their sausage rolls, and some people use shortcrust, some reckon you can only make decent banana bread with fruit so ripe it's threatening to dance a conga out the door, and some say that's rubbish — you get the idea.

Although it's nice to get everything just right, such details won't usually make or break a meal — what really makes me angry are recipes which just don't work, or aren't half as good as they should be. Having put our trust in big name chefs, spent money on their books, to say nothing of the ingredients, we deserve better than careless mistakes.

For example, a batch of chicken Kiev in which every single drop of butter has leaked out (gentle reader, it's happened to me) is enough to send you running into the arms of the bland supermarket version, and I wouldn't blame you – an empty Kiev is little short of a tragedy. Greasy, split macaroni cheese, pork too tough to slice let alone pull, chocolate fondants so dry you're forced to serve them up as cakes; these are all disasters I've navigated on your behalf, and they made me very cross indeed.

Thankfully, once you've made a dish six times, you get a pretty good idea where the pitfalls lie – and I can promise you that all the recipes in here have been triple tested in their own right: I'd stake my favourite knife on them. Where something seems like more of a matter of personal preference than culinary life or death – what spices to add to a hot chocolate, if any, for example, or whether anchovies have any place in gratin dauphinoise – I've tried to indicate this, so you can make your own choice according to taste.

These dishes may not be cutting-edge food – you'll search in vain for a daikon dust or a foie gras foam, and not a single jus was drizzled in the writing of this cookbook – but I promise you, they deliver. When sous vide machines have gone the way of the melon baller, and dehydrators are two a penny at car boot sales, we'll still be enjoying steak and ale pie and crème brûlée. Trust me.

A FEW TIPS

I have to admit, without wanting to do myself out of a single ounce of respect, that there's no great magic to cookery: as long as you've got that rare thing, a reliable recipe, and follow it fairly faithfully (a little more or less oil, or a generous hand with the chilli, is unlikely to kill a dish), very little can go wrong.

You can, however, make life easier for yourself in the kitchen: those happy souls who seem to find it all a breeze are usually just organized.

1. Check you've got all the ingredients, and equipment, before starting. I cannot stress this enough – thinking vaguely that you've seen some ground almonds in the cupboard somewhere is not good enough if you're considering embarking upon macarons. (That said, confident cooks can usually find a decent substitute for most things; it's all a matter of practice.)

2. Read the recipe carefully all the way through before starting, too: just in case, while the stew's simmering on the hob, you should be making dumplings, rather than reading the paper.

3. Get all the ingredients out, measured in the correct quantities if possible, and put them close by where you'll be working. The art of mise en place, or 'putting in place', meaning getting all the ingredients ready before embarking on a recipe, is practised in professional kitchens for good reason; it's all too easy for the garlic to burn while you're ferreting around for the bay leaves or tinned tomatoes.

4. Taste early and often (where practical), and always, always before serving something up (unless it's a cake or a tart where a sneaky sliver is going to be obvious). Remember that seasoning can alter during the cooking process, so what tastes right when you add it might seem bland on the plate. Keep a load of teaspoons handy by the hob for this purpose. (Or use your fingers, it's what they do in most professional kitchens. Sorry.)

5. Most disasters can be salvaged by a bit of lateral thinking. With sweet dishes, as long as it's cooked, there's very little that can't be turned into a delicious dessert by mixing it with ice cream or crème fraîche. Savoury — well, a generous sprinkle of herbs, or grated Parmesan, or a jaunty fried egg garnish will hide a multitude of sins. And if all else fails, check out the quick fixes on page xxiii.

LAYOUT AND EQUIPMENT

You really need very little to be a decent cook: an oven or a hob (although some people swear by microwaves for melting butter, steaming vegetables and so on, they're really not essential; I use mine more as an extra surface than a cooking tool), and a few basics, so it's better to spend money on good-quality items like knives, pans, et cetera, rather than buying a lot of stuff you'll use once in a blue moon.

Think practically: I'm not one of those food writers who gets sniffy about garlic presses, but if you've got a knife, you don't need one. The same, strictly speaking, goes for a colander: a large sieve will do the job just as well.

Always go for sturdy-looking cookware, the duller the better, rather than flashy celebrity-chef endorsed ranges — professional catering suppliers are an excellent place to start, because their stuff is designed to work, and work hard, rather than looking pretty on a shelf. Rarely cheap, it is usually good value.

If you're building up a kitchen from scratch (lucky you!), here are the basics that'll come in useful; you can acquire everything else as you go along. The list is much the same as in *Perfect*, but I've made a few re-evaluations over the last couple of years:

- BASIC Heavy-duty chef's knife and sharpener: sharp knifes will not only make your life easier, but are actually safer because they're less likely to slip

  Also Useful Smaller paring knife, kitchen scissors, bread knife, cleaver (a recent discovery on my part, but already indispensable for stuff like pumpkins and squashes, as well as for jointing meat), knife roll or block (keeping them in drawers is both dangerous and counterproductive, because they'll blunt)

- BASIC Wooden chopping board (kinder on knives), and scourer to clean

  Also Useful More chopping boards, so you can keep onions away from strawberries. A couple of smart ones (i.e. not pock-marked by use, or charred by carelessness) are handy for serving stuff like cheese and bread on

- BASIC Silicone spatula: a great multi-tasker, will stir, flip and scrape out the pan or bowl

  Also Useful Wooden spoon, fish slice, tongs (my favourite), slotted spoon, ladle, palette knife, metal skewer for testing doneness

- BASIC Grater (preferably a super-sharp Microplane or similar box grater with multiple sides for zesting citrus, finely grating Parmesan, etc.), vegetable peeler

Also Useful Mandoline for thinly slicing vegetables for dauphinoise, salads and the like, apple corer

- BASIC Balloon whisk

Also Useful Hand-held electric beaters, stand mixer, pan whisk

- BASIC Pestle and mortar and potato masher

Also Useful Stick blender, food processor

- BASIC Large, heavy-based frying pan, with lid

Also Useful Griddle pan, omelette pan (small frying pan), wok

- BASIC Heavy-based small, medium and large saucepans, with lids

Also Useful Stockpot for cooking stocks, jams, and stuff in quantity

- BASIC Ovenproof casserole dish, roasting tin

Also Useful Cast-iron dishes to go from hob to oven, baking dishes smart enough to go straight on to the table (Falcon Enamelware is sturdy and good value for money)

- BASIC Baking tray

Also Useful Grill pan, cake tins (a 23cm round springform tin, plus two 20cm sandwich tins, would be a good start), muffin and fairy cake tins, tart tin, loaf tin, cooling rack

- BASIC Scales, preferably electronic, measuring jug, reliable timer (your phone will do)

  Also Useful Measuring spoons, food thermometer, oven thermometer, ruler

- BASIC Fine sieve

  Also Useful Colander, coarse sieve, steamer

- BASIC Large mixing bowl (Pyrex, stainless steel or ceramic rather than plastic, which tends to scratch), smaller heatproof bowl to fit over a saucepan and act as a bain-marie, ramekins

  Also Useful More bowls of various sizes! One is never enough

- BASIC Tin opener, corkscrew, pastry brush, greaseproof paper

  Also Useful Baking beans (you can use dry rice or pulses otherwise), rolling pin (a clean, empty wine bottle is an acceptable substitute at a pinch), biscuit cutters, clingfilm and foil, freezer bags

- BASIC Dark-coloured apron (unless you want to wash it every day), kitchen roll for blotting fried food and mopping up spills, thick tea towels to do everything from drying your hands to getting hot things out of the oven (hang a clean one from your apron when you start cooking, so it's always handy)

  Also Useful Sturdy oven gloves and more tea towels (like the bowls, they're endlessly useful)

A word on non-stick

For some people, non-stick technology is the enemy: although it's safe when used properly, if over-heated, that magic coating emits what Bee Wilson describes in her fascinating history of culinary technology, *Consider the Fork*, as 'several gaseous by-products', which can be harmful if ingested. Also, because food doesn't stick if your pan is working efficiently, you never get the lovely little crusty brown bits which make things like fry-ups so tasty.

You can achieve a non-stick effect without chemicals by seasoning a cast-iron pan, but it takes dedication: wash the pan in hot soapy water, then rub it with fat or oil, and heat it very gently for several hours. Eventually it will develop a coating as slick as the newest Teflon number, which every meal cooked in it thereafter will add to. Don't scour it, and avoid anything too acidic, and you won't even need to re-season it as often as you ought to replace a non-stick pan.

That said, I still own non-stick cookware too. It's useful for scrambled eggs and the like, and I'm a short-termist.

GETTING THE MOST FROM YOUR OVEN

Beyond occasionally sweeping out the crumbs from the bottom, most of us pay very little attention to this workhorse of the kitchen, but a little meditation on how limited cooks were before the advent of the domestic oven should set you straight. Anyone can turn an oven on, but to get the best from yours, you need to get to know it.

For a start, is it conventional or fan-assisted? In other words, does it have a great big fan in it? My oven does, but if yours doesn't, then you should use the higher temperatures indicated in the recipes that follow (though, to be honest, after a spell in a professional kitchen recently, I realized that unless you're baking, the oven temperature makes surprisingly little difference, save for time: when food looks done and feels done, it generally is).

Unless you want to spend your evening staring through the glass to check whether your cake is cooked, however, invest in an oven thermometer: many older ovens run either hotter or colder than their temperature gauge suggests, so this will help you adjust the timing accordingly. Make sure too that you can actually see into the oven: opening the door unnecessarily will cool it down so the food takes longer to cook, and will be the death of things like soufflés or Yorkshire puddings. If you have to peep in, do so quickly but gently.

As even the most basic qualifications in science will have informed you, heat rises, so it makes sense that the higher you place food in the oven, the quicker it will cook. Most food should go in the middle, but if, for example, you're preparing a roast, it's better to put potatoes above the joint so they brown, while the meat cooks more gently beneath. Decide how to arrange the shelves before you switch the oven on: fiddling around with hot metal is the kind of fraught activity you don't need when you're trying to enjoy yourself in the kitchen.

Most ovens have a grill as well — I prefer a griddle pan, but if you do use it, remember that grilling has a tendency to dry food out. Make sure it's well basted with oil before cooking (and don't put it too close to the element: grill fires are scary).

Again, not an appliance that really requires an instruction manual, but still, one that can benefit from a few pointers.

Don't overfill your fridge if possible: it interferes with the ventilation, so it won't work efficiently – and cool things to room temperature before chilling to avoid bringing the temperature up inside.

Conduct regular audits to remind yourself what needs using up and ensure nothing's mouldering at the back, and wipe the whole thing out with hot soapy water once every couple of months. (Ensuring that you cover everything well should help keep it clean in the interim, as well as preventing that Thai shrimp paste from tainting the gooseberry fool.)

The door will be slightly warmer than other parts, so if you're chilling wine fast, put it in the main body of the fridge. Ditto the salad drawers, which have a lower humidity, and so are also ideal for storing hard cheese if it's too warm to leave it out somewhere dry and cool, like a garage.

Always get meat out of the fridge a good half hour or so before you want to use it, to take the fridge chill off it so it cooks more evenly – the same goes for things like cheeses and many dairy products, which come alive as they warm up.

If you've got anything more than a tiny freezer drawer, make the most of it: as well as storing stuff like frozen peas (double bagged, to prevent escapees), you can use it to thriftily squirrel away breadcrumbs from that old loaf that's too stale to eat, excess stock, leftover portions of lasagne, emergency rations like prawns, berries, mince and so on, ready for a rainy day when you can't face a trip to the shops. (NB: Never refreeze something that's already been frozen and defrosted.)

Wrap food well (if you can run to it, a vacuum-packing machine, available online, is an amazing boon for this) so it doesn't dry out, and label it clearly with a description of what's inside and the date, so you can eat up older things first. I find it useful to divide stuff like packs of bacon or loaves of bread up — that way you can just defrost what you need for breakfast.

Lastly, defrost raw food in the fridge, on a plate, overnight; pre-cooked food can be reheated from frozen if necessary, though I think you get better results if you have time to defrost that first too.

FOODS YOU NEED

These are the ingredients you'll find it prudent to keep close to hand — not only because you'll probably find yourself reaching for them a lot, but because, with them in the house, you're never far away from a decent meal. Try to build up as well stocked a larder as possible, so you're good for a pretty long bout of flu, a flurry of unexpected guests or, indeed, an unexpected siege.

Storage-wise, remember to keep everything clearly labelled; buying spices in bags from the 'foreign foods' section of the supermarket, or the appropriate grocers, has its benefits in terms of price, but it's easy to decant them into jars and then forget what they are, and ditto, tubs of different flours have the tendency to look pretty similar. (From bitter experience I'd advise storing anything that might be vulnerable to rodent attack in sturdy containers — you'd be surprised at the eclectic tastes of the common house mouse.)

On the subject of spices, deep drawers are ideal, so you can see at a glance what you've got, but in the absence of such luxuries, I keep mine in boxes, vaguely ordered by sweet, Oriental, etc.: so much easier to slide these off the shelf than it is to ferret around in a forest of jars in a dark cupboard. (If you're the kind of person who alphabetizes their record collection or library, then spices are another worthy candidate; I've tried, but I'm inherently too messy to sustain the order for more than a few weeks.)

Indeed, if your kitchen layout allows it, organize all your ingredients into broad categories: baking stuff in one cupboard, condiments in another, basics (oil, salt, pepper, garlic, etc.) within easy reach of the hob and so on. Eliminating time wasted searching for risotto rice or soy sauce will speed up the cooking process considerably.

Pantry

- *Plain flour, cornflour, baking powder, bicarbonate of soda, dried yeast*
- *Caster sugar, soft brown sugar, golden syrup, honey*
- *Cocoa powder and plain chocolate*
- *English mustard powder, Dijon and wholegrain mustards*

- Red and white wine vinegar, cider vinegar, rice vinegar, balsamic vinegar

- Decent chicken, vegetable and beef stocks (liquid concentrates and organic stock cubes are more to my taste than those oversalted jelly pots)

- Soy sauce, Thai fish sauce, Tabasco

- Olive oil, extra virgin olive oil and a neutral oil such as vegetable or groundnut

- Anchovies, capers, olives, Marmite, Worcestershire sauce

- Tomato purée, good-quality tinned tomatoes, tomato ketchup

- Black pepper, sea salt (both fine and flaked), chilli flakes, bay leaves

- Basmati and risotto rice

- Long and shaped pasta

- Couscous, Oriental rice or egg noodles

- Dried or tinned chickpeas, lentils and split peas

- Dried fruit — raisins, currants, mixed peel, fancy jar of fruit in alcohol or syrup for emergencies

- Nuts — flaked almonds, pine nuts, peanut butter

- Breadcrumbs, preferably panko

- *Onions, garlic, potatoes*
- *Eggs*

Freezer

- *Peas and whole leaf spinach*
- *Berries*
- *Puff and shortcrust pastry*
- *Vanilla or plain ice cream*

Fridge

- *Parmesan cheese (or vegetarian alternative)*
- *Butter*
- *Milk*

HELP!

SOS!

My melting chocolate has become a thick, grainy mass!
Chocolate 'seizes' when it comes into contact with water (steam from the bain-marie is usually the culprit). Strangely, however, adding liquid in larger amounts, such as hot cream or hot water, should rescue the situation, leaving you with a tasty chocolate sauce if nothing else.

My pastry won't roll out!
If your pastry is sticky and hard to roll, it may well be too warm, or too wet. Wrap it in clingfilm and chill for 20 minutes, then try again on a floured surface. If it seems dry and cracked when rolled out after chilling, then it may well be too cold. Gather it together into a ball and knead to warm it up slightly.

My cream won't whip!
Place the mixing bowl, cream and whisk in the fridge for 15 minutes to chill — it's easier to whip cream cold from the fridge.

My egg whites won't form stiff peaks!
I hate to be the bearer of bad news, but either there's some yolk in there, or your bowl or whisk were dirty. In either case, unfortunately you'll have to start again with thoroughly scrubbed and dried equipment and meticulously separated eggs.

My mayonnaise has curdled!
Pour it into a food processor, or use a hand mixer to whiz it and see if it comes back together. If that doesn't work, start afresh with a new egg yolk mixed with 1 tablespoon of water, and very gradually whisk the broken mayonnaise into it.

My flour-thickened gravy/sauce is lumpy!
If it's already thick enough to use, simply strain it through a fine sieve. If not, mix 1 teaspoon of warm butter with 2 teaspoons of flour, then beat this into the hot sauce. Simmer for a couple of minutes until thickened, then strain before serving.

My gravy is bitter!
Sounds like those lovely browned bits on the bottom of the roasting

tin may in fact have been burnt. You can try to rescue the situation by stirring in something sweet, like port, or redcurrant jelly, or brown sugar, but you may still have to throw it away and reach for the Bisto.

My sauce is too salty!
People suggest adding potatoes or rice to soak up the salt, but in fact, the best thing to do is to dilute the sauce with water, wine, cream or any other non-salted liquid (stock is usually not a good idea) and then thicken it again with a roux or cornflour.

Dinner gone wrong?

Don't panic if things don't quite go to plan: a carefully stocked pantry has always got your back. To whip up a quick spaghetti aglio e olio, cook 100g of spaghetti per person in well-salted water until al dente, and meanwhile fry a finely chopped clove of garlic and a generous pinch of chilli flakes per person in 4 tablespoons of olive oil. Toss the drained pasta in the oil with a little of its cooking water, scatter with some chopped parsley if you happen to have it, and ta-da, dinner. Also nice with other pantry stalwarts like olives, anchovies, breadcrumbs, lemon zest, capers, sun-dried tomatoes, Parmesan and so on.

For pudding, keep good ice cream in the freezer, and a jar of fruit in booze on the shelf. They last for ages, and the two just need a scattering of chopped nuts to turn them into a sundae. And everyone loves sundaes.

CHAPTER 1

Breakfast

*L*et's face it, most breakfasts in life will be nothing to write home about – a quick bowl of muesli, an apple on the train, a sad little yoghurt at our desk – if it really is the most important meal of the day, then frankly we're in trouble.

All the more reason, then, to make the most of the ones you can do justice to: the leisurely weekend brunches, the holiday feasts – the day you're snowed in and 'working from home'. Make a pot of tea, rather than the usual tannic mug, stick the radio on, and indulge yourself with a crispy, buttery hash brown, a stack of pancakes, or a proper bacon sandwich (or, in this case, roll). Basics like scrambled eggs, and bread, are dealt with in *Perfect* – though how I waited so long to discover how to make perfect porridge is quite beyond me.

Indeed, such a breakfast is eminently achievable before work, and well worth getting up ten minutes earlier for; after all, even so-called instant oats actually take 3 minutes to cook, plus 5 wiping them off the inside of the microwave.

A canny cook always thinks ahead: if you devote a Sunday to making your own marmalade or jam, then you'll always have the ingredients of a good day in the cupboard, ready for those mornings that need a little extra help. Happy is the man who gets up to find a stash of homemade hot cross buns waiting to be toasted.

Lastly, any breakfast is made better by freshly squeezed orange juice (of the kind you squeeze out of oranges yourself, rather than the stuff from Florida sold in bottles under that name), good tea or coffee, and a newspaper. Conversation, however, is entirely optional.

Perfect
Porridge

Simple to prepare, high in fibre and protein, and proven to lower cholesterol, porridge is the trendy modern face of the classic British breakfast – it's even (sound the bells!) low GI, which means the oats release their energy slowly, propelling you painlessly towards lunchtime. Or, at least, to the 11 a.m. tea break.

But, though it's simple to prepare, that doesn't mean it's easy – porridge making is an art. Apparently it is possible to produce a decent bowl from the microwave (although I've never managed it), but to even approach the foothills of perfection you need a pan, and a nice low heat. Anna Louise Bachelor, AKA 'the porridge lady', and winner of the 2009 Golden Spurtle* award for her spotted dick variation (yes, she takes it seriously), uses a porringer, or bain-marie, to ensure the oats cook super slowly, but, heathen that I am, I haven't found this makes a significant difference to the end result.

What does, however, are the oats themselves. Aficionados sneer at the standard rolled or jumbo oat; indeed, Sybil Kapoor pronounces it 'tasteless and pappy'. For real flavour and texture, you need oatmeal – oats in their less processed, more nutritious form, superior in both flavour and texture. Like Sue Lawrence, the author of a number of books on Scottish food, I use a mixture of nutty, nubbly pinhead oats, and finer oatmeal for optimum texture: go

---

* A spurtle is a traditional Scottish porridge stirrer.

down the all-pinhead route, and you'll still be chewing it on the bus to work.

Dour traditionalists also insist that porridge should contain nothing more than oats, water and salt, but after reading in the *Oxford Companion to Food* that it's a descendant of that 'thoroughly English institution' the medieval pottage, I've decided milk is a permissible decadence. All-milk versions are delicious, but a bit queasily rich first thing, so I've plumped for a combination of milk and water — plus the mandatory milk moat to finish, naturally.

Soaking the oats overnight does help to speed up the cooking time, but not significantly: do it if you remember, but it's no disaster if it slips your mind. More important is toasting them beforehand, as if making the Scottish dessert cranachan, which gives the dish a glorious nuttiness.

I'll allow the Scots their salt, as it brings out the flavour of the oats, but there's no point adding it too early: it doesn't seem to do much to toughen the oats as Nigel Slater believes, but it is easier to judge the seasoning later in the cooking process.

What you top them with is, of course, up to you: I've included a few suggestions below, but if you're feeling really adventurous, there's a recipe for kedgeree porridge online . . . I go for chopped dates and nuts on a weekday, and a good sprinkling of crunchy demerara sugar and some Jersey milk at weekends, but *Guardian* readers recommend golden syrup and a knob of butter, while Gordon Ramsay shows how far he's come from the Lowlands with Greek yoghurt and honey.

Per person

¼ cup pinhead oatmeal (about 25g)
¼ cup medium oatmeal (about 25g)
½ cup (about 100ml) whole milk
1 cup (about 200ml) cold water
A generous pinch of salt
Demerara sugar, golden syrup, chopped dates, etc.
A little more cold milk, to serve

1. Heat a frying pan over a medium-high heat and dry toast the oats until aromatic. Put into a bowl, cover with water and leave to soak overnight if time permits, draining them before cooking. Otherwise, use immediately as below.
2. Put the drained oats into a medium saucepan with the milk and 1 cup (about 200ml) of cold water and bring gradually to the boil, stirring regularly with the handle of a wooden spoon.
3. Turn down the heat and simmer, stirring frequently, for about 10 minutes, until the porridge achieves the desired consistency. After about 5 minutes, add the salt.
4. Cover the pan and allow the porridge to sit for 5 minutes, then serve with the toppings of your choice and, of course, a moat of cold milk.

A few topping suggestions
The Moorish: chopped dates or dried figs or
     apricots with roughly chopped pistachios, cashews
     or flaked almonds and a sprinkle of cinnamon,
     ginger or nutmeg

The Diet Can Wait: butter or double cream, and golden syrup (as suggested by *Guardian* readers)

The Scot: raspberries and heather honey

The Compote: stewed plums, rhubarb, apple or any other seasonal fruit, with a grating of orange zest

The Berry Ripple: a handful of fresh berries (stir them in for the last 5 minutes of cooking so their vivid juices ripple through the porridge)

The Bircher: grated apple and natural yoghurt

The American: maple syrup and pecans

The Elvis: peanut butter, stirred into the hot porridge, topped with sliced banana (grilled bacon optional)

The West Country: clotted cream and raspberry or strawberry jam

The Congee: thinly sliced spring onions, soy sauce, soft-boiled egg

The Deep South: grated Cheddar and a knob of butter stirred into the cooking porridge, and topped with plenty of black pepper or chopped chives

Perfect
Marmalade

I feel fiercely protective over marmalade, in the same way as I do about hedgehogs and water meadows, and other endangered, quintessentially British things.

There are as many recipes for 'perfect marmalade' as there are jars in your average WI sale. I've tried cooking the oranges whole, then chopping the squidgy poached peel as Jane Grigson suggests in *English Food*, but though the results were good, the whole operation was horribly fiddly. Adding the peel at the end of cooking, however, as in Johnny Acton and Nick Sandler's book *Preserved*, left it annoyingly chewy; the kind of thing you'd still be fishing out of your teeth come lunchtime.

Best, I decided, to follow the wise counsel of Delia Smith, and chop the peel from the raw oranges (so much easier), then boil the pith and pips in a muslin bag, which you can just fish out at the end.

She's right on the subject of pricey preserving sugar too: intended to give you a lovely clear set, it's a waste of money when peel's involved. Unlike Delia, however, I've used a mixture of brown and white sugars: Tamasin Day-Lewis says the refined stuff leaves a 'toxic froth' behind it, but I just think it has a less interesting flavour.

Once you've mastered the basics, it's easy to customize marmalade to your own taste, adding whisky, cardamom seeds, chilli – or even bacon. Personally, however, I prefer it in that other British classic, the bacon sandwich (see page 13). Give it a try: I promise you won't regret it.

Makes 3 x 1½lb/700g jars

1kg Seville oranges
1 lemon
1 piece of muslin
1kg light muscovado sugar
1kg granulated white sugar

1. Place a sieve over a preserving pan or a very large, non-aluminium saucepan – you should have enough room in the pan to allow the marmalade to bubble vigorously without boiling over. Cut the fruit in half and squeeze the juice into the pan, using the sieve to catch any stray pips and pith.

2. Put the piece of muslin into a bowl and spoon the pips and pith into it. Slice the peel of the oranges to the desired thickness, tearing off any last large pieces of flesh and adding them to the muslin in the process. Put the shredded peel into the pan (any remaining flesh will dissolve during cooking), then tie the muslin up into a tight bag and add that to the pan too. Pour over 2.5 litres of water, bring to the boil, then allow to simmer gently for 2 hours, by which point the peel should be soft.

3. Take out the muslin bag and leave to cool in a bowl. It needs to be cool enough for you to give it a good squeeze, so unless you have heatproof gloves, you can leave the marmalade to sit

overnight at this point if it's more convenient. Sterilize your jars by washing in hot soapy water and cooling in a low oven before you embark on the next step.

4. Bring the marmalade back to a simmer, and vigorously squeeze the muslin bag into it — a satisfying quantity of gloopy juice should ooze out. Stir this in, add the sugars and stir well until dissolved. Put a few saucers into the freezer.

5. Turn the heat up and boil the marmalade rapidly until it reaches setting point — a sugar thermometer is ideal here (start checking when it reaches 104°C), but to confirm this, put 1 teaspoon of the marmalade on to one of your cold saucers and refreeze for a minute or so. If it wrinkles when you run a finger through it, and your finger leaves a clear line in its wake, it's ready. If not, check it at 5-minute intervals.

6. Once it reaches setting point, turn off the heat and allow it to sit for 15 minutes, then spoon into clean jars and seal immediately. Unopened, it should keep well for at least a year.

Perfect
Strawberry Jam

*P*roper strawberry jam, by which I don't mean the bright red stuff with the texture of jelly and nary a piece of fruit to the jar, always reminds me of the summers of my childhood, crouching in the straw at the pick-your-own farm, stuffing my face with fruit so squishy that I always feared the tell-tale juice would give me away to the farmer, though now I suspect such greed is factored into the economics of the business.

Even allowing for the rose-tinted spectacles of nostalgia, I don't seem to come across fruit like that these days, teetering precariously on the line between ripe and rotten. The fresh stuff is all too handsome.

Perhaps I need to get back to the farm, but in the meantime, there's jam. The fruity, slightly syrupy sweetness and the mushy, almost leathery fruit hits the spot perfectly, both on freshly baked scones on a summer's afternoon, or on a piece of toast on gloomy autumn mornings.

Because strawberries are low in pectin, the substance that helps jam to set, they need a little extra help. You can just use jam sugar, which is enriched with the stuff, as Jamie Oliver does, but I found his version overpoweringly sweet, even for jam. The alternative is to add something that's got more pectin – lemon juice, for example, like Nigella Lawson, or redcurrants, like the Ballymaloe Cookery School. Though I agree with 'Pam the Jam' in the *River Cottage Preserves Handbook* that the resulting acidity really helps the jam 'to come alive', I found both of them yielded too soft a set for my liking. If you want to guarantee a jam that stays obediently on your scone, rather than sliding on to your shirt, hedge your bets and use jam sugar as well.

Although some recipes, like that from Thane Prince's book of *Jams and Chutneys*, call for days of preparation, macerating the fruit, maturing the jam in the pan and so on, I found the fresh flavour of the Ballymaloe version, simmered for a mere 15 minutes, the most pleasing. The other jams, richer and more complex, seemed to hide the freshness of the berries themselves.

Those berries should, I think, be mashed into the jam, as Jamie Oliver suggests, leaving just a few small ones intact as proof of its provenance. Nigella's whole fruit version felt more like a compote.

You can add extra flavourings if you so wish: Jamie goes for vanilla seeds and Nigella sticks in balsamic vinegar, which certainly doesn't feature in my childhood memories. Black pepper would also work well, but I'm going to stick with the lemon juice. Sometimes the simplest pleasures are also the best.

Makes 4 x 200g jars

2kg small ripe strawberries
1.7kg jam sugar
Juice of 2 lemons

1. Hull the strawberries and chuck away any slightly rotten ones. Keeping back about 10 of the smallest berries, roughly mash the

rest up into a chunky pulp. Put this into a wide, thick-bottomed pan, add the sugar and the lemon juice, and bring the mixture to the boil. Add the reserved whole strawberries to the pan, and put a saucer into the freezer.

2. Boil the jam for about 15 minutes, stirring it frequently and checking the setting point every minute or so during the last 5 minutes. To do this, put a little jam on your cold saucer, then return it to the freezer to cool for a minute. If the surface wrinkles when you push it with your finger, then it's done. (NB: Strawberry jam is unlikely to ever set as solid as something like a marmalade, even when cooled.)

3. Take the pan off the heat and skim off the pink scum. Pour into sterilized jars and cover with a disc of waxed paper to seal.

Perfect
Bacon Sandwich

I can think of no other dish that unites the UK like the bacon sandwich. It sustains hungry builders in the B&Q car park, paper-reading pensioners in the local caff, and footsore students in ballgowns as the sun comes up over dreaming spires. They even served them at William and Kate's royal wedding extravaganza – Harry's idea, apparently. If you're British, and you partake of the pig, nothing else quite hits the spot.

As with all such popular dishes, however, passions run high – we are one nation divided by sauce. And bread – and even bacon actually; I've seen sleeves rolled up defending the honour of back over streaky.

After eating an awful lot of both in the interests of research, I took learned advice from Tim Hayward, author of *Food DIY*, who informs me that at his Cambridge café, Fitzbillies, they use a mixture. It makes sense – on its own, crisp, juicily fatty streaky, as favoured by Nigel Slater, is almost too much of a good thing, but meaty back is dry and dull on its own. Why not start the day with the best of both worlds? (And the best means the best you can afford, naturally. Even great bacon will hardly break the bank.)

Grilling gives the meat a lovely flavour, but is a criminal waste of all that flavoursome fat. Frying works better, but best of all is the smoky, charred stuff that comes out of Jamie Oliver's griddle pan. It reminds me of breakfast barbecues the morning after a big summer party, to fuel all that walking round in a daze, on the hunt for discarded glasses and stray cans.

Such sandwiches are generally made with what Nigel describes as 'plastic bread' — white, sliced, and suspiciously cheap. He reckons this is optimum for a bacon sarnie, but I can't agree: it's pappy, squidgy and altogether unworthy of this noble snack.

After much experimentation, I've settled on a fluffy homemade bap, lightly toasted on the griddle to soak up a little of the bacon grease. If you don't have the time or the energy to make your own on a weekday morning, a robust white roll, or even a ciabatta, will do. But do give it a try next weekend: you won't look back.

A slick of creamy, unsalted butter and you're good to go: sauces are entirely up to you. Though, if you ask me, you can't go wrong with a combination of marmalade and English mustard.

Per person

2 rashers of dry-cured smoked streaky bacon
1 rasher of dry-cured smoked back bacon
Unsalted butter

For the rolls (makes 6)
450g plain white flour, plus extra for dusting
1 teaspoon salt
½ teaspoon brown sugar
100ml milk, plus extra for glazing
200ml water
2 teaspoons dried yeast

1. Sift the flour into a large mixing bowl and stir in the salt and sugar. Heat the milk and water until tepid, then stir in the yeast. Mix the liquid quickly into the dry ingredients to make a fairly soft dough, adding a little more milk or water if necessary. Cover and put in a warm place for 1½ hours until well risen.

2. Preheat the oven to 220°C/fan 200°C/gas 7. Divide the dough into 6 and shape each piece into an oval (the best shape to accommodate the bacon), then place, well spaced out, on a floured baking tray. Cover and leave for 15 minutes.

3. Brush the tops with milk, dust with flour, and poke a small dent in the top of each one to keep them flat. Bake for 15–20 minutes, until lightly golden. Allow to cool.

4. Heat a griddle pan over a high heat until almost smoking, then add the bacon (depending on how many you're feeding, you may need to do this in batches, in which case have the oven on low so you can keep the cooked bacon warm while you griddle the next lot). Cook, without moving it, until the fat begins to char and turn golden, then turn over. As each piece is cooked to your satisfaction, shift it to the edge of the pan.

5. Tear each roll in two (the rougher the cut, the crisper the toasted side will be) and toast the cut side on the griddle for about 30 seconds, until lightly charred. Butter, stuff with 2 rashers of streaky and 1 rasher of back bacon per person, and serve immediately.

- -

Lunchtime already?
To turn your perfect bacon sandwich into a perfect BLT, mix a couple of spoonfuls of decent mayonnaise (in an ideal world this would be homemade too: see *Perfect* for my recipe) with

English mustard and black pepper to taste. Spread a generous layer on the base of your toasted roll, and top with a couple of torn slices of crunchy cos lettuce and a few slices of sweet tomato. It doesn't really matter what kind of tomato you use, as long as it's got flavour, but I'd recommend big beef tomatoes on the strength of their higher than average proportion of flesh to seed. Arrange the bacon on the tomato, spread the rest of the mayonnaise on the top of the roll, crown it, and consume quickly, while everything's still crisp.

Perfect
Hash Browns

I'm a big fan of potatoes at any time of day, but I think they're criminally underrated at breakfast time. Comfortingly carby if you're feeling a little the worse for wear, and a more satisfying way to take your vitamin C than a glass of orange juice, they're an excellent vehicle for soaking up the grease of a fried egg. The Scottish have their tattie scones, the Indians aloo tikki, and the Americans — well, they saddle up on a hash brown.

They often tend towards the rösti-like (see page 208), but the big difference between the hash brown and that Swiss classic is that the American version seems to have started life as a handy way to use up previously cooked potatoes. Both Nigella and the iconic American cookbook *Joy of Cooking* ignore this important distinction, with disastrously soggy results — raw spuds have no place in a hash brown.

If you're cooking potatoes specifically for the purpose of making hash browns, rather than using up leftovers, boil them in their skins for extra flavour, and make sure you let them cool and dry out before use to avoid dampness. Finely chopping them once cool, as older American recipes suggest, rather than grating them, steers neatly clear of dangerous rösti territory, and makes for a fluffy interior with a deliciously crisp outer crust.

That crust is, I'm afraid, at its most delicious seasoned with bacon drippings, à la *Joy of Cooking*, but as few of us have a little pot of them hanging around these days, clarified butter is the next best thing (the process doesn't take long, and is well worth it in this case, because there's nowhere for burnt butter to hide). Bland vegetable oil, suggested by Nigella, is a crying shame, and even I find Nigel Slater's duck fat a bit rich first thing in the morning.

Onions are optional, but I think their sweetness makes a lovely counterpoint to the salty fattiness of the potato, and whatever else you're serving it with – add cayenne, like Nigella, or parsley, as *Joy* suggests, if it takes your fancy, but the only thing I tend to flavour my hash brown with is the golden yolk of a crisply fried egg. The weekend starts here.

Serves 2–3

> 500g floury potatoes, scrubbed and
>   cut into large chunks
> 35g butter or 25g bacon drippings
> ½ an onion, thinly sliced

1. Put the chopped potatoes into a pan of cold, salted water and bring to the boil. Turn down the heat and simmer until tender, then drain well, put back into the hot pan for a couple of minutes to dry out, and set them aside to cool completely.
2. If you're using butter, clarify it by putting it into a small pan over a medium heat. Once it starts to bubble and foam, skim off that foam and discard. When it stops, pour the remaining liquid through a fine sieve or cheesecloth to strain off any solids, then set aside.

3. Heat a small, heavy-based frying pan on a medium heat, and add half the clarified butter or dripping. Add the onion and cook until soft and golden. Meanwhile, finely chop the cooled potatoes and season generously.

4. Turn up the heat to medium-high and add the potatoes to the pan in one layer, stirring to mix them with the onions. Push down with a spatula on the top to make a cake, then cook for about 15 minutes, until crisp and nicely browned on the bottom.

5. Tip on to a plate and add the rest of the fat to the pan. Slide the hash brown back into the pan, the other way up this time, and cook for about another 10 minutes. Cut into portions and serve hot.

Perfect
American Pancakes

Americans may get a few things wrong in the breakfast department — the sugar-glazed doughnut and bitter black coffee offered gratis at every motel from San Antonio to Seattle for a start — but give me a pillowy stack of maple-drenched pancakes, topped with a lattice of brittle bacon, and I'll forgive them anything. Even Lucky Charms.

Despite eating my first stack at the age of twenty, pancakes still remind me of my childhood: kids in the Judy Blume books and Steve Martin films I devoured over my Weetabix seemed to live on the things.

Perhaps fortunately, given the quantities they tend to be served in, American pancakes, unlike our own Shrove Tuesday fare, chase an ideal of fluffy lightness. This is usually achieved with baking powder, but I've taken a tip from the television show *America's Test Kitchen* and added bicarbonate of soda as insurance. This reacts with the acid in the buttermilk I've included for its tangy flavour, creating bubbles of carbon dioxide for an extra featherlight result.

When creating this recipe I thought that I'd leave the pancakes unsweetened, and let the toppings do the talking, but after much tough testing, I decided to add a little sugar — maple syrup is pretty pricey stuff over here, so plain pancakes are the surest way to bankrupt yourself.

I've also allowed myself a bit of melted butter, like Nigella, to give the pancakes extra richness; after all, unlike the happy families of Hollywood, we're not eating these every day. Vanilla extract, as used by the Oklahoma blogger Ree Drummond, AKA the Pioneer Woman, was a step too far for my taste though.

I am, however, completely sold on her suggestion to use a mixture of flour and cornmeal: it gives the pancakes a deep golden colour which makes them look hot-diggety wholesome, and, more importantly, a far more interesting flavour and texture — the toasted crust has crunch, while the insides are slightly gritty. (In a good way, I promise.)

One of the most important lessons I took from my research is not to overmix the batter — this will develop the gluten, leaving you with a breakfast of old shoe leather, rather than the melt-in-the-mouth feast you've got up early for. Be lazy about it, and you'll reap a rich reward.

Makes about 10

45g butter
115g plain flour
115g fine cornmeal
¼ teaspoon salt
2 tablespoons caster sugar
1 teaspoon baking powder
½ teaspoon bicarbonate of soda
1 egg
300ml buttermilk
100ml whole milk

1. Turn the oven on low to keep the pancakes warm, and prepare any bacon or other accompaniments. Melt the butter in a pan or microwave, and leave to cool slightly.

2. Put the flour, cornmeal, salt, sugar, baking powder and bicarbonate of soda into a mixing bowl and stir together with a whisk.

3. Put the egg, buttermilk and milk into a smaller bowl and whisk together, then stir in 2 tablespoons of the melted butter. Add this to the dry ingredients and mix briefly until just combined – then stop.

4. Put a heavy-based frying pan on a medium heat and brush the base generously with melted butter. Use a large spoon to dollop circles of batter into the pan (you'll probably need to do this in at least two batches) and cook them until they begin to look dry and bubbly on top; depending on the heat of your pan, this should take about 3 minutes.

5. Turn them over and cook for another couple of minutes, until golden. Put into the oven to keep warm while you cook the remaining pancakes (unless you have customers ready and waiting).

6. Serve, along with any toppings, and devour immediately, while they're still hot.

Some topping ideas
- Streaky bacon and maple syrup
- Banana and honey
- Fresh berries and Greek yoghurt
- Fruit compote and ice cream
- Ricotta, honey and lemon zest
- Melted chocolate and flaked almonds

- Sugar and cinnamon
- Lemon curd and blueberries (add the curd while the pancakes are still hot, so it melts a little)
- Chopped strawberries macerated with sugar and crème de cassis for half an hour, plus a dollop of clotted cream

Perfect
Hot Cross Buns

As someone who relishes an annual rant on the impropriety of purchasing hot cross buns before Good Friday, I have mixed feelings about including this recipe here.

There is a real risk, I suppose, that it could be used in February, or on a picnic in July – or even, God forbid, during a dull moment on Boxing Day. But then, surely a homemade bun at any time of year beats a thousand dry old mass-produced versions at Easter.

I've tried an old, old recipe included in Dorothy Hartley's masterful survey, *Food in England*, which uses lard and beaten egg and, though I missed the currants (apparently replaced by yellow candied peel for Eastertide), I found the results beautifully light and fluffy. I preferred the slightly denser butter, milk and egg version favoured by Nigella Lawson, however: soft and moist, it tastes like a real treat – and is much quicker and easier than the pre-ferments favoured by serious bakers online. It also seems in the celebratory spirit of the season.

Variations on the classic hot cross bun abound – Dan Lepard uses milk stout for a dark and malty result, but this doesn't taste like a hot cross bun to me, and I'm not keen on his tea-soaked fruit either, which seems almost obscenely juicy. Not very godly.

Nothing is as outrageous, however, as the American suggestions of piping the traditional cross on in icing or 'cream cheese frosting'.

No, the defining feature of the hot cross bun should be formed from muscularly plain dough, seasoned with a pinch of salt to contrast with the sweetness of the rest.

At all other times of the year, you can leave it off — or, of course, shape it into any old shape you like. Just do me a favour: please don't call it a hot cross bun.

Makes 16

200ml milk, plus a little more for glazing
3 cardamom pods, bruised
1 cinnamon stick
2 cloves
¼ teaspoon grated nutmeg
A pinch of saffron
20g fresh yeast
50g golden caster sugar, plus extra to glaze
450g strong white flour
100g cold butter
½ teaspoon salt
½ teaspoon ground ginger
3 eggs
150g currants
50g mixed peel
3 tablespoons plain flour

1. Gently heat 200ml milk in a pan along with the cardamom, cinnamon, cloves, nutmeg and saffron until threatening to boil, then turn off the heat and leave the mixture to infuse for 1 hour.

2. Strain and discard the spices, then bring the milk back up to blood temperature (warm, but not hot) and mix it with the yeast and I teaspoon of sugar.

3. Sift the flour into a large mixing bowl and grate over the butter. Rub this in with your fingertips, or in a food mixer, until well combined, then add the remaining sugar and the salt and ground ginger. Beat together 2 of the eggs.

4. Make a well in the middle of the flour, and pour in the beaten eggs and the milk/yeast mixture. Stir in to make a soft dough – it shouldn't look at all dry. Knead for 10 minutes, until smooth and elastic, then put the dough into a lightly greased bowl, cover and leave in a warm place until doubled in size – this will probably take a couple of hours.

5. Tip the dough out on to a lightly greased work surface and knead for about a minute, then flatten it out and scatter the fruit and peel over the top. Knead again to spread the fruit out evenly, then divide the dough into 16 equal pieces.

6. Roll these into bun shapes. Put them on to lined baking trays and score a cross into the top of each, then cover loosely and put in a warm place to prove until doubled in size.

7. Preheat the oven to 220°C/fan 200°C/gas 7 and beat together the last egg with a little milk. Mix the plain flour with a pinch of salt and just enough cold water to make a stiff paste. Paint the top of each bun with the eggwash, and then, using a piping bag or a steady hand and a teaspoon, draw a thick cross on the top of each. Put them into the oven and bake for about 25 minutes, until golden.

8. While they're baking, mix I tablespoon of caster sugar with I tablespoon of boiling water. When the buns come out of the oven, brush each with this glaze before transferring to a rack to cool. Eat with lots of butter – they're pretty good the next day too, toasted carefully under the grill until golden and crisp.

Perfect
Blueberry Muffins

I have a confession to make: I don't actually like muffins. Or, at
least, I don't like 99 per cent of American muffins. Give me a flat,
bready English muffin any day, topped with hollandaise and a nice
poached egg.

These, however, are different. And not just because I
made them myself. They use a creaming method,
as suggested by Thomas Keller in his *Bouchon
Bakery* book, which gives a better rise than the
classic combining method, in which the wet
ingredients are simply stirred into the dry.

Keller's strict about beating the butter into submission first, until it's
the consistency of mayonnaise, which gives the muffins an even
fluffier result – be sure not to overmix the batter once the wet
ingredients have been added, because this encourages gluten
formation, which will yield a tough muffin. Even worse than a tough
cookie.

I've also sided with the wonder-chef on raising agents: he uses both
baking powder and bicarbonate of soda, which certainly helps on the
lightness front, while his buttermilk adds a tanginess to balance the
sugar, while being lighter than the magazine *Cook's Illustrated*'s sour
cream, which I find rather cakey.

That sugar should, I think, be demerara: a compromise between the caramel flavour provided by the light brown sugar in *Joy of Cooking*'s recipe, and the crunch supplied by Keller's granulated stuff.

Buy the smallest blueberries you can find (wild bilberries would be even better, if you happen to live near a source and the season's right), and freeze half of them to prevent them bleeding too much as they cook.

Tossing them in a little flour before adding them to the mix stops them sinking to the bottom during cooking, and I've also added a few mashed berries to the batter to supply an extra hit of blueberry flavour in every bite.

Unlike most muffin recipes, which urge you to bake them without delay, Bouchon rests his batter for up to 36 hours 'to allow the flour to hydrate'. I don't feel the results, though delicious, warrant such a pause, but at least you know there's no harm in making it the night before: then all you have to do is switch on the oven, dollop them into cases and go and have a shower while your house fills with the scent of blueberry muffins. A prospect even I can embrace.

Makes 9 muffins

75g **frozen blueberries**
75g **fresh blueberries**
240g **plain flour, plus a little extra**
110g **butter, softened**

200g demerara sugar
1 egg, beaten
1 teaspoon baking powder
1 teaspoon bicarbonate of soda
½ teaspoon salt
240ml buttermilk

1. Preheat the oven to 190°C/fan 170°C/gas 5 and line a muffin tin with 9 paper cases. Toss the frozen blueberries with a little flour and put back into the freezer until ready to use. Roughly crush the fresh blueberries with a fork.

2. Beat the butter with a hand or stand mixer until it is very soft — the consistency of mayonnaise. (NB: You may need to warm the bowl in a pan of hot water first if your butter is still quite hard.)

3. Beat the sugar into the soft butter, followed by the beaten egg, and mix until well combined. Stir in the mashed blueberries.

4. Sift together the flour, baking powder, bicarbonate of soda and ½ teaspoon of salt in a new bowl and mix together.

5. Fold half the dry ingredients into the mix, then half the buttermilk, then the remaining flour and buttermilk. Add half the frozen blueberries and mix in until just combined, but be careful not to overwork the batter. (At this point, the batter can be refrigerated for up to 36 hours.)

6. Spoon into the prepared tin and dot the remaining frozen blueberries on top. Bake the muffins for about 25–30 minutes, until well risen and golden.

7. Allow to cool slightly before serving, but these don't keep well, so don't wait too long.

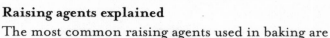

Raising agents explained

The most common raising agents used in baking are yeast, bicarbonate of soda and baking powder.

Yeast, as you probably know, is a living organism that eats sugar and emits carbon dioxide as it reproduces furiously in your dough — those bubbles of gas then expand to give the finished product an airy, fluffy lightness.

Bicarbonate of soda is an alkali that reacts with acids to produce bubbles of carbon dioxide which, again, will make your baking rise. Bicarb is always used in conjunction with something like lemon juice or buttermilk, both acidic liquids that will kickstart the reaction.

Baking powder simply puts the alkali and acid together in one tub; a mixture of bicarbonate of soda and cream of tartar, an acidic by-product of the winemaking process, all it needs to get going is moisture.

CHAPTER 2

Snacks and Nibbles

OK, so some of the recipes below might seem a little excessive for a mere mid-afternoon snack, and are certainly too hefty to qualify as a nibble (although I do like the idea of someone daintily picking at a Scotch egg) — but the spirit of this chapter is the kind of food that doesn't quite qualify as a meal on its own, or would do for lunch or a lazy supper, but not for a proper dinner.

The croque monsieur, Welsh rarebit and pizza fall neatly into this category, and dips like hummus could also qualify, with a nice round of toasted pitta or some raw vegetables if you must.

Then there's the kind of thing you might take on a picnic, or for a packed lunch — portable food like sausage rolls, Scotch eggs and salsa, for example. And party food, from cheese straws to garlic bread, blini and tapas: food for drinks, if you will.

31

None of this stuff really counts as grown-up, balanced eating, but it's all the more delicious for it. Because, just occasionally, you don't need steamed broccoli to make it a meal.

Perfect
Croque Monsieur

Although I like a nice Cheddar and baked ham toastie (or, when in Rome, a speck and Taleggio panino), the appeal of sweet, nutty Gruyère and soft, salty *jambon blanc* wrapped in crisp, buttered bread cannot be denied. Unpatriotic it may be, but I'd give this good odds as the world's best cheese and ham sandwich.

Sadly, however, the very simplicity of the dish has led to some heinous crimes against croques, the versions served up at French service stations being the prime offenders. Happily, they're very easy to make at home. (Although, I must note, not as easy as the toastie. The French do have a culinary reputation to uphold, after all.)

As this is a sandwich, the choice of bread is of paramount importance. I dislike the sweet, disconcertingly soft *pain de mie* which is the usual choice in the dish's homeland: it's liable to dissolve under the weight of its contents. Raymond Blanc's wholemeal bread feels depressingly worthy, however, while *Jamie* magazine's crusty version is too chewy for the classic croque: indeed, *Larousse Gastronomique* orders the crusts cut off, which suggests that, in this recipe, the bread should be as soft and yielding as a ripe Brie. A good-quality white sandwich loaf seems the obvious choice.

Gruyère, a firm and slightly sweet and nutty mountain cheese, is the classic topping, but Wikipedia France declares Emmental is more commonly used, probably because it's significantly cheaper. It tastes it too – mild and depressingly underwhelming, it's almost as bad as Julia Child's 'mozzarella or rather soft Swiss'. Mozzarella may melt well but it's far too bland and milky for a croque monsieur.

What sets this particular cheese and ham sandwich apart from its rivals is the topping of béchamel sauce: Raymond Blanc and Julia Child both leave it out, and their croques are dry and dull in comparison. I like the versions with added cheese, though I find the heretical Parmesan in *Saveur* magazine's version too salty: Gruyère gives a more pleasingly mellow result.

That said, you can't have a ham sandwich without mustard: *Jamie* magazine stirs it into the béchamel itself, but I spread it generously on the bread like Blanc and *Saveur*, to ensure even coverage.

Larousse dictates only that the croque is browned on both sides, whether by grilling or frying in butter. I love the fried version, obviously: butter makes everything more delicious, but practically, it's easier to grill a sandwich coated in béchamel sauce.

The best compromise seems to be to toast the bread, as *Jamie* magazine suggests, but only on one side, so you get the same simultaneously soft and crunchy texture you would from frying, brushing it with butter to make it as robustly crisp on top as possible while still yielding to the feast of melted cheese within.

Makes 2

50g butter, at room temperature
4 slices of good white bread, crusts cut off
1 tablespoon plain flour
100ml milk
80g Gruyère, grated
Nutmeg, to grate
2 tablespoons Dijon mustard
2 slices of good ham

1. Preheat the grill to medium-high and line a grill tray with foil. Melt the butter in a pan over a medium-low heat, and then use to brush one side of each piece of bread – generously. Grill the bread, butter side up, until golden and crisp, then set aside.
2. Stir the flour into the remaining melted butter to make a paste, cook for a couple of minutes until the flour loses its raw smell, then gradually whisk in the milk until you have a smooth mixture. Simmer this on a low heat for a few minutes, stirring all the time, until it has thickened, then remove from the heat and add 30g of the cheese, stirring vigorously until melted. Grate in a little nutmeg, stir and season lightly.
3. Spread the untoasted sides of the bread with mustard, then top 2 of them with the ham followed by the cheese, and grill for a couple of minutes until the cheese has melted completely.
4. Top with the other 2 slices of bread, making sure the buttery toasted side is uppermost, push down firmly, then put the sandwiches back on to the grill tray and top with the béchamel sauce. Grill for about 5 minutes, until golden and bubbling, and serve immediately.

5. To turn your monsieur into a madame, fry an egg per sandwich while they're under the grill, then drape these fetchingly on top before serving. (If only life was always that simple, eh?)

Perfect
Pizza

*E*veryone – absolutely everyone – likes pizza. It's surely the
epitome of the American dream, imported to the States by dirt-
poor Italian immigrants, transformed into enormous pies loaded
with an embarrassment of toppings, then re-exported around the
world.

But it's the Neapolitan version that's still held up as a model
of pizza perfection. Not as crisp as the Roman variety, or
as doughy as a Chicago pie, the base should be
soft and light, yet charred and chewy around
the edges, and topped with the bare
minimum – tomatoes, garlic and olive oil,
with perhaps mozzarella if you're feeling really indulgent.

Cooking an authentic pizza requires a blisteringly hot, wood-fired
oven – somewhere around the 485°C mark – but as most of us aren't
lucky enough to have one of those in the garden, this is the best
version you can make in a domestic kitchen.

Certainly far better than the takeaway variety, as Giorgio Locatelli
explains in *Made in Italy*, pizza has to be eaten 'within 5–6 minutes of
it coming out of the oven or it will be soggy and spoilt'. Hence, he
claims, in Italy 'not even if they threatened you with six years in
prison, would you eat a . . . pizza delivered on a motorbike'.

There are a few things you can do to help your oven out: turning it on to heat for an hour beforehand (pizza may be cheap, but the fuel to cook it is sadly not), and cooking the pizza on a hot pizza stone, or a terracotta tile, so it crisps on the bottom.

If you can find strong '00' flour, that's the best thing to use: the double zero indicates it's been finely milled, which will give you a softer result, with just a hint of chewiness thanks to the higher gluten content. Dusting the pizza base with semolina not only makes it easier to slide in and out of the oven, but gives it a bit of extra crunch.

If you're really patient, you can ape Heston Blumenthal and make a small batch of dough the day before: the longer fermentation gives it a tangier flavour, which works well with milky mozzarella. Indeed, the longer the ferment, the more complex the base will taste. Four hours seems like a good compromise: long enough to be interesting, but not so long that the base starts to compete with the toppings for your attention.

The Associazione Vera Pizza Napoletana permits only four ingredients in a pizza base: flour, water, yeast and salt, which rules out Locatelli's extra virgin olive oil, or the River Café's milk, or indeed Heston's malt extract (which apparently helps the dough to brown). Fortuitously, I find all of them also make the dough more difficult to work with, so I'm going to kowtow to the Neapolitans and keep mine simple: you can always add olive oil on top. Indeed, I'd go so far as to suggest you must.

Add the toppings just before you slide the pizza into the oven, or they'll make the base soggy, especially if you're using mozzarella, and slide it in as quickly as possible so you don't let too much heat out. Then all you can do is wait, pray . . . and get out the napkins.

Makes 6—8, depending on size

    10g fresh yeast (or 7g instant dried,
       made up as on the packet)
    ½ teaspoon sugar
    320ml warm water
    500g pizza flour (or half '00' flour and
       half strong white flour), plus extra to dust
    1 teaspoon salt
    Olive oil and semolina/cornmeal/polenta,
       to serve
    Your chosen toppings (see below)

1. Mash together the yeast and sugar in a small bowl and leave for 1 minute. Stir this mixture into the warm water. Put the flour in a food processor, add the yeast mixture and mix on the lowest speed for about 4 minutes, until it comes together into a soft dough. Tip in the salt, turn the speed up slightly and mix for another 4 minutes. Alternatively, mix the yeast mixture and flour together with a wooden spoon, then turn the dough out on to a lightly floured work surface, add the salt, and knead for 10 minutes until springy.

2. Put the dough into a large, lightly greased bowl, and turn until coated in oil. Cover the bowl with a damp cloth, shower cap or clingfilm, and leave it in a warm place for 4 hours.

3. Divide the dough into satsuma-sized bits and use the palm of your hand to roll these into balls on the work surface. Place, well

spaced out, on a lightly oiled baking tray, then cover and store somewhere cool until you're ready to cook (if you don't want to use it all, the leftover dough should keep at this point for about 2 weeks in a sealed container; in this case, don't divide it up until just before use).

4. Meanwhile, turn the oven to its highest setting, and put your seasoned (a new stone should come with seasoning instructions) pizza stone, terracotta tile or heavy baking tray on a high shelf. Allow the oven to heat for about an hour to make sure there are absolutely no cold spots.

5. Dust a work surface lightly with flour and put a ball of dough on to it. Flatten the ball with the heel of your hand, then use your fingertips to knock the air out of it. Lift it up on to your fingertips and rotate it, stretching it out as you do so, until the dough is as thin as possible, leaving a slightly thicker rim of dough around the edge.

6. Slide the base on to a rimless baking tray, chopping board, or pizza paddle dusted with semolina, then add the toppings and a drizzle of olive oil.

7. Working as quickly as possible, slide the base on to the hot stone, tile or baking tray and bake for about 8 minutes, keeping an eye on it, until crisp and golden. Devour immediately.

- -

Some toppings
CLASSIC
- Torn mozzarella, roughly chopped cherry tomatoes, basil leaves to finish
- Tomato sauce, anchovies, capers, oregano
- Tomato sauce, torn mozzarella, baked ham, roasted artichokes in oil, mushrooms, egg
- Caramelized onions, anchovies, black olives

NEAPOLITANS LOOK AWAY

- Tomato sauce, roasted aubergine slices in oil, ricotta, mint to finish
- Dolcelatte cheese, sliced poached pears, thyme
- Tomato sauce, crumbled sausage, sprouting broccoli, smoked mozzarella
- Tomato sauce, fried pancetta, egg, crumbled black pudding

Perfect
Cornish Pasties

*L*et's get one thing out of the way from the off: I'm not Cornish. In my defence, however, pasties were once common throughout the country – it's just that the Cornish, with typical grit, have hung on to their packed lunches more stubbornly than the rest of us.

Indeed, they've now got them European Protected Geographical Status, which means that, to qualify for the name, a Cornish pasty must be a robust, savoury pastry filled with raw beef, swede, potato and onion (and, of course, be made west of the Tamar).

That robust pastry is important: according to the *Oxford Companion to Food*, traditionally all pasties would have been prepared 'in a way that made [the pastry] too tough to be eaten' – the shell was just there to protect the filling during transportation.

This makes Gary Rhodes' puff pastry utterly impractical – I certainly wouldn't want that in my pocket all morning in the tin mine. A plain shortcrust is far preferable, made with strong bread flour, as Richard Bertinet explains, because you 'need the extra strength in the gluten to produce strong, pliable pastry'.

Lard gives a crisp, flavoursome result (though if you don't eat pork, replace it with the shortening used by the Cornish Pasty

Association), while margarine contributes a slight flakiness — it's important, as the CPA stresses, to rest and chill it well before rolling out, so the pasties keep their shape in the oven.

On to the filling. Chuck is the usual cut recommended for pasties, but I find it too dry — and Mark Hix's rump, if you will, has the wrong texture, as well as being rather extravagant for this dish. Skirt has an excellent flavour, and when cooked slowly, a tenderness chuck lacks.

Potatoes should be waxy, so they don't dissolve in the cooking process, and there's no need to pre-cook anything as Hix suggests — the slight harshness of the raw onion is an essential part of the pasty's flavour. Carrots are obviously sacrilege, as the CPA observes: swede provides all the sweetness the filling needs.

Adding a little bit of liquid is a good idea: though the meat and vegetables will cook in their own juices, a little bit of gravy is a lovely thing with all that robust pastry — a drop of water is quite sufficient, but if you're feeling extravagant, a knob of butter à la Gary Rhodes, or a dollop of clotted cream, is even nicer. Just make sure it's Cornish.

Makes 2 large, or 3 small

For the pastry
500g strong white flour, plus extra to dust
115g lard or shortening, chilled
20g margarine
I teaspoon salt
Cold water

For the filling
200g beef skirt
175g waxy potatoes, peeled
125g swede, peeled
2 small onions, peeled
Clotted cream or butter

Also
1 egg, beaten with a little water

1. Start with the pastry. Sift the flour into a mixing bowl and grate in the lard or shortening. Add the margarine and salt, then rub the fat in until the mix looks like breadcrumbs.

2. Stir in just enough cold water (approximately 175ml should do it) to bring the mixture together into a dough – a food mixer is useful here if you have one. You'll know the pastry's ready when it comes cleanly away from the side of the bowl. Wrap in clingfilm or greaseproof paper and chill for 2 hours.

3. Preheat the oven, and a baking tray, to 200°C/fan 180°C/gas 6. Chop the beef and vegetables into evenly sized dice, then mix them together in a bowl and season well.

4. Roll out the pastry on a lightly floured surface until it's about 5mm thick, and cut out circles of your desired size.

5. Divide the filling mixture between the pastry circles, leaving a few centimetres of space around the edge of each, and top the filling with a dollop of cream or butter.

6. Brush the edge of the pastry circles with eggwash, then bring one edge over the top of the filling to meet the opposite one, and pinch the two edges together to seal. Crimp according to skill (there are some good videos available online to demonstrate the proper technique), and cut a small hole in the top of each pasty.

Put the pasties on a hot baking tray, brush with eggwash and bake for 20 minutes, until golden brown. Turn the heat down to 160°C/fan 140°C/gas 3 and cook for another 20 minutes. Allow to cool slightly or completely before serving. Burnt tongues are strictly for emmets.

Perfect
Welsh Rarebit

*R*arebits (a corruption of the original rabbit) are generally made with Cheddar, purely because that's what most of us tend to have hanging around in the fridge on the kind of lazy Sunday evenings the dish was made for. Mark Hix keeps things Welsh with Caerphilly instead, but in fact, according to Simon Hopkinson and Lindsey Bareham in *The Prawn Cocktail Years*, traditionally a rarebit would have been made with hard English cheeses, 'Cheddar, double Gloucester, Cheshire and Lancashire'.

I'm with Nigel Slater: Caerphilly doesn't have enough of a tang to make it interesting here — it just gets lost amongst the other ingredients. Mature Cheddar is too strong for my liking though — and I'm not sure what Delia was thinking of with the intensely salty Parmesan. Lancashire, however, as suggested by Jane Grigson, has just enough bite to remain the star ingredient, without steamrollering everything else in the process.

Bread-wise, I like a seedy wholemeal for a really savoury flavour, but I respect your right to use whatever you like, as long as it's robust enough to stand up to the weight of the topping: toasting it on both sides, as Hix does, helps with this. (The edges may char slightly during the final grilling, but as they'll be covered in molten cheese, you're unlikely to mind too much.)

Most rarebit recipes demand some sort of liquid to loosen the cheesy topping: ale or milk for Jane Grigson, cider for the Cheese Society, port for Mrs Beeton and stout for Hix, Hopkinson and Bareham. I find the cider too acidic, and port turns the cheese a slightly scary colour – the ale's not bad, but the moment I taste the stout versions, I'm sold. It gives the dish a rich maltiness which works fantastically with the salty, tangy cheese – and what's more, there are a number of good Welsh stouts on the market to soften the blow of that Lancashire.

If the cheese isn't to turn rubbery the minute it's whipped from the grill, you either need a tabletop 'cheese toaster', as recommended by Mrs Beeton, or some other fat in the topping. Too much butter, as used by Nigel Slater and Jane Grigson, makes things greasy, and Mark Hix's double cream is too liquid. Egg yolks are by far the best option, adding richness while softening the cheese to a spreadable consistency.

English mustard (surely enjoyed in Wales too) adds a bit of kick, and Worcestershire sauce is a must for any cheese on toast – you could top it with a sprinkle of cayenne pepper too if you like, but frankly, that's quite enough flavour for me.

Serves 2

    I teaspoon English mustard powder
3 tablespoons stout
30g butter
Worcestershire sauce, to taste
175g Lancashire cheese, grated
2 egg yolks
2 slices of bread

1. Mix the mustard powder and a dash of stout to a paste in the bottom of a small saucepan. Stir in the remaining stout and add the butter and about 1 teaspoon of Worcestershire sauce to the pan — you can always add more later if required. Heat gently until the butter has melted.

2. Tip in the grated cheese and as it begins to melt, stir to encourage it. Do not let the mixture boil. Once it's all melted, taste for seasoning and adjust if necessary, then take the pan off the heat and allow the cheese to cool until it's only just warm, checking regularly that it hasn't solidified.

3. Preheat the grill to medium-high, and toast the bread on both sides. Beat the egg yolks into the warm cheese mixture until smooth, then spoon this on to the toast and grill until bubbling and golden. Eat immediately.

Perfect
Scotch Eggs

*R*obustly portable, conveniently hand-sized, and absurdly delicious, Scotch eggs are the perfect snack.

The egg question is a simple one of preference: I like mine to be soft, but not runny, particularly if they're destined for a picnic, so I've plumped for a 5-minute boil, but you can cook yours for a couple of minutes more or less if you prefer. Rolling the peeled eggs in flour, as Angela Hartnett suggests, will help the meat to stick when you come to the assemblage.

The meat casing is more tricky. Many recipes just call for sausagemeat, which is an easy way to do things, but I find the all-sausagemeat eggs from Hartnett, Gary Rhodes and Heston Blumenthal a bit greasy for my liking. Tom Norrington-Davies' semi-lean pork mince, however, ends up a bit dry. You could mix the mince with pork fat, as the Ginger Pig suggests, but if you don't have an obliging local butcher, a mixture of sausagemeat and mince provides the perfect compromise.

As with a sausage itself, you can play around with the seasonings to suit the occasion: I find Hartnett's garlic and thyme too Mediterranean for a classic Scotch egg, while Heston's American mustard and smoked paprika is just confused. Instead, I'm plumping for traditional sausage seasonings like mace and mustard, with lots of fresh chopped herbs, as Norrington-Davies suggests, which gives the meat a bright, spuriously healthy appearance.

Less traditional, perhaps, are the panko breadcrumbs I'm using to coat it all — but if Yorkshire's Ginger Pig has embraced these super-crisp Japanese crumbs then so can I. In fact, I like them so much that, like Gary Rhodes, I'm going to go for a double coating, for extra crunch. Assembling them is a case of practice makes perfect: flouring the eggs, as Hartnett suggests, will help the mixture to cling to them, while rolling the sausagemeat out between clingfilm is a great tip from Gary Rhodes, helping, as it does, to ensure an even thickness.

Now for the bad news. Scotch eggs are so delicious because they're deep-fried, and sadly there's no way around it: baked versions are a tragedy waiting to happen. Instead, embrace the oil: as occasional treats go, these will knock your socks off.

Makes 4

6 eggs
200g plain sausagemeat
200g pork mince
3 tablespoons chopped mixed herbs
   (I like chives, sage, parsley and thyme)
A pinch of ground mace
1 tablespoon English mustard
A splash of milk
50g flour, plus extra to dust
100g panko breadcrumbs
Vegetable oil, to cook

1. Put 4 of the eggs into a saucepan, cover with cold water and bring to the boil. Reduce the heat and simmer for 5 minutes, then drain the eggs and put them straight into a large bowl of iced water. Leave to cool for at least 10 minutes.

2. Put the meats, herbs, mace and mustard into a bowl, season and then mix together well with your hands. Divide into 4 balls while you've still got sausagey hands.

3. Carefully peel the eggs (rolling them gently on a hard surface to crack the shells is a good way to start). Beat the 2 remaining raw eggs together in a bowl with a splash of milk. Tip the flour into another bowl and season, then tip the breadcrumbs into a third bowl.

4. Put a square of clingfilm on the work surface, and flour it lightly. Place one of the meatballs in the centre, and also flour it lightly, then place another square of clingfilm of a similar size on top. Roll out the meat until it's large enough to encase an egg, and remove the top sheet of clingfilm (it can be reused for each subsequent egg).

5. To assemble the Scotch egg, roll 1 peeled egg in flour, then put it in the centre of the rolled-out meat. Bring up the meat to completely encase it, using the clingfilm underneath to help you, then smooth it into an egg shape with damp hands. Dip each egg in flour, then egg, then breadcrumbs, and then into just the egg and breadcrumbs again.

6. Use a deep-fat fryer or fill a large pan a third full of vegetable oil, and heat it to 170°C (or when a crumb of bread dropped in immediately sizzles and turns golden, but does not burn). Cook the Scotch eggs a couple at a time, for 7 minutes each, until crisp and golden, then drain well on kitchen paper and season

lightly before serving; I like mine with English mustard for dipping, but brown sauce, ketchup, mustard mayonnaise and tartare sauce (not just for fish!) all have their devotees. As a rule, if it goes with a sausage, it'll go with a Scotch egg.

Perfect
Cheese Straws

*T*he cheese straw is the sine qua non of party food — easy to eat with
one hand, simple to prepare in advance, popular with all ages and,
most importantly, just the kind of fatty, salty thing people eat in
quantity after a glass or too many of wine. They're the grown-up
version of a big bag of Wotsits, and, gratifyingly, rather less likely to
stain your hands a tell-tale orange.

Bought versions tend to disappoint, being made in the continental
fashion with puff pastry — Michel Roux's homemade puff pastry
twists are wonderfully light, but soften quickly as they cool,
which is not ideal unless you've got a Michelin-star kitchen
at the ready to churn out a fresh batch. Shortcrust, more
traditional in this country, is far better: crisp, but
dangerously light, especially when made with a mixture
of lard and butter, as suggested by Rose Prince. (Use
the same weight of butter if you'd prefer to keep them
vegetarian friendly.)

Another feather in the cheese straw's cap is that it will happily accept
just about any hard cheese you happen to have hanging around — the
older the better, in fact, because as Mark Hix observes, 'to get them
thin and thoroughly cheesy the cheese needs to be as strong as you
can get it'. If you're buying it new, however, I'd go for Parmesan, as
Hix does — Roux's Emmental and Prince's Gruyère are too mild,
and most Cheddars too damp. If you'd prefer to use a British

cheese, go for a really mature Cheddar, and leave it unwrapped somewhere cool to dry out a little before use.

Cheese straws can, of course, be made with ready-bought pastry, and the cheese folded in in layers, as Hix suggests (sprinkling it on top, as Michel Roux does, means much of it falls off before it even reaches the oven), but one of the advantages of making your own is that you can mix it into the dough itself, which is much easier, and gives a more even distribution.

You could just leave it at that, but as this is party food, I add a little English mustard for heat, a pinch of nutmeg for a festive flavour — and a final scattering of cheese, just to hammer home the point. Smoked paprika or cayenne pepper would also work well.

Finally, a good tip from Ireland's Ballymaloe Cookery School: although cheese straws are best eaten warm from the oven, if you must make them in advance, leave them to crisp up in a cool oven (100°C) before storing in an airtight container — they'll keep better, as long as you don't eat them all in the process.

Makes about 50 straws

150g cold lard
150g cold butter
450g plain flour
150g Parmesan, finely grated
½ teaspoon mustard powder
A pinch of freshly grated nutmeg
1 egg, beaten

1. Grate the cold lard and butter into a large mixing bowl, and tip in the flour. Rub the fat into the flour until you have a breadcrumb-like mixture, then stir in all but 2 tablespoons of cheese, plus the mustard powder and grated nutmeg.

2. Add just enough iced water to the mixture (you'll probably need 2–4 tablespoons) to bring it together into a firm dough, then wrap the dough in clingfilm or greaseproof paper and refrigerate for 30 minutes.

3. Preheat the oven to 220°C/fan 200°C/gas 7. Roll out the pastry to 5mm thick, then brush it with beaten egg and sprinkle with the remaining Parmesan. Cut into rectangular strips about 1cm wide and 10cm long, and arrange these on a lightly greased baking tray. (You can cover and refrigerate the dough at this point, until you're ready to cook.)

4. Bake the straws for about 15–20 minutes, until they're golden brown, then cool them briefly on a rack to firm up, and serve. They are best eaten warm from the oven, but if you need to make them ahead, leave them to crisp up in a cool oven (100°C) instead before removing to an airtight container — they're less likely to soften.

Perfect
Blinis

While cheese straws might be the ideal party snack, sometimes you're after something a little more . . . sophisticated. Which is where blinis, the little black dresses of the canapé world, step in.

Served to mark the beginning of Lent in their Eastern European homeland, they've become a byword for year-round indulgence in the West, and with good reason — more interesting than pastry, more impressive than bruschetta, these fluffy little pancakes are the ultimate one-bite feast. Sadly, however, they're only really worth eating if you make them yourself: the ready-made sort available in more aspirational supermarkets tend to be disappointingly damp and chewy.

What sets blinis apart from most other forms of pancake is that they contain yeast, hence the fluffiness. One of the downsides of this, as any baker knows, is that yeast requires a fair degree of patience, but it's well worth it: I try Thomas Keller's yeast-free potato blinis, which are impractically heavy for a pre-dinner snack, and Darina Allen's cheat's version, using cream of tartar and bicarbonate of soda, but neither reaches the heights of lightness I get from yeast.

Richard Bertinet employs a fancy double-rise method for his blinis, which take nearly 4 hours to ferment, but the results are well worth it — they almost melt in the mouth. Patience is clearly a virtue.

For an authentically Eastern European flavour, use a mixture of buckwheat and strong white flour: all-buckwheat versions, like Sophie Dahl's, are overpoweringly earthy to the western palate, and the higher gluten content of the bread flour will also help the blini to rise. (Keller's potato versions, made with just 2 tablespoons of flour to a whole pound of spuds, are delicious, but more like rösti than the blini we're familiar with here.)

Some recipes add beer to the batter, which gives the blini an aggressively malty note that might work better with vodka than wine – I prefer the tangy richness of sour cream, especially as the rest of the pot can be used as a topping. I've added caraway seeds as well, which are a great match with smoked fish, but also make the blini delicious enough to eat solo if you're not a fan.

Don't be put off by the time this recipe takes: it's very light on effort, and when you're preparing for a party, sticking a bowl of batter in the airing cupboard and forgetting about it for a few hours doesn't add much to the to-do list. And the results really are worth it, I promise.

Makes about 35

150ml milk
70g buckwheat flour
70g strong white flour
1 teaspoon salt
2 teaspoons caraway seeds
2 eggs
4g dried yeast
100g sour cream
25g butter

1. Gently heat the milk in a small pan until just about to boil. Meanwhile, combine the flours, salt and caraway seeds in a large mixing bowl and separate the eggs.
2. When the milk begins to boil, take it off the heat, allow to cool to warm, then stir in the yeast, followed by the egg yolks and the sour cream — you'll need to stir vigorously with each addition.
3. Pour the milk mixture slowly into the bowl of flour, stirring as you do so. When you have a smooth paste, cover and leave in a warm place for an hour, or until spongy-looking — the mixture won't rise dramatically, but it should have expanded slightly, and you should be able to see a few bubbles on the surface.
4. Whisk the egg whites to soft peaks and very gently and slowly fold them into the mixture using a rubber spatula or metal spoon. Once you can no longer see any streaks of egg white, cover, and leave for another 2 hours.
5. When you're ready to cook the blinis, melt the butter in a large frying pan over a medium-high heat, then add the batter in teaspoonfuls to the pan to create small circles.
6. Cook until bubbles rise to the top of each, then flip them over and cook for another minute or so on the other side, until golden brown. You'll probably need to do this in batches, so keep them warm while you cook the rest — these are best eaten hot from the pan if possible.

Blini bling: a few quick topping ideas
- Sour cream, smoked salmon, and beautiful orange lumpfish or jet black herring roe (or, of course, caviar, should you be in possession of a winning lottery ticket)

- Black olive tapenade, half a cherry tomato and a basil leaf
- Soft, creamy goat's cheese, shredded, cooked beetroot and a sprig of dill
- Ripe avocado and crumbled feta, mashed together and topped with a thinly sliced radish
- Crème fraîche mixed with hot horseradish, and topped with a sliver of rare roast beef

Perfect
Hummus

*F*or a nation generally suspicious of pulses, Britain has really taken hummus to its bosom. Yet despite its popularity very few people actually make their own, which is a shame, because sour supermarket hummus is a world away from the fresh stuff, which is simplicity itself to make.

Although, in extremis, passable hummus can be made from tinned chickpeas, purists frown upon these abominations: all wrong texturally, apparently. I try Claudia Roden's recipe with both tinned and dried, and find the latter indeed give a nuttier, slightly grainier texture which I prefer, although as Anissa Helou admits in *Modern Mezze*, 'you can now buy jars of excellent ready-cooked chickpeas, preserved in water and salt, without added artificial preservatives'. They're expensive, at almost four times the price of the tinned sort, but have a lovely buttery flavour: if you need to cheat, please, do it properly.

Nigella Lawson has bravely spoken out before about the global conspiracy to pretend chickpeas cook far quicker than they do, and it's true: despite lengthy pre-soaking, even the ones from my local 'Mediterranean supermarket', which I suspect has a fairly high turnover of the things, just aren't soft, even after 4 hours.

You can use a pressure cooker, but it's much easier to do as Helou and Yotam Ottolenghi recommend, and add a little bicarbonate of soda to the soaking water. This stops the calcium in my hard tapwater from glueing together the pectin molecules in the pea's cell walls — in fact, the newly alkaline water actually encourages them to separate. Too much can give the hummus an unpleasant soapy flavour, however, so err on the side of caution.

Homemade hummus can run the risk of clagginess; Nigella adds Greek yoghurt to match the 'tender whippedness that you get in restaurant versions' but it doesn't quite taste right to me, and I discover a similar texture can be achieved with chickpea cooking water, as suggested by Paula Wolfert.

Otherwise, I'm sticking to the classic recipe: chickpeas, tahini, lemon juice and garlic — with just a pinch of cumin. It may not be exactly standard in the Middle East, but it's by no means unknown, and it really livens up the end result, though purists may wish to leave it out.

Save any other embellishments for the topping: make it into a meal with minced lamb, caramelized onions and pine nuts, as the *Moro* cookbook does, or a salad with hard-boiled eggs and onion as Ottolenghi likes it, top with a little lemony za'tar — or just stick to a splash of olive oil and a few toasted flatbreads. Sometimes, simple is best.

Serves 4

200g dried chickpeas
1½ teaspoons bicarbonate of soda
6 tablespoons tahini
Juice of 1 lemon, or more to taste
3 cloves of garlic, crushed, or according to taste
A pinch of ground cumin
Salt, to taste
Olive oil, to top
Paprika or za'tar, to top (optional)

1. Put the chickpeas into a large bowl and cover them with twice the volume of cold water. Stir in 1 teaspoon of bicarbonate of soda and leave them to soak for 24 hours.
2. Drain the chickpeas, rinse them well and put into a large pan. Cover them with cold water and add the rest of the bicarb. Bring to the boil, then reduce the heat and simmer gently until they're really tender – they should be easy to mash, and almost falling apart, which will take between 1 and 4 hours depending on your chickpeas. Add more hot water if they seem to be boiling dry at any point.
3. Leave the chickpeas to cool in their cooking water, and then drain well, reserving the cooking liquid, and setting aside a spoonful of chickpeas as a garnish.
4. Beat the tahini with half the lemon juice and half the crushed garlic – it should tighten up – then stir in enough of the cooled cooking liquid to turn it into a loose paste. Put this paste into a food processor along with the chickpeas and whiz until smooth.
5. Add the cumin and a generous pinch of salt to the food

processor, then gradually, with the motor still running, tip in enough cooking water to make a soft paste — it should just hold its shape, but not be at all claggy. Taste, and add more lemon juice, garlic or salt if you think it needs it. Serve at room temperature, rather than fridge-cold.

Perfect
Salsa

Salsa is a dish that relies so heavily on freshness that it's impossible to capture it in a jar — especially this simple tomato and chilli version, which is versatile enough to pair with grilled meat, rice and beans, scrambled eggs or a big bowl of salty tortilla chips. Make it once, and you'll never pay a visit to Old El Paso again.

It stands or falls on its tomatoes, which according to Chicago chef and Obama favourite Rick Bayless, who's devoted his career to spreading the word about authentic Mexican food north of the border, are 'a critical ingredient in Mexican cuisine, second only to chillies'. I try a number of different approaches, simmering them with onion and garlic until 'well thickened' like Elisabeth Lambert Ortiz in her *Complete Book of Mexican Cooking*, which gives a rich flavour, but not the punchy fruitiness I'm after, roasting them like Thomasina Miers, which gives a lovely smokiness, but doesn't feel fresh enough, and using them raw, like Bayless. This, the simplest method, is also, happily, the most delicious: along with the lime juice, they give just the acid hit I'm looking for. (Vinegar is often suggested as a substitute, but, though wine vinegar is fine at a pinch, you really can't beat the citrussy zing of lime.)

Bayless suggests using either plum or round tomatoes: unless it's high summer, I find it difficult to source either with a sufficiently intense flavour, so instead I decide to use the sweet little cherries which seem to taste better all year round.

Making a fresh tomato salsa rules out most of the almost infinite array of chillies deployed in Mexican cuisine, essentially reducing me to a choice between jalapeños, which Lambert Ortiz describes as 'very flavourful as well as hot', and serranos which, according to Bayless, have a 'pure and simple' heat. (See glossary below for a bit more info about different types of chillies you might come across in this country.)

I prefer the herbaceous quality of the jalapeño, but those available in this country tend to be unpredictable in terms of heat, so don't worry too much – if all the examples you can find are bland and watery, swap in a Scotch bonnet or a bird's-eye instead. (Don't be tempted to substitute pickled jalapeños, however – they'll muddy the flavour here. Save them for your nachos.)

Onions add a different sort of heat – a white onion, which, as Bayless notes, is a quite different beast from the yellow ones we get over here, would be most authentic, but given the difficulties in sourcing them, I'm forced to try other options. The fresh green tang of spring onions works wonderfully, though, as this makes ideal party food, I'm going to marinate them briefly in lime juice to soften their bite.

You can use a pestle and mortar, as Miers does – though even Bayless concedes that careful pulsing in a food processor can produce a 'decent salsa' – but actually, if your tomatoes are sufficiently ripe, simple chopping produces the most satisfying texture for scooping.

Note that the quantities below are all to my taste, and will vary according to yours, and the ingredients you have to hand, so do play around until you're happy – in which case you can call it your perfect salsa.

Makes 500ml

3 spring onions
Juice of 1 lime
500g ripe cherry tomatoes
1–2 jalapeño or other green chillies,
    depending on taste
A small bunch of coriander
¼ teaspoon salt

1. Finely chop the spring onions and put them into a serving bowl. Stir in the juice of half the lime. Chop the tomatoes into rough 5mm dice, and deseed and finely chop the chilli.
2. Add these to the bowl along with the roughly chopped coriander – you might want to add the chilli gradually and keep on tasting as you do so, until you achieve your ideal level of heat, especially as they vary so much according to provenance and season.
3. Season the salsa to taste with salt, leave to sit for half an hour, then serve, with a spritz more lime juice if you think it needs it – it should be fresh and punchy, so don't be tempted to make it too far ahead.

Chillies: a field guide
The range of chillies available in supermarkets has improved greatly in the last few years, although some

areas are still better than others. For obscure varieties you'll still need to visit specialist suppliers, or look online (southdevonchillifarm.co.uk is a good source), but you might well find this lot more easily:

Bird's-eye: these pointy, diminutive red and green chillies, popular in South-East Asian cookery, are viciously hot.

Jalapeño: sold either green (unripe, with a herbaceous flavour) or red (ripe and sweeter), these bulbous carrot-shaped chillies vary wildly in heat, but most of the ones in British supermarkets tend towards the milder end of the spectrum. You'll also find them pickled for topping nachos and the like, and once dried and smoked, they're known as chipotle, a spice widely used in Mexican cookery.

Habanero: pumpkin-shaped orange or red chillies with a fiery, fruity flavour, these, like Caribbean Scotch bonnets, should be treated with caution and, preferably, rubber gloves.

Serrano: similar in appearance to the jalapeño, serranos have a hotter, sharper flavour, and are usually used in an underripe, green state.

Perfect
Sausage Rolls

*T*he sausage roll lives a double life. Borne aloft, hot from the oven, by the hostess of a drinks party, or produced from Tupperware at a picnic, it's the finger food they eat in heaven. Emerging from a plastic wrapper at a service station, however, they're enough to drive you in the direction of an egg and cress sandwich. This is one of those foods which is always better fresh — and unless you have a decent bakery in the vicinity, that means homemade.

Not that this is any great chore: even sausage rolls made with bought pastry and split sausages are pretty good, but to really hit the jackpot, it's worth expending a little extra effort. You can make great sausage rolls with rich, crumbly shortcrust, but Delia's quick flaky pastry, spiced up with a little mustard powder, is a winner in the lightness stakes — even better than the real puff pastry from Simon Hopkinson and Lindsey Bareham's *The Prawn Cocktail Years*, which I find too delicate for the filling, and which droops sadly on cooling. (NB: Shortcrust can work better for picnics, however: it stands up more bravely to transportation.)

Ready-prepared sausagemeat can be rather salty — useful in extremis, but in comparison to Simon and Lindsey's pleasingly rustic-looking filling, made from lean belly pork, lean shoulder, streaky bacon and fat, it lacks texture and substance. Theirs is just more interesting both in texture and taste: it's meatier, and less greasy and salty.

I don't think the filling needs the extra fat, however — good bacon has quite enough of that. Ideally, ask your butcher to mince the meat for you; otherwise, patience and a sharp knife will do the trick.

Herbs and spices are a matter of personal preference, so feel free to muck about as you wish — sage and thyme are traditional partners with pork, as is the sweetness of nutmeg or mace, but the lemon zest is rather more novel. I think it really lifts the flavour of the filling, making the sausage rolls dangerously moreish — which is, of course, just what you want.

Makes about 25 small rolls

For the pastry
225g plain flour, plus extra to dust
A pinch of salt
2 teaspoons English mustard powder
175g very cold butter
ice-cold water
1 egg, beaten with a little water and salt

For the filling
**300g pork belly, skin removed, minced or
    finely chopped**
**300g pork shoulder, minced (this can often be
    bought ready minced if you don't have a good butcher)**
200g smoked streaky bacon, rind removed, finely chopped
Zest of 1 lemon

Nutmeg, to grate
2 tablespoons roughly chopped thyme leaves
8 sage leaves, roughly chopped

1. Sift the flour into a mixing bowl, add the salt and mustard powder and grate in the butter. Stir them all together with a knife, so the strands of butter are well coated with flour — it should look like a rough crumble mixture. Pour in just enough ice-cold water to make a dough that comes away cleanly from the bowl — do this very cautiously though, it shouldn't be at all sticky — and bring it together into a ball. Wrap in clingfilm or greaseproof paper and chill for 30 minutes.

2. Put all the meats into a large bowl and mix them well with your hands. Tip in the rest of the ingredients and mix in, seasoning well with black pepper and a little salt (remember the bacon will be salty, so don't go mad — you can always fry a little of the mixture to check the seasoning if you like). Preheat the oven to 220°C/fan 200°C/gas 7.

3. Roll out the pastry on a floured surface to a thickness of about 5mm, and cut into 3 lengthways. Divide the meat into 3 sausages, as long as your pastry, and place one slightly off-centre down each strip.

4. Brush one edge of each pastry strip with beaten egg and then fold the other side over to enclose the sausagemeat. Press the edge down to seal, and then go along it with the back of a fork to decorate. Brush the top with more eggwash, cut the rolls to the desired size, and prick each one with a fork.

5. Put the rolls on a baking tray and bake for 25 minutes, or until golden brown. Cool on a rack, and serve warm.

Perfect
Garlic Bread

'Anyone who says they don't like garlic bread must be fibbing' —
never have I agreed with the authors of retro recipe bible *The Prawn
Cocktail Years* more than this.

Garlic bread is the perfect food for the kind of party that's gone
beyond the cheese straw and blini stage: where people congregate
around the oven like vultures, and burn their tongues
in their eagerness to eat the smell — Nigel Slater's
ridiculously good Parmesan and garlic baguette was
such a fixture at the annual Christmas parties I used
to throw with my ex that people would request it on their
RSVP. But times they have a-changed, and I'm prepared to
move on — can Nigel's bread be bettered?

The answer is, happily, yes it can. Having tried a number of
different recipes in my selfless quest for perfection, from Nigel's
baguette to Jamie Oliver's pizza, Giorgio Locatelli's focaccia to
Nigella's 'hearthbread' (a sort of puffy deep-pan pizza base), I
slightly guiltily realize that it's Ina Garten's ciabatta that's stolen my
heart. The American Barefoot Contessa's bread stands up to the
copious amounts of garlic butter rather better than soft baguette, so
the finished loaf is chewier and more satisfying to eat. Sorry, Nigel.

One thing he and I do agree on, however — well, actually, I reckon
I'd agree with Nigel about most things in life, truth be told — is the

importance of raw garlic. Nigella roasts a whole bulb and then purées it before adding it to the top of her hearthbread, while Locatelli confits it in milk and sugar until it's almost jammy. Even the Contessa drops it into hot olive oil to neutralize the flavour, which seems quite mad — garlic bread should taste of garlic! If you're worried about your breath, then believe me, they're almost certainly not worth it.

For maximum impact, that garlic needs to be incorporated into the butter (and only the richness of butter will do here, I'm afraid — recipes using oil are a greasy disappointment). Sprinkle it on top instead, as Jamie and Nigella do, and it will burn in the hot oven, giving the loaf an acrid flavour.

Nor is cutting the loaf laterally, as Garten suggests, a good idea: the garlic simply soaks downwards, leaving the top half dry and dull. Ciabattas might be rather flat, but it is possible to slice them vertically (especially if you take the pursuit of perfection really seriously, and bake your own — Richard Bertinet has an excellent recipe in his book *Crust*).

I can't now countenance garlic bread without Slater's generous helping of salty Parmesan — enough so 'that the cheese forms thin strings as you tear one piece of bread from the next' — but otherwise, I don't like many of the other additions: Garten's oregano in particular is too pungent. One modification I will be adopting, however, is Richard Bertinet's squeeze of lemon juice: a slight hint of citrus tanginess works brilliantly with the garlic and parsley.

Be warned: this bread is almost molten straight out of the oven, so be patient, and you will be rewarded.

1 ciabatta loaf
100g salted butter, at room temperature
4 cloves of garlic, crushed
A small bunch of parsley, finely chopped
40g Parmesan, grated, plus a little extra for topping
A squeeze of lemon juice

1. Preheat the oven to 220°C/fan 200°C/gas 7. Very carefully cut
    the ciabatta into slices roughly 4cm apart, making sure not to go
    right through the loaf so it holds together at the base, and place
    it in the middle of a piece of foil large enough to enclose it.
2. Beat together all the other ingredients, apart from the extra
    Parmesan, until well combined and distributed, then gently
    force the butter between the slices of bread (this is messy work,
    but you won't regret it).
3. Sprinkle the top of the loaf with the remaining Parmesan, and
    seal the foil fairly loosely around it. It will sit quite happily for a
    few hours at this point.
4. Bake the bread for about 20 minutes, then open the foil and
    bake for another 5 minutes, until golden on top. Devour as
    soon as it's cool enough to tear into.

Perfect
Ham Croquetas

Fried, starchy and assertively salty, croquetas are an almost peerless accompaniment to a few drinks, and my favourite tapa by a country mile.

Obviously, you can stick pretty much anything you like in croquetas – David Eyre of London's Eyre Brothers restaurant reckons the salt cod version is as good as they get, while Hugh Fearnley-Whittingstall recommends them as a vehicle for leftover roast chicken, but for me, it has to be ham. Specifically savoury, nutty Spanish cured ham, encased in buttery béchamel and crisp breadcrumbs: just add a glass of chilled fino sherry, and I'm in heaven.

The stiff béchamel filling means they're best eaten so hot you burn your fingers on the crisp breadcrumbs in your hurry to get to the molten core. Some recipes add potatoes to further firm them up – I find a recipe on the website of a Spanish ham producer which mixes them with lard, cream and eggs to make the filling, but the results are stodgy and bland in comparison to the béchamel.

Which isn't always just béchamel, of course: I try infusing the milk with a *jamón* bone and herbs (underwhelming for the effort), adding onion (too assertive), Manchego (ditto, Martha Stewart), hard-boiled egg white (lumpy, unsurprisingly), and using olive oil rather than butter, but in the end, the only thing I think could be added to the near perfect recipe in the *Barrafina* cookbook is leeks. It may sound a surprising ingredient, but having tried them in José Pizarro's recipe, I'm sold: their sweetness makes the perfect contrast to the saltiness of the ham.

I notice in the course of my testing that the ham seems to lose some of its salty punch when cooked, so I've added it in two batches: one to infuse the béchamel, and the other right at the last minute, so it retains as much of its own flavour as possible.

Chilling the finished béchamel well makes it easier to roll into shape and coat, at which point Japanese panko breadcrumbs, though definitely not authentically Spanish, add extra crunch. And, having pooh-poohed Martha Stewart's cheesy filling, I've added a little grated Manchego to the coating — just a hint.

And then, extravagant though it may seem, I've decided to fry the croquetas in olive oil. You don't need any more than a litre bottle, and the flavour is so complementary that it seems a shame not to: you can always filter it and reuse it for further croquetas should you develop a taste for them.

These are great for parties: make the béchamel filling in advance, and then simply coat and cook them to order — and, of course, make sure you get one from each batch as reward. It's only fair.

Makes about 15

100g cured Spanish ham, preferably in
   a large chunk
2 tablespoons olive oil
60g unsalted butter
½ a small leek, finely diced
60g plain flour, plus extra to dust
500ml whole milk
Nutmeg, to grate
2 free-range eggs, beaten
150g panko breadcrumbs
25g Manchego or other hard cheese,
   finely grated
1 litre olive oil, to fry

1. Dice the ham as finely as you can. Heat the oil and butter in a
   medium, heavy-based saucepan over a medium heat. When the
   butter melts, add the leek and fry gently for a minute or so, then
   add 70g of the ham and cook until the leek has softened, and the
   fat on the ham has begun to melt.
2. Reduce the heat and gradually stir in the flour. Cook very gently,
   stirring regularly, until the flour loses its raw flavour – this will
   take about 8–10 minutes. Meanwhile, heat the milk until hot but
   not boiling.
3. Gradually beat the hot milk into the flour mixture until you have
   a smooth paste. Cook this gently for another 15 minutes, until
   it's the consistency of smooth mashed potato, then fold through
   the rest of the chopped ham and season the mixture to taste with
   a grating of nutmeg and some black pepper (you shouldn't need
   any salt).

4. Cool the béchamel in a bowl, then cover, pressing clingfilm on to the surface of the sauce to stop a skin forming, and chill for at least 2 hours.

5. Beat the eggs in one bowl, and combine the breadcrumbs and grated cheese in another. Use floured hands to roll the mixture into croqueta-sized cylinders. Dip these in the egg, then roll them in the breadcrumbs until well coated.

6. Heat the olive oil in a large pan to 180°C, or until it begins to shimmer. Line a plate with kitchen paper. Fry the croquetas in batches for a couple of minutes, until golden all over, then lift them out with a slotted spoon, drain on the kitchen paper and serve at once.

Perfect
Patatas Bravas

*F*or a long time, I didn't get the point of patatas bravas. They're so often just chunks of fried potato in a ketchup-sweet sauce that they seemed like a waste of an order when delicious morsels of morcilla, or crisp calamari, or even the calming weight of a Spanish omelette were on offer instead.

I stand by the fact they can be disappointing in the extreme, in this country at least — apparently no one cooks patatas bravas at home in Spain. This makes recipes hard to come by, and one of the ones I try, from Simone and Inés Ortega, authors of the classic *1080 Recipes*, doesn't even involve frying or tomatoes, instead tossing boiled potatoes with a spicy vinaigrette to make something more like a potato salad. This is how they do bravas in Valencia, apparently, but it's not what I'm after.

It strikes me the dish as we know it would be more interesting if the potatoes weren't so soggy, and I find the secret to keeping them crisp from a surprising source. Mary Cadogan's recipe for *BBC Good Food* magazine roasts the spuds rather than fries them, which not only cuts down on the grease but really brings out their flavour and keeps them wonderfully crunchy — until I add the sauce.

How to keep them that way stumps me until I chance upon a recipe from Asturian-born US chef José Andrés, who claims to have spent sixteen years perfecting his bravas. He serves the sauce separately, so the potatoes stay crisp right up until the last minute — it may not look authentic, but it's undeniably a great improvement.

I find his sauce too sweet, however — I prefer the smoky spice of José Pizarro's recipe, with its earthy smoked paprika and fresh chilli. But the real breakthrough comes when I discover, via Andrés, that in many of parts of Spain bravas are served with a creamy, garlicky allioli sauce to balance the spiciness of the tomato base.

This is what makes the dish as far as I'm concerned, complementing the crunchy potatoes and sweet, piquant sauce perfectly. Paired with a cold Spanish beer, I finally see what all the fuss is about.

Serves 4–6

500g waxy potatoes
300ml olive oil
1 small onion, finely chopped
1 red chilli, finely chopped
1 x 400g tin of chopped tomatoes
½ teaspoon sugar
½ teaspoon salt
1 teaspoon smoked paprika
2 tablespoons sherry vinegar
1 egg
1 clove of garlic, crushed
Chives, to serve

1. Preheat the oven to 200°C/fan 180°C/gas 6. Peel the potatoes and cut them into rough 2cm chunks. Pour 2 tablespoons of olive oil into a roasting tray and heat it in the oven for 5 minutes before tossing the potatoes in the hot oil, and baking them for about 45 minutes until crisp and golden.

2. Meanwhile, make the sauces. Put another 2 tablespoons of oil into a heavy-bottomed pan on a medium heat, add the onion and cook for about 7 minutes, until soft. Stir in the chopped chilli and cook for another couple of minutes, then add the tomatoes, sugar, salt and smoked paprika and stir well to combine. Bring to the boil, reduce the heat and simmer the sauce for about 20 minutes until thick and dark. Take off the heat, add 1 tablespoon of sherry vinegar, and season to taste.

3. For the allioli, put the egg into the small bowl of a food processor with the garlic and 1 tablespoon of sherry vinegar. Add 1 tablespoon of olive oil and whiz until incorporated, then, with the motor still running, slowly drizzle in the remaining olive oil until you have a creamy mayonnaise-style sauce. Season to taste. (You can also use a hand blender, but it's harder to drizzle and hold it at the same time.)

4. Take the crisp potatoes out of the oven and sprinkle them with a little sea salt. Spread the tomato sauce on a serving plate, arrange the potatoes on top, then add a big dollop of allioli and a sprinkle of chives, and serve immediately.

CHAPTER 3

Soups and Salads

*Y*ou might be forgiven for dismissing this as the boring chapter — after all, what soup could hope to compete with pulled pork, and which salad stacks up to a syrup sponge? As someone who habitually skims past the 'light bites' section of any menu, I sympathize: few things tempt me less than a badly made salad, all limp leaves and too much dressing, or a generic soup of the 'guess the vegetable' variety. So, naturally, I haven't included any here.

Instead, you'll find the real hard-hitters of the genre: the kind of dishes that you can happily tuck into without worrying you should have got a side of chips too. Which is not to say they're all rib-stickers: alongside the hearty French onion soup, cockle-warming cullen skink and the classic chicken penicillin for the soul there's fruity tomato, spicy tom yum (which, at the risk of shocking Jewish mammas everywhere, is my cold remedy of choice) and the sunny Mediterranean flavours of a proper niçoise salad.

What they all have in common, however, is the simplicity of flavour — if you're making a tomato soup, I think it should taste of tomatoes. It may sound obvious, but there's no need for rich stocks or spoonfuls of spice if the raw ingredients are good enough — and that goes as much for the humble tomato as it does for the anchovies in your Caesar salad.

Rather than trying to confuse the issue, I've always tried to enhance the dish's natural assets — whether that's using pea pods to amplify the sweetness of a pea soup, or steering clear of boiled potatoes and tinned tuna to keep the niçoise as sunny and fresh as a Provençal morning, and I must say, I'm pretty pleased with the results. These are soups and salads to stake your appetite on. Delicate souls need not apply.

Perfect
Pea Soup

*T*he humble pea is one of our most under-appreciated vegetables – not under-used but very rarely allowed to be a star in its own right. Which is a bit of a crime. Fight back against this injustice with a classic pea soup – a little taste of summer available from the freezer all year round.

Because of the very ubiquity conferred by such technology, we tend to take peas for granted – and it's true that the frozen kind tend to be of such a quality that the two are basically interchangeable in the recipe below. (Indeed, the pea converts its sugars to starch very rapidly, so unless you can buy them very fresh, you're probably better off going with Clarence Birdseye.)

For a really intense flavour in season, however, simmer at least a few pods along with the other ingredients: both Jane Grigson and Tamasin Day-Lewis recommend it, and it does seem to heighten the natural character of the peas themselves. (Don't purée the pods with the peas as Mrs Grigson suggests, though: you'll go mad trying to sieve all the stringy bits out.)

Many recipes use stock – having tried both ham and chicken, I decide that here, I'm with Marcel Boulestin, who writes in his 1931 work *What Shall We Have Today?* that 'when made with the addition of stock [soups] lose all character and cease to be what they were intended to be. The fresh pleasant taste is lost.' More robust ingredients can, I think, stand up to and be complemented by stock, as other recipes in this chapter prove, but with peas, his point stands: Delia and Jane Grigson's water is a much more satisfying way to loosen the soup.

That said, bacon works so well with peas that I couldn't resist adding a little at the beginning, so it releases its savoury flavour as the fat gently melts in the pan: vegetarians should feel easy about leaving it out, however.

Puzzlingly, the majority of recipes I try enrich the soup with cream of some sort; certainly not the first ingredient that springs to my mind for a light, summery supper. I think it blunts the fresh sweetness of the peas, although I will permit a little Delia-style crème fraîche at the end as a tangy garnish. (Rose Elliot thickens her version with potato instead, which, while a better bet flavour-wise, gives it a warming, wintery texture I'm none too keen on here.)

As this is a summer soup, in style at least, I've eschewed onions and shallots in favour of Jane Grigson and Delia Smith's spring onions: they give the soup a fresher character, which I don't even want to muddy with garlic.

Mint is a must for much the same reason, but simmering it with the peas, as Lindsey Bareham and Rose do, dulls its flavour: instead I stir the leaves in at the end, as Tamasin, Jane and Delia suggest.

A spritz of lemon juice, as recommended by Lindsey, further enhances the fresh flavours of the other ingredients. Delicious hot, but for maximum refreshment, serve chilled.

Serves 4

30g butter
4 spring onions, chopped
2 rashers of smoked streaky bacon,
   chopped (optional)
450g shelled peas (about 1.2kg of pods),
   plus 5 pods if available
750ml water (or vegetable stock if
   you're omitting the bacon)
A squeeze of lemon juice
A pinch of sugar (optional)
A small bunch of mint, chopped,
   and crème fraîche, to serve

1. Melt the butter over a medium heat in a large pan and sweat the
   spring onions and bacon until cooked, but not browned.
2. Tip in the peas, and the pods if using, stir well, then pour in
   750ml of water. Bring to the boil, then simmer until the peas
   are tender.
3. Remove the pods if necessary, then purée the soup using a
   blender or hand blender until smooth. Squeeze in the lemon
   juice and season to taste – you may also want to add a pinch of
   sugar depending on the sweetness of your peas, or a little more
   water if you'd prefer a thinner soup.
4. Reheat the soup if serving hot, chill if you'd prefer it cold, and
   serve garnished with chopped mint and a swirl of crème fraiche.

Perfect
Chicken Soup

*T*he answer to everything, according to the archetypal Jewish mamma —
I hesitate to describe my recipe as penicillin for the soul, but it is very
definitely Wholesome. For a start, it comes in big steaming bowls, a
sight infinitely more restorative than anything you can get over the
counter. Secondly, there's some evidence to suggest it may have anti-
inflammatory properties, though no one quite knows why. And thirdly,
making your own is thrift par excellence, which always lifts the spirits.

Claudia Roden makes the soup with a whole bird, but
although she has kosher credentials, I'm not sure this is a
good idea unless you're lucky enough to be able to lay
your hands on a stringy old boiling fowl. Younger
chickens don't boast enough flavour in the carcass, while
the meat is too tender to benefit from prolonged
simmering — it just goes rubbery.

A better and cheaper idea is to use wings, as Heston Blumenthal
does — although there will be plenty of flavour in any bony bits, so
feel free to swap — and only add a chicken carcass if you happen to
have one left over from a Sunday roast or similar.

Purists may sneer, but to guarantee a good, chickeny flavour, I've
also used chicken stock: if you make your own, this isn't really
cheating, and if Lindsey Bareham uses beef stock, then chicken must
surely be acceptable.

Stock is as nothing to the heresy of adding fresh vegetables, however — but I think the vitamins they bring with them are quite in the spirit of the soup (after all, in the days when chicken fat was believed to be a cure-all, chicken soup wasn't chicken soup without golden coins of oil floating on the top: carrots are simply the modern equivalent).

To be truly comforting, a soup needs body: you could make matzo ball dumplings (recipe below), or stick in some vermicelli, but wholegrain barley seems more in keeping with the rest of the ingredients: chewy, nutty, and pleasingly filling, it'll warm you from the inside out.

To finish, I won't be adding Heston's star anise (too Oriental), Skye Gyngell's mint, coriander and lemon (too Middle Eastern), or thyme, bay or decadent saffron: all this resolutely savoury soup needs is the peppery tang of parsley to set it off to perfection.

Serves 6

1kg chicken wings or drumsticks or a mixture,
   plus a leftover chicken carcass if you happen to have one
2 sticks of celery, chopped
2 onions, skin on and quartered
3 carrots (2 roughly chopped,
   1 peeled and more finely chopped
   and kept separate)
3 leeks (2 roughly chopped, 1 more finely chopped and kept
   separate)
A small bunch of parsley, separated into stalks and leaves
750ml chicken stock, cold
200g wholegrain barley, cooked

1. Place the chicken in a large pan or stockpot and pour in just enough cold water to cover. Bring to the boil and skim off any scum that rises to the top – important because otherwise your soup will have a horrid, greasy flavour.
2. Add the celery, quartered onions (if they're clean, there's no need to peel these), the roughly chopped carrots and leeks, parsley stalks and stock to the pan. Season generously with pepper, then turn down the heat and leave to simmer gently for a couple of hours.
3. Strain the soup through a fine sieve; you can pick the meat off the bones and add it to the soup if you wish, although it may be rather chewy, but discard the vegetables.
4. Return the soup to the pan, add the finely chopped carrot and leek and cook for 10 minutes, until soft.
5. Tip in the cooked barley, season the soup to taste, and serve with the chopped parsley leaves on top.

Simple matzo ball dumplings

60ml sparkling water
2 large eggs
1 tablespoon neutral oil (or liquid chicken fat, should you happen to have some knocking about)
100g matzo meal
1 tablespoon finely chopped parsley or dill

1. While the soup is simmering for a couple of hours, whisk together the water, eggs and oil, then stir in the matzo meal and herbs. Season generously and chill for half an hour.
2. Roll the dough into small balls about 1.5cm in diameter. Once you've strained the soup and returned it to the pan, add the

dumplings and simmer for 10 minutes before adding the carrot and leek.

3. Cook for another 10–15 minutes, until the dumplings are cooked through.

Perfect
Cullen Skink

*T*hough the name may sound more like a Dickensian villain than anything you might want to put in your mouth, cullen skink is, in fact, one of the world's finest seafood soups, a comfortingly rich mixture of smoked haddock and starchy spuds, named after the fishing town on the Moray Firth.

(The skink bit apparently comes from the German word for shin, suggesting the soup would originally have been made from beef — fish was simply the local twist, albeit one of no little genius.) Smokier than chowder, heartier than a French bisque, it's the ultimate winter lunch.

Although it's traditionally made with smoked haddock, as the *River Cottage Fish Book* points out, any smoked white fish will do. Go for the undyed stuff, if you're not keen on that lurid yellow colour, but don't bother investing in fancy Arbroath smokies, as Nick Nairn suggests. Headless, gutted haddock, hot-smoked over a wood fire, they're utterly delicious on their own, but the intense smoky flavour completely overpowers the soup.

Using a proper fish stock as a base, as Mark Hix suggests in *British Regional Food*, is also too strong: much better to copy Sue Lawrence, Scottish cookery expert, and use the haddock poaching liquid to flavour the soup instead. The River Cottage boys and Gary Rhodes poach their fish in milk, rather than adding the dairy at the end, but I find this makes the soup itself too rich – this is a Scottish fishwives' dish, to be eaten in big, steaming bowls, rather than tiny restaurant portions.

Many cooks simply use leftover mash to thicken their soup, but I prefer a few chunks of potato for texture. You could roughly mash the cooked spuds in the pan, as Lawrence suggests, but puréeing the majority into the body of the soup, as in Rhodes' recipe, makes the soup itself silkier, and provides a more interesting contrast of textures. Leaving the skins on the potatoes, as Hix does, gives the whole thing a better flavour – as well as relieving you of a job.

Both onions and leeks are common additions; Nairn's shallots are too delicate. Leeks alone, however, as in Hix's soup, lack the sweetness of onions, while those onions don't provide the same fresh, green flavour I love leeks for. A mixture of the two, as in Rhodes' soup, seems like the best bet. And, for good measure, I've added a sprinkle of chives too. Just the thing to warm your cockles after a hard day's fishing – or, indeed, at the office.

Serves 6

500g undyed smoked haddock, skin on
A bay leaf
A knob of butter
1 onion, peeled and finely chopped
1 leek, washed and cut into chunks
2 medium potatoes, unpeeled,
   cut into chunks
500ml whole milk
Chives, chopped, to serve

1. Put the fish into a wide pan large enough to hold it comfortably, add the bay leaf, and cover with about 300ml of cold water (you may need more if your pan is very wide). Put it on a medium heat. By the time it comes to the boil, the fish should be just cooked – if it's not, give it another minute or so. Remove the fish from the pan and set aside to cool, retaining the cooking liquid.
2. Melt the butter in a large saucepan on a medium–low heat, and put in the chopped onion and leek. Cover and sweat, without colouring, for about 10 minutes, until softened. Season with black pepper.
3. Add the chunks of potato to the pan and stir to coat with butter. Pour in the fish poaching liquid and the bay leaf, and bring to a simmer. Cook until the potato is tender.
4. Meanwhile, remove the skin and any stray bones from the haddock, and break it into large flakes.
5. Use a slotted spoon to lift out a generous helping of potatoes and leeks, and set aside with half the flaked fish. Discard the bay leaf. Add the milk and the remaining haddock to the pan, and either mash or blend until smoothish. Reheat and season to taste.
6. To serve, put a spoonful of the potato, leek and haddock mixture in each bowl, pour in the soup and top with a sprinkling of chives.

Perfect
Tom Yum

*T*he name means 'hot and sour' in Thai, and that just about sums
up this soup which is, as far as I'm concerned, possibly the best cold
remedy not to contain whisky. Searingly spicy, and wonderfully
sour, it will wake up even the stuffiest of heads.

This recipe uses prawns, because I prefer to keep things light
when I'm feeling ill, but you could substitute anything
from beef to crab, depending on your mood — the
important thing is the hot and sour base.

Though punchy, I've kept that base relatively
simple: making your own nam phrik phao, or chilli jam, as Rosemary
Brissenden recommends in *South East Asian Food*, is not only far too
time-consuming for anyone in need of a reviving meal, but the rich,
sweet, toasty flavours spoil the freshness of the soup for me.

The basics every recipe has in common are aromatic lemongrass and
lime leaves, sour lime juice, savoury fish sauce and hot chillies — you
can add coriander root and tamarind like David Thompson in his
book *Thai Street Food* if you want to get fancy, or up your vitamin
content with Allegra McEvedy's mushroom and tomato
combination, but a good tom yum doesn't really need any of them.

The only concessions I've made are for galangal, which works well
with the chilli, and a little palm sugar as a sop to my no doubt

westernized palate — although the idea came from blogger MiMi Aye, a native of Burma, so it at least has South-East Asian provenance.

If you're feeling very pure, you can dilute this base with water, but I like the more assertive flavour of a quick prawn stock, as in Rosemary Brissenden's recipe.

Really, any stock will do, however, as long as it's robust enough to stand its ground: David Thompson uses chicken, which gets a bit lost amongst all the other ingredients. Be careful of using bought fish stocks with prawns, however: they tend to be too savoury, and obscure the sweet nuttiness of the crustaceans.

Hot, fragrant and sour, this soup will clear your head in no time — for a more filling meal for those not at death's door, I sometimes add pak choi or rice noodles to bulk it out.

Serves 4

16 raw shell-on king prawns
A dash of oil
4 lime leaves, roughly torn
2 lemongrass stalks, cut into
   5cm pieces and crushed
2 slices galangal (optional)
2 bird's-eye chillies, finely sliced
1 tablespoon palm sugar
Juice of 1½ limes
2 tablespoons fish sauce
A handful of coriander or Thai basil leaves, torn, to serve

1. Shell the prawns, setting the meat aside for later. Heat the oil in a saucepan on a medium-high flame, and fry the prawn shells until pink. Add 1 litre of water, bring to a simmer, leave to cook for 10 minutes, then strain and discard the shells.

2. Pour this prawn stock into a clean pan and add the lime leaves, lemongrass and galangal, if using. Bring it back to a simmer and leave to infuse for 5 minutes, then add the chopped chillies and simmer for another couple of minutes.

3. Add the prawn meat to the pan and cook until pink, then take the pan off the heat and stir in the sugar, lime juice and fish sauce. Taste for seasoning and adjust if necessary, then pour into bowls. Garnish with coriander or basil and serve immediately.

Thai basics

Thai food is frequently described as a delicate balance of hot, sour, salty and sweet, but relatively little is written about the ingredients doing the balancing, which can be confusing when you're blundering around an Oriental supermarket squinting at Cantonese labels and trying to discreetly sniff out the galangal. Here's a brief guide to the less familiar cornerstones of Thai cuisine:

Basil: three varieties are commonly used in Thai kitchens, none of them interchangeable with the broad-leafed Italian sort. Thai basil (*bai horapha*), with its aniseedy flavour, is the most commonly found in the UK, although spicy, peppery holy basil (*bai grapao*) or zesty lemon basil (*bai manglaek*) may be found in specialist shops.

Chillies: the most common varieties used are long chillies (*prik chii faa*), lime-green, less hot banana chillies (*prik yuak*) and the fearsomely piquant little bird's-eyes (*prik kii nuu suan*). Dried versions can be found in Oriental grocer's.

Coconut milk and cream (*hua gati*): obviously the tinned or dried sort is easier to come by here than fresh coconuts. David Thompson recommends looking for a brand without added stabilizers.

Coriander (*pak chii*): Thai cooks use the roots and stems as well as the leaves, though you might have to go to a specialist to find a bunch with these still attached.

Dried prawns (*gung haeng*): add a savoury depth to dishes. Look cool in the jar.

Fish sauce (*nahm plaa*): again, intensely savoury, and best used with discretion.

Galangal (*khaa*): looks like a ginger root, but tastes more peppery and less sweet.

Kaffir lime leaves (*bai makrut*): Thompson describes these as 'hauntingly aromatic', which hits the nail on the head nicely.

Lemongrass (*dtakrai*): peel off the tough outer leaves and use the tender inner white part.

Palm sugar (*nahm dtarn bip*): caramel-coloured, with an almost fudge-like flavour, this gives a distinctive sweetness that makes it well worth hunting down in the specialist section of big supermarkets.

Shallots (*horm daeng*): the small red (actually pink) kind are more commonly used in

Thailand, but European versions aren't a bad substitute.

Shrimp paste (*gapi*): richly aromatic; don't be put off by the smell.

Tamarind (*makaam bliak*): intensely sweet and sour, it's better to buy the dark pulp than the ready-made paste if you can find it, and dilute it yourself.

Turmeric root (*kamin*): these vividly orange little roots taste like . . . well, turmeric. Often found in Indian specialists as well.

Perfect
Tomato Soup

Although we may not be famous for our tomatoes, this is, I think, the finest possible dish for the British summertime. For a start, it makes use of seasonal produce: you have to wait until they're so ripe they're almost splitting. Secondly, it acknowledges that there are summer days — many, many summer days — which are in need of warming up.

There are good recipes using tinned tomatoes of course, and, having road-tested both Mark Bittman's wintertime tomato soup, as published in the *New York Times*, and one from the American department store chain Nordstrom, which apparently enjoys 'something of a cult following for those who love tomato soup', I can recommend both for a cold weather fix. But neither are a patch on the sweet and sour pleasures of the fresh version.

In really warm climates, no doubt fresh tomatoes are flavourful enough to need no special treatment, but I find recipes which simply simmer them in stock produce a sadly bland result. For a really tomatoey result, you need to roast the tomatoes, as Lindsey Bareham suggests — it concentrates the sweetness.

As it's a vegetable soup, you could use a matching stock here, but I always find them too assertively herby — better, if you don't mind meat, to substitute a good chicken stock, which will add savoury richness without contributing any distinct flavour of its own. My recipe uses less stock than many: although it shouldn't be thick, a tomato soup should still have presence on the spoon.

That said, you don't need much in the way of added thickeners — cream of tomato soup is a classic, the natural wateriness of the fruit lending itself to a little added luxury, but too much double cream makes the Nordstrom recipe a bit sickly. Jamie mixes his double cream with egg yolks, which gives his soup a beautifully silky texture, but it's *Larousse*'s seasonally light fromage frais which seems to work best with the dish's summery flavours — and tangy crème fraîche is even better, pointing up the sweet and sour flavour of the tomatoes. I'm not sure *Larousse*'s potatoes are entirely in keeping though — they make the soup far too cosy and fluffy.

Carrot and onion both accentuate that sweetness (helped along by a pinch of sugar), but I've eschewed their traditional companions celery and bouquet garni — they seem too wintery here, somehow. Garlic, however, is a natural match for tomatoes, as is fresh basil.

My final touch is a dash of balsamic vinegar — inspired by a River Café tomato sauce using both vinegar and sugar to amplify the natural assets of the fruit, it makes up for any deficiencies in the tomatoes themselves, and adds a depth of flavour all of its own.

Note, though it's lovely hot in a summer rainstorm, this soup also goes down a treat chilled, should the weather forget itself for a few hours.

Serves 4

1kg ripe tomatoes
4 tablespoons olive oil
A pinch of sugar
1 onion, chopped
1 carrot, peeled and diced
2 cloves of garlic, finely chopped
A small bunch of basil, separated into leaves and stalks
600ml chicken stock
1 tablespoon balsamic vinegar
2 tablespoons crème fraîche
Extra virgin olive oil, to serve

1. Preheat the oven to 190°C/fan 170°C/gas 5 and cut the tomatoes in half laterally. Place them, cut side up, in a baking dish, drizzle with 2 tablespoons of olive oil and season with salt, pepper and a pinch of sugar. Bake them for about an hour, until thoroughly softened and just beginning to blacken around the edges.

2. Once they're nearly ready, pour the remaining oil into a large, heavy-based pan over a medium heat and add the chopped onion, carrot and garlic. Fry, stirring regularly, for about 7 minutes, until thoroughly softened. Meanwhile, roughly chop the basil stalks. Add these to the pan and cook for another minute.

3. Tip in the baked tomatoes, plus any juices from the dish, and pour in the stock. Stir and bring to the boil, then turn the heat down, cover the pan and leave to simmer for 25 minutes, until all the vegetables are soft.

4. Use a blender to purée the soup, then stir in the vinegar and crème fraîche and season to taste. Reheat, then serve with a pinch of torn basil leaves and a drizzle of olive oil on top.

Perfect
French Onion Soup

Onions are at their best in the autumn and winter months, which is handy, because this French classic, with its crown of melted Gruyère, is not well suited to warm weather. Beefy, boozy and deliciously cheesy, it's fancy enough for guests, but simple enough to make an excellent, if self-indulgent, solo supper.

Anthony Bourdain makes the important, if obvious point in the *Les Halles Cookbook* that 'onion soup, unsurprisingly, is all about the onions' — yet makes no further recommendations. Only Raymond Blanc is willing to stick his neck out with specifics, naming pink Roscoff onions as the ones with the necessary blend of sweetness and acidity for this dish. They're available online from Brittany, but I find yellow onions work fine, as long as they're in good condition (never buy them in plastic bags — you'll always find some rotten ones hidden inside), and treated with respect.

This means proper caramelization — 'a nice, dark even brown colour', as Bourdain describes it. As often seems to be the case, he's cheerfully dishonest about how long this will take: he may be a great cook, but no one can get onions to that stage in 20 minutes. It'll probably take an hour and a half to achieve the desired result, depending on your pan and hob, but they don't need constant attention, so you can always read the paper at the same time.

Adding a pinch of sugar to help things along, as Lindsey Bareham cunningly suggests in *A Celebration of Soup*, shouldn't be entirely necessary if you put in the time, but there's no harm in adding it at the end if your onions aren't quite as sweet as you'd like.

Beef stock supplies the traditional liquid element — Blanc uses water, which smacks of peasant frugality for the sake of it, and Bourdain a rather underwhelming chicken stock, but I think you need the rich, savoury flavour of a good beef reduction to stand up to the sweetness of the onions.

There's also a fine tradition of adding booze to onion soup: white wine is a decent choice, but cider is even better, supplying a certain rustic acidity. Bourdain, never one to toe the line, goes for port, and I'm surprised to find the sweetness goes very well, so I'm plumping for a medium-dry cider rather than Michel Roux Jr's dry version.

A dash of brandy, meanwhile, adds a distinctly French flavour to the dish, while some vinegar supplies a little balancing acidity. French wine vinegar would do, but if you don't mind the rather un-Gallic intrusion, sweet, rich balsamic is even better.

A roux, made directly in the pan to save on washing-up as in Raymond Blanc's recipe, gives the soup more body.

Le Gavroche whisks an egg yolk and a teaspoon of crème fraîche into its onion soup — delicious, but far too rich to eat in the kind of portions it deserves. Save your efforts for the all-important raft of toast and cheese instead, toasting the bread to slow the sogging process, rubbing it with garlic for that authentic French flavour and loading it with as much cheese as it will take. If you can still see soup beneath, you haven't got enough.

Serves 4 as a starter

80g butter, plus a little extra for the toasts
4 onions, peeled and thinly sliced
1 tablespoon plain flour
3 sprigs of thyme, leaves picked
1 tablespoon balsamic vinegar
400ml medium cider
600ml good-quality beef stock
8 slices of baguette
1 clove of garlic, halved
A dash of Calvados or other brandy
100g Gruyère, grated

1. Put the butter into a large, heavy-bottomed pan over a low heat and, once melted, add the onions. Season and cook, stirring regularly, until they're a deep, rich caramel colour. (Once they've softened, you can turn up the heat a little, but keep a watchful eye on them.) This process will probably take between 90 minutes and 2 hours, depending on your nerve.

2. Stir the flour and thyme into the onions and cook for a couple of minutes, stirring constantly, then mix in the vinegar and a third of the cider, stirring and scraping all the brown bits from the bottom of the pan as you do so.

3. Whisk in the remaining cider and the stock, and bring to the boil. Simmer it for about an hour. Right at the end (if serving immediately), heat the grill and rub the slices of bread with the

cut side of the garlic clove. Melt the remaining butter, brush this on to the bread and toast on both sides. Leave the grill on.

4. Add the brandy to the soup and check the seasoning, adjusting if necessary. To serve, ladle the soup into ovenproof dishes and top with 2 croutons each and a mound of cheese. Grill the cheese until golden and bubbling, and serve immediately.

Perfect
Salade Niçoise

*U*ntil I went to Nice, I thought I didn't like salade niçoise — mulchy tinned tuna, floppy green beans and rubbery black olives are hardly the stuff of Mediterranean fantasy. Turns out that, in the Alpes-Maritimes, the ingredients are far more of a lottery, with my personal bête noire, tinned tuna, far less popular than the far more handsome little anchovy. As Nigel Slater observes, 'whenever I say "hold the tuna" I am invariably told that I wasn't going to get any anyway'.

I do try Delia's niçoise recipe using the best quality tinned tuna I can find, in the interests of balance, but even the most committed tuna lovers admit that it doesn't have a hope against the stridently salty anchovies — it's just too mild. If you must use it, leave the anchovies out instead. Gary Rhodes uses fresh tuna, which seems very 1990s to me (Simon Hopkinson, less kind, describes it as 'a notion only to be entertained by the permanently bewildered' in *A Good Cook*): a fine, if extravagant choice, but chopping up and tossing it with the salad is a criminal waste.

Potatoes are another British classic pooh-poohed by the French — indeed, the former mayor of Nice, Jacques Médecin, pleads in his cookbook, 'never, never, I beg you, include boiled potato or any other boiled vegetable'. Now he may have been a convicted fraudster, but he has a point: the sunshiney flavour of the other ingredients is spoilt by the potatoes, and even crunchy French beans: juicy, sweet little broad beans are better in season, adding body to the salad without weighing it down. If you can't get them fresh, however, French beans are a better bet. Similarly, spring onions taste fresher than Delia's shallots or David Lebovitz's thinly sliced red onion.

The sweetness of red pepper is welcome with the saltiness of the anchovies, and cucumber adds a refreshing crunch, although deseeding is essential, so it doesn't make the salad too watery, and peeling the tomatoes isn't just a cheffy affectation on the part of Rowley Leigh – it helps them absorb the vinaigrette better.

And it should be a vinaigrette: however good the Provençal olive oil, it demands the balancing kick of vinegar, although not Delia's mustard: you really don't need it if you have salty anchovies (pounded into the dressing too, as Gary Rhodes cleverly suggests) and the inevitable French garlic.

Fresh basil adds the final, very Mediterranean touch to a dish that's worlds away from the petrol station favourite. Give it a try: even if, like me, you don't like salade niçoise, I promise you'll like this.

Serves 2

    2 eggs
    500g broad bean pods or 50g
       French beans
    4 ripe tomatoes
    ¼ of a cucumber
    2 spring onions, finely chopped

½ a red pepper, thinly sliced
50g small black olives, pitted
1 tablespoon capers
4 anchovies, cut into slivers
A few basil leaves, roughly torn

For the dressing
1 small clove of garlic
A pinch of coarse salt
2 anchovies, finely chopped
A small handful of basil leaves, torn
4 tablespoons extra virgin olive oil
½ tablespoon red wine vinegar
Black pepper

1. Put the eggs into a saucepan large enough to hold them in one layer, cover with cold water and bring slowly to the boil. Turn down the heat and simmer for 7½ minutes, then drain and cool in a bowl of iced water.

2. Meanwhile, pod and then peel the broad beans (if using French beans instead, top and tail them, then cook in salted boiling water until just tender and drop immediately into iced water to cool). Drop the tomatoes into a pan of boiling water, leave for 15 seconds, then scoop out, peel, slice and deseed. Peel the cucumber in stripes, then scrape out the seeds from the centre and cut it into half-moons.

3. To make the dressing, pound the garlic to a paste in a pestle and mortar along with a pinch of coarse salt. Add the chopped anchovies and then the basil, and pound it all to a paste, slowly dribbling in the olive oil and the vinegar along the way. Season generously with black pepper.

4. To assemble the salad, toss the beans, tomatoes, cucumber, chopped spring onion and sliced red pepper with two-thirds of the dressing and decant it on to a serving plate. Carefully peel the eggs, cut into quarters and arrange on top of the salad, along with the olives, capers, anchovy strips and remaining basil leaves. Drizzle the rest of the dressing over the salad and serve immediately.

Perfect
Caesar Salad

Not a Roman dish, or even an American one, but a salad created by a Mexican restaurateur struggling to cope with the number of thirsty visitors propelled across the border by Prohibition. The genius of Caesar Cardini's recipe was that it could be prepared at the table by waiters, taking the pressure off the kitchen — Julia Child recalls the sheer theatre of it: 'I remember the turning of the salad in the bowl was very dramatic. And egg in a salad was unheard of at that point.'

The man himself may have been big, but that hasn't protected his creation — bacon, grilled chicken, even salmon are all common interlopers in modern Caesar salads, despite his original version containing nothing but leaves, dressing, croutons and cheese.

That's not to say there's no room for improvement: Tamasin Day-Lewis includes the original recipe in her book *All You Can Eat*, and I find it a bit underwhelming — pleasant enough, but hardly likely to cause a stir these days. For a start, though Caesar never thought of adding anchovies, I wouldn't dream of leaving them out: the salty, intensely savoury umami flavour makes the dish for me, although I do confine them to the dressing; having them draped across the lettuce like so many eyebrows is a step too far.

The dressing itself also contains, as Child noted, egg yolk; most recipes, apparently in obedience to the creator himself, lightly cook it, but I can't really see the point. It doesn't help thicken it, and it won't protect you against salmonella if that's what you're worried about — best to leave it out altogether if so.

Whisking the egg with the garlic-infused oil, lemon juice and Worcestershire sauce may lack the theatre of tossing each ingredient into the bowl individually, but it does help the dressing to emulsify so it coats the leaves better, which seems more important to me.

Those leaves don't need to be whole: Day-Lewis reports that the salad was originally finger food, but with this much garlic and anchovy involved, I think a fork is preferable, and Cardini himself apparently came to the same conclusion, if the *Dictionary of American Food and Drink* is to be believed — the recipe evolved to call for bite-sized pieces of lettuce. Tearing gives a more haphazard, rustic look to the dish, especially if you're attempting some 'tableside' drama.

Baked croutons are crunchier, and less greasy than the fried versions — but to be honest, they're not going to turn the dish into a health food. Salty, creamy and crisp, Caesar salad started life as a drinking companion, so please don't stint on the cheese or the oil. Refined it isn't, but by Caesar it's good.

Serves 4

> 2 cloves of garlic
> 150ml olive oil
> 4 thick slices of day-old white sourdough
>   or other robustly textured bread

2 anchovy fillets, rinsed
1 egg yolk
Juice of ½ a lemon
2 cos lettuces, torn into rough pieces
A large handful of finely grated Parmesan

1. Crush the garlic and whisk it into the oil. Leave them to infuse for at least an hour before starting on the rest of the salad.

2. Preheat the oven to 220°C/fan 200°C/gas 7 and cut or tear the bread into rough crouton-sized cubes. Toss these with a little of the garlic-infused oil to coat, then bake for about 15 minutes, until golden and crisp.

3. Mash the anchovies against the bottom of your salad bowl to make a paste, then beat in the egg yolk and, little by little, the rest of the garlic-infused oil until you have a thickish dressing. Add the lemon juice and taste – season if necessary.

4. Put the leaves into the bowl and toss until thoroughly coated with the dressing. Add the grated cheese and toss well again. Top with the croutons and serve.

Perfect
Panzanella

*B*read and butter pudding (see page 252) is the perfect final
resting place for stale bread when it's cold outside, but in summer
and early autumn, this thrifty Italian classic pips it to the post. Anna
del Conte has written evocatively of eating panzanella in the shade of
a spreading fig tree at her farmhouse in Chianti, washed down with
wine cooled in the icy water of the well, but happily, even without
such a magnificent setting, it's a dish that proves far more than the
sum of its parts.

The bread, of course, is all-important: I'm afraid most soft
British loaves will simply disintegrate under such treatment. A
ciabatta or an ordinary sourdough will do at a pinch, but for the
best results you need some stale country bread, of the sort sold
in Italian grocers and proper bakers. (Don't try and make it with
anything fresh either, it needs to be robustly stale.)

Chewy and dry, your elderly bread needs soaking to soften it; the
late great Marcella Hazan uses plain water, but as we're no longer
Tuscan peasants, I think we can afford to upgrade to Giorgio
Locatelli's wine vinegar, which gives it an invigorating zip.

The other principal ingredient of panzanella is tomatoes; Del Conte
seeds hers, but I think it's a shame to strip them of their juices, so,
like Jamie Oliver, I'm going to salt them and then whisk the
resulting juices into the dressing.

Cucumber is surprisingly common, and Oliver uses celery heart, but I'm not sure either are necessary unless, like the bread, you have some that needs using up. Instead, red onion, soaked as Del Conte suggests, to blunt its bite and bring out the natural sweetness, and charred peppers, a stroke of genius from Jamie given the ripeness of many British peppers, bulk out the salad. The sweetness of basil makes it the obvious choice as a garnish.

Because the salad itself should be quite sweet with ripe summer produce, I've gone for a punchy vinaigrette, made from tomato juices, anchovies and garlic — Oliver's whole anchovies are overpowering, but used like this they bring a more subtle, savoury note to the dish.

There's no need to let the salad stand overnight as Locatelli suggests: it'll just go mushy. However, it does benefit from being left to stand and mingle for 15 minutes or so before serving, though it will be fine for up to an hour. Don't be tempted to chill it though, however warm the weather — remember, it's Italian and it can take it.

Serves 2–4

½ a red onion, thinly sliced
I red pepper
I yellow pepper
8 ripe tomatoes
200g stale country bread
4 tablespoons white wine vinegar
I tablespoon capers
2 anchovies, finely chopped

1 small clove of garlic, crushed
6 tablespoons extra virgin olive oil
A small bunch of fresh basil

1. Soak the onion slices for an hour in cold water with a pinch of salt. Meanwhile, blacken the peppers on a gas hob, barbecue or using a kitchen blowtorch. Tie up in a plastic bag or put into a bowl covered with clingfilm and leave for 20 minutes.
2. Chop the tomatoes into large dice, sprinkle lightly with salt and put in a colander set over a bowl to drain.
3. Tear the bread into chunks of a similar size to the tomatoes, put into a serving bowl and moisten with vinegar. Drain the onion well and add the slices to the bowl along with the capers. Use a sharp knife to scrape as much black skin off the peppers as you can, then cut the flesh into long strips. Gently press the tomatoes to squeeze a little more juice into the bowl beneath, then tip the diced flesh into the salad.
4. Add the chopped anchovies and crushed garlic to the tomato juice and whisk in the olive oil. Season to taste – you probably won't need any salt.
5. Pour the dressing on to the salad and toss thoroughly to coat. Roughly tear the basil leaves and sprinkle them on top. Allow to sit for between 15 minutes and an hour before serving.

CHAPTER 4

Fish and Seafood

I think we're getting over our rather bizarre fear of all things fishy in this country — you see a lot more seafood on the menu these days, and some of it doesn't even come encased in batter. (Though I'm not about to send it back if it does; see page 126.)

Most fish and seafood is best cooked very quickly and simply: squid, octopus and the like aside, the delicate flesh doesn't stand up well to the rigours of heat, and you're much more likely to over- than undercook it, so always err on the side of caution. After all, if your fish is fresh, eating a piece that's still slightly raw in the centre is unlikely to do you much harm.

To check whether a piece of fish is cooked, there's no need to faff about with a thermometer: once the flesh has turned opaque, a gentle prod with the finger to assess firmness will do the trick. And, as ever with cooking, practice makes perfect.

Gentle cooking methods, like poaching, or steaming in a foil parcel in the oven, tend to be safer bets than baking or frying when you've got yourself a nice fillet of gurnard, or a whole bream. That said, such dishes are so simple they don't really lend themselves to much perfecting, so the recipes in this chapter tend towards the more . . . if not complicated, then more interesting side of seafood. The crispy squid, smoky pâtés and potted prawns which, if I'm honest, I prefer to the poshest hunk of turbot or sole bonne femme.

As usual, if you have a fishmonger in the vicinity, I'd urge you to use them when you can. If a supermarket's all you have, then cruise the sell-by dates (the fresher the better, obviously), rather than just sticking the first piece you see into your trolley – and bear in mind that Oriental supermarkets tend to be an excellent and good value source of frozen seafood in particular.

When choosing fish and shellfish, always have sustainability in mind: the Marine Conservation Society website is a good place to check the status of whatever's on your list, and offers a handy list of good alternatives should it fall foul of their guidelines. I've developed a real fondness for gurnard and pollack, and would now choose them over their pricier rivals, but if there's something I haven't heard of on the slab, then I'll generally give it a try instead. After all, when it comes to variety, there are always plenty more fish in the sea.

Perfect
Calamari

I know there are still sad, benighted souls out there who haven't warmed to squid, and my heart goes out to them, really it does. That sweet, firm flesh, the way the tentacles crisp up obligingly in the heat . . . oh sorry, was it the t-word that put you off?

Admittedly, the squid is a beast that needs to be prepared with care: either slow-cooked until meltingly tender, or flash-fried to hot and crunchy – anything in between and you'll still be chewing when they bring the bill. Calamari, obviously, fall into the second camp, and are quite possibly the best thing you can eat with a cold beer at a beach bar. Or, indeed, at home with a cold beer, dreaming of beach bars.

Tiny squidlets, fried whole, are annoyingly hard to get hold of in this country – if you're using the bigger sort, then freezing them first will help to keep them tender, although they'll probably have been frozen for transport anyway, so do check.

You can also help your squid along the path to perfection, by marinating them in milk, which softens them slightly. (Squid soaked in milk will also have a browner, slightly sweeter batter, which can't be a bad thing either.)

Most calamari recipes differ only in the coating, from Marcella Hazan's simple plain flour to Nigel Slater's egg and mineral water tempura batter. I found the latter a little too heavy and voluminous, while Nigella's cornflour and semolina was too gritty for my liking.

She's on to something with the cornflour though: after playing around with Mitch Tonks' superfine '00' flour and cornflour mixture, I decided that it's this that makes his calamari so deliciously light. Patting the rings dryish, but not as completely as Mark Bittman suggests in the *New York Times*, helps that batter to stick.

You can add any seasonings you fancy — but after experimenting I concluded that all the squid really needs is salt.

Sadly, although I've had a go at shallow-frying the calamari, turning them midway as Marcella suggests proves a hazardous exercise — better to embrace the inevitable and deep-fry them. Don't overcrowd the pan though, or they'll steam rather than fry, and you'll lose that delectable crispness which is the whole point of the exercise.

People seem to like a squeeze of lemon, but for me, you can't beat a really garlicky bowl of mayonnaise or aioli for dipping — happily, many of the same people who can't stand suckers also run a bit shy of excessive garlic too, so with any luck you won't have to share that either.

Serves 4 as a starter, 2 as a main course

400g cleaned squid, tentacles and all
Milk, to cover
4 tablespoons cornflour

4 tablespoons plain flour
1 teaspoon salt
Sunflower, vegetable or groundnut oil, to cook
Salt flakes, to serve
Lemon wedges or aioli, to serve
  (optional – see page 80 for a quick aioli recipe)

1. Separate the tentacles from the squid, and cut the bodies into thick rings, about 1cm wide, and large triangles. Use a sharp knife to score the triangles lightly with a criss-cross pattern. Put the pieces and tentacles into a bowl and cover with milk, then cover and refrigerate for up to 8 hours (even 30 minutes is better than nothing).

2. When you're ready to cook, combine the flours and salt in a shallow container. Fill a large, heavy-based pan a third full with oil and heat over a medium-high flame until a pinch of flour sizzles when it hits the oil.

3. Drain the squid well, perfunctorily pat dry with kitchen paper, then drag each piece through the flour and shake off the excess.

4. Fry the pieces in batches for about a minute or so, until crisp, and slightly golden. Drain on to kitchen paper, sprinkle with salt flakes, and serve each batch as soon as it's ready, with lemon wedges or aioli.

Perfect
Ceviche

*O*n the face of it, it's little surprise that ceviche has taken a while to catch on outside its Latin American homeland. Raw fish, marinated in citrus juice and chilli, doesn't even have the immediate appeal of sushi, with its familiar rice, and that happy disguise of soy and wasabi which means you can look all cosmopolitan without tasting anything the slightest bit fishy. Ceviche, by contrast, is a little bit more uncompromising — sure, in Ecuador they often add tomato sauce, while in Central America it comes with tacos or tostadas, but essentially, it's all still bits of raw fish.

The effect of that citrus juice marinade on said raw fish is quite extraordinary, however: the flesh turns opaque, the texture firms, yet the flavours remain bright and zingy. It's the perfect summer lunch — and, if such things are of interest, remarkably low in calories too.

Even in South America, there's no particular species that's earmarked for ceviche: it makes sense to use whatever's available locally. Henrietta Clancy, chef at the wonderfully named Peruvian pop-up The Last Days of Pisco, experimented with a number of different species before settling on sea bass — unlike more delicate white fish, it doesn't fall apart or become rubbery in the marinade, and she tells me it's the closest thing to the tilapia she enjoyed so much in Peru.

To help the texture, I've cut the fish into largeish chunks — slicing it thinly, as *olive* magazine suggests, gives a boringly uniform texture, while dicing creates a pleasing contrast between the 'cooked', citrussy outer layer, and the raw, squidgy middle.

You can also adjust the consistency by varying the marinating time: Tom Aikens serves his right away, which gives it a sashimi-like quality, while the *River Cottage Fish Book* suggests leaving it for a 'minimum of an hour and a maximum of 12 hours'. After 4 hours, I abandoned the experiment: the fish is chalky and dry.

Henrietta tells me she prefers a shorter gap, to maximize the contrast 'between what your dish tastes like at the beginning of the meal compared to what you get at the end'; 10 minutes feels about right to me, but play about until you find your perfect point. Whatever you decide, salting the fish before marinating seems to help the flavours marry better.

The limes in this country tend to be less sweet than those in South America, so to try and recreate the authentic flavour I've used a mixture of lime and orange juice. It's also vital to be generous with the juice so you get a good spoonful along with the fish. (Peruvians apparently drink the leftover juices after they've finished the ceviche — surely a hangover cure in the do-or-die category.)

It's well worth hunting down the aji amarillo chilli online: the fruity, almost pineappley flavour is quite different to any other variety I've tried, though a bird's-eye will do the job at adding heat and colour if you've left it a bit late. Finely chopped red onion provides sweetness; I like to soak it briefly in iced water as Martin

Morales, the man behind the aptly named Ceviche restaurant, suggests to prevent it from overpowering the other flavours on the plate.

Fresh coriander adds a certain herbaceousness — and if you're feeling really adventurous, be daring and stick in a pinch of mixed peel, as Clancy does in some of her recipes. Yes, the stuff you put in your Christmas cake — trust me on this one.

Serves 2

> ½ a red onion, finely chopped
> iced water
> 250g skinless and boneless sea bass or sea bream fillets
> ½ teaspoon salt, plus extra to season
> Juice of 4 limes
> Juice of ½ an orange
> 1 red chilli, shredded, or
>   1 teaspoon aji amarillo paste
> A small bunch of coriander, roughly chopped

1. Soak the finely chopped onion in iced water for 5 minutes, then drain well and put on kitchen paper to dry.
2. Rub the fish with the salt and cut it into 1.5–2cm cubes. Leave for a minute. Add the citrus juices and the shredded chilli or paste, toss together and leave to marinate for 10 minutes. Check the seasoning and tweak if necessary.
3. Divide the fish and marinade between bowls, scatter with chopped coriander, and serve immediately.

Perfect
Smoked Mackerel Pâté

We're always being told how healthy oily fish are for us, but for some reason, they have a bad rep — too fishy, apparently, which is an odd accusation to level at a fish. Anyway, this recipe, one of my mum's favourites, is entry-level mackerel, the risky gateway to increased consumption of omega-3 oils and their super healthy ilk.

You need hot-smoked fish: the cold-smoked sort is too delicate, and making it into a pâté would be a crime. Add this to cream cheese — Delia gets too exotic with her grainy ricotta, and David Cameron (yes, *that* David Cameron)'s homely cottage cheese recipe, which he's submitted to a number of charity collections, is weirdly lumpy.

Cheeseless recipes, like those from the *River Cottage Fish Book* and Matt Tebutt, are too emphatically mackerelly to eat in any quantity. Cream cheese, favoured by no lesser person than my mum herself, provides the silkiest of textures.

To stop the pâté becoming claggy, something more liquid is needed, and preferably also tangy to cut the richness, like Delia Smith's sour cream, or the River Cottage boys' crème fraîche; *Country Life* magazine's double cream is far too bland for the task.

I must salute mackerel: it's a rare fish that stands up so well to spice. Cameron goes for Tabasco, and Delia for cayenne, but I've decided to add both heat and flavour with fresh horseradish: cleaner than the creamed sort, and a brilliant pairing with the smoke.

Dill is another obvious match: the sweet, aniseedy flavour works wonderfully with both the oily fish and the heat of the horseradish — it's not an essential, but it does look pretty (and let's face it, a dish that, unadorned, has a tendency to look a bit like a bowl of Polyfilla can use all the help it can get in that direction).

I've also left a few flakes of fish whole for texture — and to remind everyone that there is mackerel in there, and actually it's really rather nice.

Delicious served on rye bread, or crisp toast, preferably with a nice watercress salad and some pickled capers or beetroot for that authentic Scandi feel.

Serves 4

3 hot-smoked mackerel fillets
150g cream cheese
100g crème fraîche
3 teaspoons freshly grated horseradish
Lemon, to squeeze
A small handful of dill, finely chopped

1. Peel the skin from the mackerel fillets and do a quick check for any rogue bones. Flake three-quarters of the fish into a food

processor along with the cheese, crème fraîche and grated horseradish and whiz until smooth.

2. Add a generous grinding of black pepper, and lemon juice to taste, check the seasoning, then fold through the dill and the remaining flakes of fish. Serve with rye bread or crisp toast.

Perfect
Battered Fish

As long as the fish isn't dry or, of course, off, then I'll forgive many things for a light, yet crunchy savoury coating, preferably standing proud on its own solid little batter legs. Utter heaven with well-salted, really potatoey chips, and a decent helping of mushy peas.

The choice of fish, therefore, is up to you — pollock, gurnard (go beyond the usual boring cod and haddock and you'll not only get points for sustainability, but you might just find a new favourite), skin-on, skin-off depending on your degree of northernness — what really matters is getting some air into the batter.

This is usually done in two ways: by adding a raising agent like yeast or baking powder to the batter, or by including something carbonated, like beer or sparkling water. Using one or the other seems to give disappointing results: Rick Stein's baking powder and still water gives a crisp, but quite solid coating, while the River Cottage plain flour and beer mixture is crunchy, dry and dense, though the beer supplies a good flavour.

Trish Hilferty, gastropub legend, uses fresh yeast, which gives her batter a quite incredible volume, but it seems to soak up more oil than the others. Simon Hopkinson's secret weapon is potato flour, which, he claims, 'retains its crispness like no other' — but actually I find it just gives the batter a weirdly grainy texture. In fact, there's no need to add anything more than plain flour, beer and baking powder — eggs and milk are both so rich that the fish can't compete on flavour.

Gary Rhodes explains that it's important that the batter is thick, 'almost too thick', to ensure that as the fish cooks, the batter billows obligingly around it. His self-raising flour and lager combination gives the lightest of results of all the recipes I try — and I'm pleased to note there's no need to rest it before use, as many of the other recipes suggest. Indeed, it seems counter-intuitive: allowing a Yorkshire pudding to stand before baking helps the flour absorb the liquid, but here we want to keep the mixture as effervescent as possible to help it rise, and as any fool knows, a fizzy drink left to stand will quickly become a flat one.

The best tip I get, however, comes from Matthew Silk, co-owner of 149 in Bridlington, winner of the Fish & Chip Shop of the Year 2011, who reckons the batter must be 'seriously cold, say 6°C, so that when it hits the fat at 185°C the reaction happens'. He's right: chilling the ingredients beforehand gives the batter an almost ethereally light texture.

I'd strongly urge you to fry the fish in dripping if you're prepared to leave the windows open for the rest of the day: the rich flavour is absolutely peerless. Otherwise, vegetable oil gives a pretty decent result at less risk to your soft furnishings — but, personally, I'd happily sacrifice a set of curtains for really good fish and chips.

Serves 4

Dripping or oil, for frying
3 teaspoons baking powder
400g plain flour, put in the freezer
for 15 minutes before using
½ teaspoon salt
550ml very cold beer
4 pieces of sustainable white fish (I used pollock)

1. Heat the fat in a deep-fat fryer or a chip pan to 185°C.
2. Whisk the baking powder into the chilled flour with the salt, then, working quickly, whisk in the cold beer to make a thick paste. This all needs to be done just before you cook the fish.
3. Place the bowl of batter next to the fryer or pan. Prepare a plate lined with kitchen paper.
4. Dip each piece of fish into the batter to coat, then carefully lower it into the hot fat and agitate the frying basket to prevent the fish sticking to it. (This will also give the batter a more craggily interesting texture.) Cook one or two pieces at a time: don't overcrowd the fryer or the fish will steam.
5. Cook the fish for about 4–6 minutes, depending on size, keeping an eye on it; it should be crisp and golden when ready. Lift out of the fat and drain on kitchen paper, then serve as quickly as possible.

Perfect
Crabcakes

*C*learly Americans don't have the monopoly on crabcakes — they make a mighty fine spicy version in Thailand, for example — but nowhere are they more revered than the Eastern Seaboard. Specifically Maryland, as watchers of *The Wire* will testify: a box is even used as a bribe in the first season of the gritty Baltimore-based drama. In Maryland, they rate their cakes on the quantity of crustacean stuffed in there — only the barest amount of 'filler' is permitted as mortar for the chunks of crab.

We also produce great crab in this country — blue crabs, the American connoisseur's crustacean of choice, aren't easy to find (indeed, they've only been sighted twice in British waters), but native brown and spider crabs are quite as delicious, and the great thing about the crabcake is that it's more crab than cake, so you'll really be able to taste them.

Unfortunately the picked variety is too finely shredded to work in a cake, and falls apart in the pan, so unless you get lucky and find great big lumps of crab for sale, you'll probably need to do the excavation yourself. Get the biggest beast you can find, and concentrate on the claws, where the largest bits of white meat hang out: blue crabs don't have the rich brown meat we're used to here, so this is a white-meat only affair I'm afraid. As a last resort, imported tinned lump crabmeat isn't a bad substitute, although the flavour is inevitably inferior.

Obviously some filler is needed to bind those lumps together, and these fall into two main camps: dry and liquid.

A dry binder is more popular for good reason: it not only makes the cake lighter, but helps it hold together in the pan. Breadcrumbs, as used by James Beard and the Old Bay seasoning company (who have featured a crabcake recipe on their iconic yellow tin for as long as anyone can remember), prove preferable to *Saveur* magazine's crushed crackers, and Mark Bittman's flour, which are both a bit soggy in comparison.

I've kept the flavourings quite austere: mustard is almost mandatory (dry powder adds heat without the slight vinegariness of the prepared sort), but the classic Old Bay is too pungent for my taste. Instead I've picked out elements of it: hot paprika, hot pepper and sweet nutmeg which, although the recipe is a secret, is definitely in there somewhere. I've also added some fresh parsley, which gives colour and a peppery freshness to the cakes.

You could leave your crabcakes uncoated, but this seems a shame: a crunchy crust makes a fine contrast to the soft crabmeat inside. Breadcrumbs stray too close to fishcake territory for my liking: James Beard's simple dredging of flour is less obtrusive, and just as effective.

Grilled crabcakes, offered by many restaurants as a sop to the health-conscious, lack the crisp crust of the fried versions — you don't need much oil here, and a flavourless vegetable variety works perfectly. Lard, butter and extra virgin olive oil all spoil the flavour of the crab, which is, after all, the whole point here.

Eat hot from the pan, with as little ceremony as possible.

Makes 4

40g breadcrumbs
½ teaspoon mustard powder
½ teaspoon salt
¼ teaspoon white pepper
A pinch of nutmeg
A pinch of paprika
2 tablespoons chopped parsley
250g white crabmeat, in chunks
1 egg, beaten
Flour, to coat
Vegetable oil, to cook
Lemon wedges, to serve

1. Put the breadcrumbs, mustard powder, seasoning, spices and chopped parsley into a bowl and stir well to combine. Add the chunks of crab and stir gently so they're evenly distributed, being careful not to break them up too much.
2. Gradually add the beaten egg until you have a firm mixture that you can form into cakes without too much trouble.
3. Divide the mix into 4, and shape each into a flat cake. Put a little flour in a flat dish, season it lightly and turn the crabcakes in it to coat. Chill them for 30 minutes, covered.
4. Cover the bottom of a frying pan with a shallow layer of oil and put over a medium-high heat. Cook the crabcakes for about 4 minutes on each side, turning carefully, until crisp and golden all over. Serve immediately, with lemon wedges.

Perfect
Potted Shrimp

*F*ood historian Bee Wilson describes potting as the more elegant descendant of the pie, in which the air-excluding pastry crust ('medieval clingfilm' as she wonderfully has it) has been replaced by a more tempting spiced butter. These days, we have much less need to preserve our food, but the practice lingers – and for good reason: it's utterly delicious.

Originally, potted foods would have been expected to last in challenging conditions – Meg Dods claims in her 1826 *Housewife's Manual* that game 'to be sent to distant places' would keep for a month if potted according to her instructions – so butter would have been clarified, to stop it going rancid. (Clarifying butter involves heating and straining it to remove the milk solids – as well as, according to Elizabeth David, expelling air so it forms a more robust seal.) Although the process is a little more complicated than straightforward melted butter, the results are well worth it, even if they'll be devoured within the hour: a thick yellow cork of clarified butter is an attractive sight, and boasts a smoother texture and silkier flavour than the ordinary stuff.

Many recipes call for you to heat the shrimps in the butter (Mrs Beeton simmers the poor things for 15 minutes, by which time they could be sold as an appetite-suppressing gum) but, as they're usually sold cooked these days, this seems unnecessary. Texture-wise, I'm with Mark Hix: the less heat they see the better.

I've kept the spicing quite delicate, in a nod to tradition: cloves seem too sweet, Tabasco and cayenne pepper too hot (though the latter makes a pretty topping), and as for the Ballymaloe garlic and thyme — Meg Dods would be horrified.

Sweet mace and subtle white pepper are quite sufficient, with just a little lemon juice to balance out the richness of the butter — and Mark Hix's trump card, a hint of Gentleman's Relish anchovy paste, as used at Scott's of Mayfair. The pairing of salty fish and sweet shrimp is a stroke of rare genius: no wonder James Bond, a spy of impeccable taste, was such a fan. And a recommendation from 007 is definitely good enough for me.

Serves 4

200g unsalted butter
Juice of ¼ of a lemon
¼ teaspoon ground mace
¼ teaspoon white pepper
½ teaspoon anchovy paste or
    Gentleman's Relish
200g cooked and peeled brown shrimps
Cayenne pepper, to serve

1. Put the butter in a pan over a gentle heat to melt, and then allow to simmer until you spot the first dark flecks on the bottom — watch it carefully, or it will burn. Strain it

through some butter muslin, or two sheets of kitchen roll, into a jug.

2. Wipe out the pan, and pour in two-thirds of the clarified butter. Add the lemon juice, mace, pepper, anchovy paste and a pinch of salt and allow to simmer very gently for 5 minutes, then take off the heat and leave to cool but not set.

3. Divide the shrimps between 4 ramekins, pressing them in tightly. When the spiced butter is just warm, but still liquid, divide it between the ramekins and put them into the fridge to set.

4. Once solid, pour over the remainder of the clarified butter and return to the fridge to set. Top with a sprinkle of cayenne pepper for colour, and serve with a lot of hot toast.

CHAPTER 5

Meat

*T*hough I'd never want to give up the greasy joys of burgers, or the sensual pleasures of slow-cooked mutton curry, I don't, truth be told, eat that much meat. (Or, at least, I don't when I'm not testing seven steak and ale pie recipes for the greater good, or pondering the thorny problem of how on earth to keep garlic butter inside a chicken Kiev.) By inclination, I'd probably only eat meat about twice a week. But when I do, I like to make the most of it.

As you'll see, that doesn't mean treating yourself to the fancy bits – with the exception of the aforementioned Kievs, and beef Wellington, almost all the recipes in this chapter make use of more economical cuts of meat. They may demand a little more skill in the cooking department, but the rewards are infinite: I love the way a slow-simmered piece of beef shin melts into its gravy, or tearing into the juicy succulence of a slightly chewy chicken thigh. Anyone can sear a rump steak in a hot pan so it's halfway decent, but making the most of stewing steak is rather more of an art, albeit an easy one to master once you realize a few basic principles.

For a start, much of that classic 'meaty' flavour is thanks to what's called the Maillard reaction – the scientific process responsible for the colour and flavour of toasted bread, chocolate, dark beer and, yes, roasted meat. Food scientist Harold McGee explains how the sugars in these foodstuffs react with amino acids when heated to produce 'a brown colouration and full, intense flavour' – the diagrams are all in his book *McGee on Food and Cooking*, but for these purposes, all you need to remember is that browning meat is a very good idea, even if you're going to go on to cook it very slowly and gently.

The benefits of so doing are the other thing I think it's very important that you know before we get cooking. To keep the meat as tender and juicy as possible, it should ideally be heated no higher than 60°C for very brief periods of time. Unfortunately, meat isn't all simple muscle – there's chewy collagen too, which won't dissolve into wobbly, unctuous gelatine below 70°C, and indeed requires prolonged exposure to such a heat in order to break down at all.

All meat cooking, then, is to some extent a compromise, the method dependent on the bit in question – but as it's the rich, melting gelatine that makes stews and casseroles and dishes like pulled pork quite so obscenely delicious, wherever possible I favour collagen-rich cuts, patiently simmered until they fall apart under the fork. No blandly tender fillet could ever hope to compete.

The other benefit of going for the less glamorous bits, the ox tails and lamb breasts of this world, is that they're relatively cheap, which means that, even if you're on a tight budget, you should be able to afford a better-quality piece than would be possible if you were buying the boring stuff.

Organic is usually a good indicator of careful, slow rearing, with ample space to breathe, but it's not the be-all and end-all: many small producers at farmers' markets, or who supply butchers, take just as much trouble over their animals without jumping through the hoops of certification. I know not everyone has such a market, or even a decent butcher, within easy reach, but good meat is easily available online, and, increasingly I must concede, in many supermarkets. If the provenance isn't clear on the packaging, then ask.

Lastly, always bring your meat to room temperature before cooking, except where specified, or it will bring the temperature of the pan or dish down, which sort of defeats the point. Oh, and remember, most things are enhanced by a good dollop of English mustard.

Perfect
Steak and Kidney Pudding

*T*he British can be justly proud of the pudding. Done well, as it so rarely is these days, it's a marvellous combination of rich and delicate – a meaty, savoury interior, steamed to perfection in its light, spongy pastry jacket, complete with the kind of gravy that can make even grown men a little damp around the eye.

But traditional puddings are thin on the ground these days, even on pub menus – sad, yes, but also an excellent reason to make your own. People seem to think that steaming anything more complicated than a head of broccoli is hard work, but in fact, as long as you remember to keep topping up the water during ad breaks, making your own pudding is gratifyingly easy.

Steak and kidney is the classic combination, although those who are still trying to suppress a smile of relief at every bite that turns out to be the former rather than the latter should bear in mind the myriad alternative options (including a rather lovely vegetarian leek pudding from the north-east). That said, if you use veal or lamb's kidney, rather than Constance Spry or Jane Grigson's ox variety, it does tend to fade obligingly into the background, providing only a hint of offaly excitement – take your pick according to preference.

The beef, meanwhile, should be neck or chuck: something with a good amount of sinew to break down during cooking. Mrs Beeton extravagantly calls for rump steak, but it turned out to be a mistaken extravagance, dry and disappointing.

The pastry must, of course, be suet — the creamy fat encasing the kidneys (a pleasing synergy) has a relatively high melting point, which means the pastry shell has already set by the time it melts away, leaving only a rash of tiny bubbles in its place. This is why something that sounds so heavy (suet pastry, a great lump of an idea) is actually so remarkably light.

If you can get the fresh stuff, which butchers will be able to order in for you, then it gives a better flavour than the dried pellets in jaunty coloured boxes. I also add mustard powder and chopped thyme to make it even more delicious.

Braising the meat before adding it to the pastry not only gives your gravy a better flavour, but also prevents the singularly unattractive grey, claggy look that bedevils Constance Spry's filling. She's also rather sparse in her flavourings — rationing's over now, and I feel confident that we're allowed to use stock and stout rather than plain old water to make a gravy, although Jane Grigson's red wine, and Gary Rhodes' garlic, may well be a step too far in the name of progress; this remains a very British dish. Which doesn't mean you have to serve it with over-boiled vegetables — unless you really want to.

Serves 4

1½ tablespoons beef dripping or oil, to cook
1 onion, thinly sliced
1 carrot, peeled and diced
1 bay leaf
A small bunch of thyme, leaves picked
1 tablespoon plain flour
400g chuck or stewing steak, cut into chunks
150g rose veal kidney
150ml stout
150ml beef stock

For the pastry
250g plain flour
2 teaspoons baking powder
¼ teaspoon salt
½ teaspoon English mustard powder
125g chopped suet
3 sprigs of fresh thyme, leaves finely chopped
Oil, to grease

1. Melt the dripping in a large, heavy-based pan over a medium heat and cook the onions and carrots along with the herbs until they are beginning to caramelize. Remove them from the pan and set aside.

2. Season the flour well, and toss the steak and kidney in it to coat. Add more fat to the pan if necessary, then brown the meat in batches: if you do it all at once, it will steam in its own juices.

3. Pour in the stout and scrape any beefy floury bits from the bottom of the pan, then add the stock, the vegetables and all the

meat. Bring the liquid to a simmer, partially cover and simmer gently for 1¾ hours, until the steak is very tender. Season to taste and allow to cool.

4. Two hours before you want to eat, sift the flour and baking powder into a mixing bowl and add the salt and mustard powder. Rub in the suet briefly to mix, then add the thyme and enough cold water to make it into a firm dough. Set a quarter of the dough aside, then roll out the rest on a lightly floured surface to about 0.5cm thick. Generously grease a 1 litre pudding basin and line with the pastry, being careful not to stretch it too much.

5. Fill the pastry-lined bowl with meat and gravy, stopping about 2cm from the top, then roll out the rest of the pastry to make a lid and seal it on with a little cold water. Cover the basin with foil, leaving enough slack for the pastry to rise, and fashion a handle out of string to lift the basin out of the water when required.

6. Put the pudding into a large pan half-filled with boiling water, cover and simmer for 1½ hours, checking the water level regularly and topping up as necessary. Turn out and serve immediately.

Perfect
Steak and Ale Pie

What a noble thing is the pie. Everyone, with the puzzling exception of my own mother, loves plunging through that pastry portal to discover the riches that lie beneath — and whether that's cheese and potato, apple and blackberry, or, as here, a classic meat and gravy number, the pie rarely disappoints.

The most important thing to bear in mind about steak and ale pie is that you shouldn't use steak. Or at least, not the kind generally recommended for pies — stewing, braising and chuck steak all came out tough in my experiments.

Much better were the shin beef recommended by Hugh Fearnley-Whittingstall and the ox cheek and ox tail deployed by the London steak restaurant Hawksmoor in their cookbook: flavoursome, rich, and yes, melt in the mouth. Generously-sized chunks of bacon add another layer of smoky flavour (lest there be any remaining doubt, this is not a dinner for dieters).

I'm not keen on the slimy mushrooms which seem bafflingly common in pie recipes, or indeed on the classic, but inevitably mushy carrots, but baby onions make the cut, adding a little sweetness to what is otherwise a defiantly savoury dish.

For the gravy, ale is obviously non-negotiable, although be sure to go for a full-bodied, slightly sweeter variety — as beer writer Melissa Cole explains, using just any old stout can make your gravy bitter. You could top it up with water, but I think the Hairy Bikers' beef stock gives a more satisfyingly meaty result.

And then, despite what I've said about the ale, I've added some cocoa powder, like chef Tom Norrington-Davies — unless you're a super-taster you'll be hard pressed to identify it in the finished gravy, but somehow it rounds things off perfectly.

Finally, to top the dish, I've eschewed the usual featherlight puff in favour of a crumbly suet version: crisp on top, soft, almost doughy beneath, and the perfect thing for soaking up all that lovely gravy. I don't, unlike Hugh, believe it's necessary to line the entire dish with the stuff, because I'm not keen on the gumminess that lurks at the bottom, but if you feel strongly that a pie ought to be encased in pastry to be worthy of the name, by all means make double the quantity and do so. Serve with steamed greens, as a nod to a balanced diet.

Serves 4

A large chunk of dripping
700g boneless beef shin or ox cheek,
    cut into large chunks
20g plain flour, seasoned
200g smoked bacon lardons
225g whole baby onions
400ml sweetish dark ale

400ml beef stock
4 sprigs of thyme, leaves roughly chopped
I bay leaf
I tablespoon dark muscovado sugar
I teaspoon red wine vinegar
I teaspoon cocoa

For the pastry
400g plain flour, plus extra to dust
I teaspoon baking powder
2 teaspoons mustard powder (optional)
½ teaspoon salt
175g suet (or chilled, grated bone
   marrow if you have it)
Iced water
A little milk, to glaze

1. Preheat the oven to 170°C/fan 150°C/gas 3. Melt a generous knob of dripping in a large frying pan over a high heat, and toss the chunks of beef in seasoned flour to coat. Sear it in batches, taking care not to overcrowd the pan, until well browned. Transfer to an ovenproof casserole once done.

2. Reduce the heat a little, and add the lardons and the onions to the pan. Cook until the bacon fat begins to melt, and the onions are brown on all sides, then tip them into the casserole along with any fat and juices.

3. Pour a glug of ale into the frying pan and bring it to a simmer, scraping the bottom to dislodge any bits, then pour the whole lot into the casserole along with the meat. Add the remaining ale, the stock, herbs, sugar, vinegar and cocoa and bring it all to a simmer.

4. Cover the dish and bake for 2¼ hours, then uncover and cook, stirring occasionally, for another 1½ hours, until the meat is tender and almost falling apart (it will cook further in the pie). Allow to cool to room temperature.

5. Meanwhile, make the pastry. Mix the flour, baking powder and mustard powder in a bowl with ½ teaspoon of salt. Stir in the fat, then add just enough iced water to make a dough. Shape into a disc, wrap in clingfilm and chill for at least an hour.

6. Preheat the oven to 190°C/fan 170°C/gas 5. Spoon the filling into a dish, and roll out the pastry on a lightly floured surface to about 1cm thick. Wet the rim of the pie dish, then place the pastry over the filling, pushing down around the edge to seal. Cut a hole in the middle to let the steam out. Brush with a little milk and bake for about 50 minutes, until golden.

Perfect
Beef Stew and Dumplings

Stew and dumplings reeks of institutional catering, when in fact, done well, it's one of the most comforting dishes around.

Stewing steak, despite the name, is not the best cut to use here – Delia Smith hits the nail on the head when she confesses that for years she was put off shin by its unattractive appearance, until she realized all the stuff that looked so off-putting would melt during cooking, adding flavour and richness to the gravy. 'Now,' she says in her *Complete Cookery Course*, 'for an old-fashioned brown stew, I wouldn't use anything else.' And on the matter of 'brown stew', Delia knows best – it may take longer to cook, but shin falls apart under the fork, and gives a gorgeously unctuous character to the surrounding sauce.

You could make that sauce with water, as recommended by *Francatelli's Plain Cookery Book for the Working Classes* (1852), but frankly, the working classes deserve better in the form of stock and stout – they both go brilliantly with beef (see also steak and kidney pudding, and steak and ale pie), to produce what is, in my opinion, an unbeatable gravy. If you can find what used to be known as 'milk stout', made in Britain, the slight sweetness gives a more well-rounded result than the ubiquitous Irish variety. Thicken the gravy with a little flour to give it a respectably robust consistency.

Add potatoes to the pot if you like, but I think that, together with the dumplings, they're carb overload. Instead I've used sliced onions, carrots and baby turnips for sweetness, the latter two added towards the end of cooking, so they keep their texture. Mushy vegetables are almost as unwelcome in a stew as gristle.

Lastly, keep an eye on the temperature. You need to cook the meat slowly, so it isn't tough, but bear in mind it still needs to bubble — as Harold McGee (him again) explains in his book *The Curious Cook*, strands of beef collagen don't even begin to unravel until the temperature gets above 60°C, and it needs to be 20° higher for them to dissolve into gelatine 'in any appreciable quantities'. In other words, to turn chewy meat into something really delicious, keep your stew hot, but not too hot: a gentle simmer is what you're after.

Apart from that, it can be happily left to its own devices for a couple of hours — bear in mind that like many slow-cooked dishes, this stew is even better reheated, which makes it the ideal thing to prepare ahead for guests. And who says you can't serve stew and dumplings at a dinner party anyway?

Serves 4—6

800g shin of beef
2 tablespoons flour, seasoned with salt and pepper
Beef dripping, butter or oil, to cook
2 onions, sliced
300ml beef stock
300ml stout, preferably British milk stout
1 bay leaf
3 sprigs of thyme

2 carrots, peeled and cut into chunky slices
2 small turnips, peeled and cut into chunks

For the dumplings
100g plain flour
1 teaspoon baking powder
50g suet
A small bunch of chives and parsley,
    finely chopped

1. Trim any outer sinew off the beef and cut it into large chunks.
   Coat these with the seasoned flour.
2. Heat a heavy-bottomed casserole or large pan on a medium heat
   and add a knob of dripping or butter, or a couple of tablespoons
   of oil if you prefer. Brown the meat well in batches — be careful
   not to overcrowd the pan, or it will boil in its own juices —
   adding more fat if necessary, then transfer the pieces to a bowl.
   Scrape the bottom of the pan regularly to prevent any crusty bits
   from burning.
3. Add some more fat to the pan and fry the onions until soft and
   beginning to brown. Put these into the same bowl as the beef,
   and then pour a little stock into the pan and scrape the bottom
   to deglaze it. Put back the beef and onions, pour in the rest of
   the stock and the stout, season, and top with the herbs. Bring to
   the boil, then partially cover, turn down the heat to a gentle
   simmer, and cook for 2 hours.
4. Add the carrots and turnips to the pan, and leave to simmer for
   about another hour, checking occasionally, until the meat is
   tender enough to cut with a spoon. Leave to cool, overnight if
   possible (this will improve the flavour), then remove any
   solidified fat from the top and bring the stew to a simmer.

5. Meanwhile, make the dumplings by sifting the flour into a bowl. Add the rest of the ingredients and just enough cold water to make a dough. Roll this into 6 round dumplings and add these to the top of the stew. Partially cover again and simmer for 25 minutes, until the dumplings are cooked through, then check the seasoning of the gravy, and serve.

Perfect
Beef Wellington

I'd always assumed this was a dish created in honour of the great duke's famous victory at Waterloo – but in fact, it seems that the name at least is almost certainly a twentieth-century invention, awarded to mark the dish's resemblance to a brown, shiny wellington boot. Rather less glamorous, isn't it?

The concept of cooking a piece of meat in a pastry case to keep it moist is much older, however – and whatever the history, this is one dinner party classic in sore need of a revival. Not only does it look and taste impressive (who doesn't love putting a great big boot on the table?) but it's surprisingly simple to prepare, and can be done ahead of time, making it perfect for the host who'd actually like to spend some time with their guests. Not always a given, I'll admit.

That said, it doesn't come cheap: fillet of beef is sadly non-negotiable – you need its buttery softness for the dish to work. Fortunately, however, you don't need pâté de foie gras (far too overpowering for the poor beef), or Parma ham, or any of the other expensive ingredients some chefs stick in.

Truffles are similarly de trop; though mushrooms are an integral part of the dish, a simple porcini duxelles, with a little Madeira for sweetness (the duke was, apparently, a fan) and double cream as a nod to the special occasion, is quite sufficient. (You can use fresh chestnut or field mushrooms if you prefer, but I think the meaty flavour of dried porcini works best with the beef.)

Chopped shallot, meanwhile, adds a subtle sweetness — Delia uses onion instead, which gives a puzzlingly pasty-like quality to her Wellington, making it about as posh as an old pair of galoshes.

The pastry should be puff — I tried a flaky alternative as suggested by *The Prawn Cocktail Years*, but found it too heavy for this rather refined dish. Unless you're weighed down with time and a yen to spend a morning chilling, folding and rolling, one of the excellent all-butter ready-made varieties will do you proud. (You can salve your conscience by decorating it with poppy seeds instead, just to make it look even less like its namesake.)

Traditionally, the pastry would be lined with crêpes, to soak up the meat juices and stop it going soggy, but as Simon Hopkinson and Lindsey Bareham observe, 'if the pastry is good and thin, buttery and rich, nothing is nicer than a meat-soaked crust', and James Martin's pancakes just add an unnecessary layer of stodge.

Add some spinach to the filling if you like, as Madalene Bonvini-Hamel of the British Larder does, but though it looks pretty, I prefer to serve greens on the side in more generous portions. The beauty of the Wellington is in its simplicity.

Serves 4

10g dried porcini mushrooms
50g butter
2 shallots, finely chopped
300g mixed mushrooms
   (e.g. chestnut, oyster, shiitake, flat black),
   roughly chopped or torn
1 sprig of thyme, leaves picked
200ml Madeira
2 tablespoons double cream
1 tablespoon vegetable oil
500g beef fillet
250g all-butter puff pastry
1 egg, beaten, to glaze
1 tablespoon poppy seeds

1. Soak the dried porcini in 150ml of boiling water for 20 minutes, then, reserving the soaking water, squeeze them out and finely chop.
2. Meanwhile, melt the butter in a frying pan over a medium heat and cook the shallots until pale golden. Add the mixed mushrooms, porcini and thyme to the pan and cook until the mushrooms have softened. Pour in 150ml of Madeira, season, turn up the heat and cook until the wine has all but evaporated. Scoop three-quarters of the mixture into a bowl. Mix in the double cream, taste for seasoning, and set aside.
3. Preheat the oven, and a flat baking sheet, to 220°C/fan 200°C/ gas 7. Heat the oil in a frying pan over a high heat and, when smoking, add the fillet and sear briefly on all sides until well

browned and crusted. Season generously and allow to cool. Don't wash the pan yet — you'll need it for making the sauce.

4. Roll out the pastry to a rectangle measuring a few centimetres wider than your fillet, and long enough to wrap it in, and 3mm thick. Brush this all over with beaten egg, then spread with the duxelles mixture. Put the beef at one end and carefully roll it up, making sure the join is on the bottom, then trim the edges and tuck them in to seal the parcel, using the tines of a fork to press the edges together. Brush with beaten egg and sprinkle with poppy seeds.

5. Put the Wellington on the hot baking sheet and bake for 30 minutes, until golden, then set aside to rest for 15 minutes.

6. Meanwhile, make the sauce. Heat the pan in which you seared the beef, pour in the remaining Madeira, and scrape the bottom to dislodge any crusty bits of meat. Add the rest of the mushrooms, plus the porcini soaking liquid, and allow the mixture to reduce slightly. Taste, season, and serve with the beef Wellington.

Perfect
Chilli con Carne

We may love chilli, but, as a nation, we haven't been particularly kind to it. Lumps of mince made fiery red with cayenne pepper, topped with kidney beans and served bursting forth from a microwaved jacket potato — hardly the proud culinary heritage so celebrated in its American homeland.

The International Chili Society, an organization devoted to the 'promotion, development and improving of the preparation and appreciation of true chili', credits the dish to south-western cattle drivers, who had to survive on what they took with them, and the raw ingredients they found along the trail. Which might, I suppose, include Nigella's tomato ketchup, but is unlikely to have taken in her cardamom pods, or Hugh Fearnley-Whittingstall's chorizo.

In this recipe, I've stripped the dish right back to its roots: meat and peppers. No tomatoes — the only recipes I find using them are British — and no cayenne, although I have kept the dubiously authentic minced meat, because, although I enjoyed Jamie's brisket, and Hugh's pork shoulder, without it, it isn't chilli to me. You won't find any lumps here though: after two and a half hours in the pot, it should almost melt in the mouth.

My spice mixture, which might seem a bit daunting if you were hoping to pick up the ingredients from the corner shop, is based on that apparently used by the long-gone Chilli Queens of San Antonio: Mexican women who once sold their highly spiced stews from street carts 'to a cadre of customers who rode in from all over the prairies to singe their tonsils'.

The coffee, meanwhile, is stolen from Jamie Oliver's American road trip — cowboys travelled on caffeine apparently, and I love the smoky, almost campfire bitterness it adds to the dish. Add sweet, charred onions and copious amounts of garlic, plus the mealy beans strictly forbidden by the Institute of Texan Cultures, and you have a meal fit for a chilli queen herself. Serve with rice, Nigella's wonderfully fluffy cornbread — or, of course, a good old jacket potato. Just call it Anglo-Texican fusion.

Serves 6—8

Beef dripping or vegetable oil, to fry
1kg minced meat
2 onions, thinly sliced
5 cloves of garlic, minced
350ml freshly brewed coffee
2 chipotle chillies
2 ancho chillies
1 teaspoon cumin seeds, toasted
1 tablespoon Mexican oregano
2 teaspoons chilli powder, or to taste
2 tablespoons dark muscovado sugar
2 fresh long green chillies
400g cooked kidney beans

1. Heat the dripping or oil in a large, heavy-bottomed pan on a high heat, then brown the mince well (to a deep brown, rather than beige) in batches, stirring regularly. Don't be tempted to do it all at once, or it won't brown properly. Remove from the pan once cooked and set aside.

2. Add the onions to the pan and stir-fry briefly, until slightly browned at the edges.

3. Turn the heat right down and add the garlic. Stir and cook until the onion has completely softened, then add the browned meat, brewed coffee, 300ml of water and a generous pinch of salt. Bring to the boil, reduce the heat again, then cover and simmer for 2 hours.

4. Meanwhile, remove the stalks and seeds from the dried chillies and discard. Grind the chillies together in a pestle and mortar, or grinder, along with a pinch of rock salt and the toasted cumin seeds. Mix in the oregano and chilli powder.

5. Add the spices to the pan along with the sugar and the whole fresh chillies, stir well and simmer, partially covered, for another 30 minutes, adding a little more water if it seems dry, or you prefer a saucier chilli.

6. Ten minutes before the end, add the drained beans, taste, and adjust the seasoning and spicing if necessary. If possible, leave overnight and reheat to serve.

Perfect
Meatballs

With apologies to Lady and the Tramp, I'd be hard pushed to describe meatballs as romantic, but there aren't many other occasions where they don't fit the bill. From our very own faggots to the Chinese lionhead variety, via Turkish koftes and Iranian sparrowheads, they're a dish with universal appeal. It's tough to pick a favourite, but, possibly thanks to those damn dogs, I'm pretty soft on the Italian variety, served with a big plate of spaghetti and what's known in America as 'red sauce'.

Beef-only meatballs are sadly dull, tasting of dripping and little else, and veal, despite claims it makes the best meatballs of all, has too delicate a flavour to stand up to such treatment. Better to do as they do in Italy, and mix in some pork for good measure.

Binding is key — there's nothing sadder than a meatball that crumbles in the pan. Egg, as used by Hugh Fearnley-Whittingstall and the *Ginger Pig Meat Book*, works wonders, but makes the finished meatballs rather dry and dense. Even just using the yolk is disappointing; far preferable to do as Angela Hartnett suggests in *Cucina* and go for breadcrumbs soaked in milk: 'the secret of making light meatballs' apparently.

Onions are a classic flavouring — I don't think you need garlic as well, although I wouldn't rule it out of the sauce — but I found classic Italian cookery bible *The Silver Spoon*'s anchovies overwhelming, and though Hugh and Angela both use Parmesan, I prefer to save it for the top. I have allowed myself one impromptu addition though: fennel seeds, which work wonderfully with the pork, and add a pleasing crunch to the cooked meatballs.

The cooking, annoying as it sounds, should be done separately; otherwise, the meatballs seem to lose their flavour to the sauce (which is fine, if you're happy to make that sacrifice: personally, I'd like both parts to taste equally fantastic). Cooked alone, they remain juicy, while also developing a tasty caramelized crust.

This is a three-pan job: one for the meatballs, one for the sauce (I'd obviously recommend the perfect tomato sauce recipe in *Perfect*), and one for the pasta. It's well worth it though, I promise.

Serves 4

> **6 tablespoons milk**
> **1 thick slice of white bread, crusts removed**
> **300g minced beef**
> **200g minced pork**
> **1 onion, finely chopped**
> **2 tablespoons finely chopped flat-leaf parsley**
> **3 teaspoons fennel seeds, toasted (optional)**
> **Olive oil, to fry**

1. Put the milk and bread into a shallow bowl and leave to soak for about 10 minutes. Meanwhile, put the other ingredients, except for the oil, into a large bowl, season generously, and mix well with your hands.
2. Use a fork to mash the bread into a milky paste and then add this to the meat and mix in well. Heat a little olive oil in a large pan over a medium-high heat and fry a pinch of the mixture until cooked through. Allow to cool slightly, then taste and adjust the seasoning of the mixture if necessary.
3. Shape the mixture into balls with damp hands – I like to make them about the size of a chocolate truffle – then add another 2 tablespoons of olive oil to the pan and fry them in batches until nicely caramelized all over. Turn down the heat and fry more gently until cooked through.
4. Serve with a tomato sauce and spaghetti.

Perfect
Jerk Chicken

*T*he international face of Caribbean cuisine (because let's face it, stew peas and hard food sound like acquired tastes), jerk, seasoned with a blend of hot peppers, sweet spices and aromatic thyme, is generally credited to the African slaves brought to the islands by their British and Spanish colonizers.

And while pork and goat are also popular candidates for the jerk treatment, if ever a meat needed a bit of help in the flavour department, it's chicken. (If you'd prefer to use something else, adjust the cooking times accordingly.) Your chicken should ideally be a good, full-flavoured bird, or it'll just end up as a vehicle for the marinade, and with the bones left in for maximum taste and succulence.

Hugh Fearnley-Whittingstall's *River Cottage Meat Book* advises taking the skin off to allow the spice to work its way into the meat, but as I think the crispy skin is one of the joys of jerk, I rub the marinade under the skin instead, as US magazine *Saveur* suggests. Be careful while doing this, though: a stray lump of chilli lurking unseen in an innocuous-looking thigh can blow your head off.

Although a dry rub is apparently 'more authentic' according to Helen Willinsky, author of *Jerk: Barbecue from Jamaica*, I found the wet variety adds more flavour, especially tangy lime juice and salty soy sauce. (If, like me, you scoff at the idea of soy in a Jamaican classic, bear in mind that it's found in 'every little one room grocery shop' on the island according to food geek site egullet.com.)

Into the soy and lime juice go fruity, fiery Scotch bonnet chillies, in a ratio of half per leg (although I find recipes which go as high as one per leg, and as low as two per 2kg of chicken, so feel free to tweak to taste), spring onions, which give a fresher flavour than the yellow sort or indeed shallots or garlic, which are also popular, woody thyme, and sweet allspice, cinnamon and nutmeg. Allspice ought to be the defining flavour, but the other sweet spices go so well with smoky unrefined sugar that I can't resist them.

The River Cottage Meat Book suggests baking the chicken before sticking it on the barbecue, which seems like a criminal waste of fuel — if the weather's foul but you must have jerk, then do the lot in the oven and finish it on a griddle pan, but otherwise, the only way is grilling.

Jerk is often cooked in foil parcels in its homeland, but this precludes the pleasure of a crisp skin, so I prefer to sear it on a hot grill, then move it to the cooler sides to cook through.

However you cook this, jerk chicken can be very little other than delicious, even if you're in Bury St Edmunds, rather than Boston Bay — but please be careful when chopping the chillies, or you won't know where you are, and frankly, you won't care. Rubber gloves are advisable.

Serves 6

1 tablespoon allspice berries
1 tablespoon black peppercorns
½ teaspoon cinnamon
½ teaspoon ground nutmeg
1 tablespoon fresh thyme leaves, chopped
4 spring onions, chopped (use the white part
    and most of the green)
3 Scotch bonnet chillies, finely chopped
1 tablespoon dark brown sugar
1 teaspoon salt
2 tablespoons dark soy sauce
Juice of 1 lime
6 chicken legs (thigh with drumstick attached),
    skin-on (or 6 thighs and 6 drumsticks)

1. Grind the allspice and the peppercorns to a powder in a pestle
    and mortar, then put them into a food processor with the
    cinnamon, nutmeg, thyme, spring onions and chillies. Whiz
    them to a purée, then stir in the sugar, salt, soy sauce and lime
    juice.
2. Put the chicken into a bowl, add the marinade and massage it
    into the meat, making sure you get it underneath the skin (and
    remembering it will be hot, so wash your hands well
    afterwards!). Cover and leave to marinate for at least 6 hours,
    or overnight.
3. Light a barbecue and allow it to cool to a medium heat – you
    should be able to hold a hand over the grill for 4 seconds
    without tears. Put the chicken on the grill and sear well on both
    sides, then move it to the edges of the barbecue, put the lid on

and cook for about 25 minutes, turning occasionally, until all the pieces are cooked through.

4. Alternatively, preheat the oven to 200°C/fan 180°C/gas 6 and bake the chicken in a roasting tray loosely covered with foil for about an hour, until cooked through. Heat a griddle pan on a high heat, then sear the legs until charred and crisp on both sides.

5. Serve with rice and peas, baked sweet potato or fluffy cornbread fritters.

Perfect
Chicken Kiev

A dish associated, in this country at least, with the 1970s in all their exotic glory, the Kiev's exact origins are, sadly, missing in action behind the Iron Curtain. Apparently immune to Cold War travel restrictions, it was a bit of a treat in my 1980s childhood: my brother was adept at spotting the inevitable leaky portion and passing it on to someone else, usually me.

I still love the Kiev today, but clearly, the leakage issue was of primary importance if I was to improve upon the supermarket version. Just plugging the hole with more chicken, as Hugh Fearnley-Whittingstall suggests, proved a disaster, with nary a drop of butter left.

Simon Hopkinson and Lindsey Bareham stick the chicken together with egg and flour in *The Prawn Cocktail Years*, which proves more effective, as does freezing the butter and securing it in its meaty prison with a cocktail stick, but the best method of all comes from Jesse Dunford Wood, a London chef who wraps the stuffed chicken breast tightly in clingfilm and freezes it for a couple of hours, then defrosts it before cooking. It's far less fiddly, and works like a charm.

Double coating the Kievs with super-crisp panko breadcrumbs provides extra insurance for my precious butter, as well as offering another layer of crunch.

The authentic dish, according to Hugh, Simon and Lindsey, is made with a chicken breast with the wing bone still attached, but Dara Goldstein suggests in *A Taste of Russia* that this is simply so it can be 'outfitted with an aluminium or paper frill to look fancy'. Not really my primary concern.

Hopeful dieters may be interested to know that American magazine *Cook's Illustrated* bake their Kievs, which gives a surprisingly tasty result, but, importantly, fails to deliver the vital crisp outer shell. It's deep-frying all the way I'm afraid — but once you cut into that well of hot, garlicky butter, you won't regret it.

Makes 2

> 50g salted butter, at room temperature
> 2 cloves of garlic, crushed
> 2 tablespoons parsley, finely chopped
> 1 tablespoon tarragon, finely chopped
> ½ a lemon
> 2 chicken breasts
> 2 tablespoons flour, seasoned
> 2 eggs, beaten
> 4 tablespoons breadcrumbs,
>   panko if possible, seasoned
> Vegetable oil, to deep-fry

1. Use a fork to mash together the butter, crushed garlic and chopped herbs, and season with black pepper, a little more salt and a squeeze of lemon juice. Shape into 2 small sausages, and wrap each in clingfilm. Put into the fridge to chill.

2. Butterfly each chicken breast by opening it out using a knife (make a horizontal cut almost, but not quite all the way through, and open it out like a book), then put it between two sheets of clingfilm and bash it with a rolling pin or meat tenderizer until it's about 0.5cm thick, being careful not to bash so hard you create holes. Season both sides well.

3. Put a sausage of butter on the edge of the chicken nearest you and begin to roll the meat up around it, tucking in the ends as you go (use a little beaten egg and flour as glue if it proves obstinate). Use the clingfilm to wrap the chicken into a tight sausage, and freeze for 2 hours.

4. Put the seasoned flour, eggs and breadcrumbs into three separate shallow dishes and roll the frozen Kievs in each in turn, then again in the eggs and crumbs. Put them into the fridge to defrost, which should take about an hour. Preheat the oven to 170°C/fan 150°C/gas 3.

5. Heat the oil in a large pan or fryer to 160°C, or until a crumb of bread turns golden in about 15 seconds, then lower the first Kiev in. Cook for 8½ minutes, then drain it on kitchen paper and put it into the oven to keep warm while you cook the next.

6. Serve immediately, once your guest has either disrobed or tucked a napkin into their collar.

The mysterious case of the Ukrainian chicken . . .
A persistent rumour, repeated by Hugh Fearnley-Whittingstall, suggests chicken Kiev was created for the opening of the Hotel Moscow in that city in the sixties, but *The Russian Tea Room Cookbook* credits it to 'the great French chef Carême at the court of Alexander I', while the food historian Vilyam

Pokhlebkin believes its decadence to be typical of the last days of the tsars. Whatever the truth, it first pops up in print in 1937, in a *Chicago Daily Record* account of that city's Yar restaurant, owned by a former officer of the Imperial Army, and became a staple of Soviet catering. Adventurous tourists venturing to the USSR were warned of the dangers a jet of hot butter might pose to their delicate western clothing. They were clearly undeterred, however: chicken Kiev was the first chilled ready meal produced by M&S back in 1979 and has never been off their shelves since.

Perfect
Southern Fried Chicken

*F*ried chicken is taking over the world. Or, at least, taking over
Britain. Deep-fried, wrapped in seasoned batter, and served in
boxes and buckets — in London, at least, you can't move for
branches of Kansas Fried Chicken and the singularly unappetizing-
sounding Chicken Spot.

Done well, it can be pretty addictive stuff: juicy meat, served on the
bone for flavour, in a crisp, spicy — and, let's be honest, ever-so-
slightly greasy — crust is always going to be
finger-licking good. But sadly, if the stuff being
eaten on the top deck of the bus is anything
to go by, it's not: flabby batter, stringy,
fat-sodden chicken — give me a jumbo
haddock and mushy peas any day of the week.

Much better to make it yourself. I'd recommend using only thighs
and drumsticks: bland breasts take ages to cook through, by which
time the batter is inevitably overcooked, and wings, in my
experience, don't offer a good enough meat to batter ratio. And —
controversially — I'd remove the skin: I know any good Southern
housewife will stop reading at this point, but it doesn't crisp up
under the batter, and chewy skin is not nice.

Marinating doesn't seem to be very traditional (and, when I try
Laurie Colwin's recipe without it, it works perfectly well — so don't

be put off if you need that fried chicken fast), but these days, you're no one if you don't have a signature soak. Though it does a good job in the juiciness department, however, I find that brining makes the chicken unpleasantly salty.

Better are dairy marinades, as recommended by Richard Ehrlich and Tim Hayward, author of *Food DIY*: I prefer the tanginess of buttermilk to the simple sweet juiciness of plain milk. There doesn't seem to be much point in adding too many spices at this stage, though; it doesn't come through in the finished dish.

I'd say the coating is what makes the dish, however — and it's a tricky business to perfect. There's a fine line between that firm, satisfying crunch, and what Ehrlich memorably describes as a 'sarcophagus of stodge'.

The flour should be plain — in substance, but not flavour, because this is where you pack in that seasoning. I like Laurie Colwin's *Home Cooking* recipe, which sticks with salt, pepper and smoked paprika, because, like her, 'I adore [it], and feel it gives the chicken a smoky taste and a beautiful colour.'

If, like me, you don't adore the mess and drama of deep-frying, you'll be relieved to know that I preferred the shallow-fried versions — deep-frying is more difficult to control, and surprisingly, yields a less crisp coating, presumably because the crust hasn't had anything to form against. Covering the pan, as Colwin suggests, is a clever idea: though, as she says, the idea 'may make many people squeal', it means the chicken cooks through quickly, before the coating has time to burn, so it stays beautifully juicy.

OK, so fried chicken will never be a health food, or even a regular occurrence, both for the sake of your heart, and your soft furnishings. As Laurie Colwin observes, 'there are many disagreeable things about frying chicken'. Eating it hot from the pan, however, is not one of them.

Serves 2–3

300ml buttermilk
1½ teaspoons salt
6 pieces of chicken
  (I use a mixture of legs and thighs)
150g plain flour
½ teaspoon freshly ground black pepper
½ teaspoon smoked paprika
Vegetable oil, for frying

1. Put the buttermilk and 1 teaspoon of salt into a container large enough to hold all the chicken, and then add the meat and toss to coat. Cover and chill for about 8 hours if possible, allowing it to return to room temperature before cooking.
2. Put the flour, spices and ½ teaspoon of salt into a large, flat dish and whisk to combine. Pour 1.5cm of vegetable oil into a wide, straight-sided pan with a lid, and heat until very hot: a cube of bread dropped in should brown almost immediately (about 170°C).
3. Wipe as much buttermilk off the chicken pieces as you can, then roll them in the seasoned flour until thoroughly coated.
4. Put the chicken in one layer in the pan (you may need to do this in batches, depending on how big your pan is) and put the lid

on. Turn the heat right down and fry the chicken for 6 minutes, then turn the pieces over, cover again and cook for another 6 minutes. Prepare a rack, and lots of kitchen paper to drain the chicken.

5. Turn the heat up and fry the chicken until it's a deep golden colour on all sides. Lift on to the rack and dry with kitchen paper. Allow to cool slightly before serving.

Perfect
Chicken Liver Pâté

I mourn the loss of pâté from our culinary repertoire. Sometime in the noughties, probably while I was busy making melba toast, it quietly dropped off menus, to be replaced by deep-fried Brie, or tempura squid with sweet chilli sauce, or, horror of horrors, something involving a foam.

Well, they've all had their time, and now, I think, it's time to return to the hearty embrace of real food. The variations are near infinite — but for silky elegance, I don't think you can beat the simple chicken liver version. Winningly easy to make, and obligingly happy to sit in the fridge for a few days, it's possibly the perfect lunch party dish or dinner party starter. Or, indeed, the best thing to have in the fridge when you come home overtired from work, and perhaps a few more drinks than you intended, and require sustenance, fast.

There's no need to soak the livers first, as Raymond Blanc does — though common practice with stronger-tasting pig or ox livers, it robs the more delicate chicken version of its distinctive offally character. You should, however, brown them in a pan: using them raw, or poaching them in stock as several recipes suggest, denies the finished dish a layer of savoury flavour. They don't need to be cooked for 5 minutes, as Delia Smith suggests, though — leaving them blushing pink in the middle will give a better texture.

Those livers can be bound together with butter, as in Delia's recipe, butter and cream, like Julia Child's, or Raymond Blanc's butter and egg combination. Butter alone makes the pâté too oily, and eggs seem to give it a moussey texture – only the cream and butter hit the silky spot.

Flavour-wise, though I'm keen to let the livers themselves take centre stage, a little booze seems appropriate for such a rich dish. Having tried brandy and port, I've settled for the subtle sweetness of Madeira as a perfect match with the chicken, and the shallots I've taken from Raymond Blanc's recipe – others use garlic, spring onions, even yellow onions and anchovies, but I prefer the sweeter flavour of shallots with the livers. Sweet spices also seem appropriate: ginger and allspice supply a pleasingly festive feel.

Raymond Blanc and Constance Spry both bake their pâtés in a water bath, which gives them a firmer, lighter consistency, but, though they look impressive, I prefer the creamier texture of the quicker set version.

A seal of butter is only necessary if you're keeping the pâté a few days, but it does look pretty – and of course, it saves real gluttons the embarrassment of having to ask for the butter dish.

Serves 4

350g chicken livers, cleaned
175g butter, diced
I shallot, finely chopped
I teaspoon thyme leaves, finely chopped
75ml Madeira
75ml double cream
½ teaspoon salt
I allspice berry, ground
¼ teaspoon ground ginger

1. Trim any stringy or green bits from the livers, and cut them into rough 1.5cm pieces. Heat a knob of the butter in a frying pan over a medium heat. Add the chopped shallot and thyme and soften in the butter, then turn up the heat to medium-high and add the livers. Sauté for a couple of minutes, until they're nicely browned on the outside but still pink within. Transfer the lot to a food processor.
2. Pour the Madeira into the same pan and bubble until it's reduced to a couple of tablespoons. Add this to the food processor, with the cream, salt and spices, and whiz it all together until smooth.
3. Add all but 75g of the butter, and whiz again until thoroughly combined. Taste and adjust the seasoning if necessary.
4. Pass the pâté through a sieve into a serving dish, or individual ramekins, and chill for half an hour. Melt the remaining butter and pour on top (you can clarify it if you have the time – see page 133), then refrigerate until set.

Perfect
Coronation Chicken

A word of warning. This isn't the kind of Coronation chicken you can knock up for an impromptu picnic in the time it takes your partner to find the rug.

The original recipe, created by the founder of the Cordon Bleu cookery school, Rosemary Hume (rather than her better-known partner in the venture, florist Constance Spry, as is often claimed), calls for a whole poached chicken, rather than the usual leftovers from Sunday's roast. Although I did try roasting one, thinking that this would give the bird a better flavour, in fact the poached version, once I've added some spices to the pot, is much nicer: juicy and subtly exotic-tasting.

Instead of using just mayonnaise, which can be rather too rich and claggy, I've gone for a half and half mixture of mayo and Greek yoghurt to make the dish creamier and lighter, after finding crème fraîche too buttery, and double cream too runny.

Generic curry powder feels like a very 1950s ingredient, but it adds just the right touch here – make sure you toast it first though, or the raw flavour will spoil the dressing.

The original Coronation chicken was a more delicate affair than we're used to today, and to be honest, rather underwhelming to a modern palate, so I've given the sweet, mildly spicy sauce a bit more oomph. Mango chutney goes in, courtesy of Hugh Fearnley-Whittingstall's recipe, to add an Indian fruitiness, and Worcestershire sauce, itself an Anglo-Indian creation, contributes a pleasing tangy, savoury flavour. Chopped apricots and toasted almond flakes finish the whole thing off nicely, giving it a more interesting texture than your average yellow gloop, while coriander adds freshness and colour.

I suspect the results would have been regarded as rather bold back in 1953, but this is a dish crying out to be dragged into the twenty-first century and given the respect it deserves. As Simon Hopkinson tartly observes, 'those cowboys who continue to think that bottled curry paste mixed with Hellmann's is in any way a reasonable substitute here need a good slap with a cold chapatti'. Try it, and you'll see why.

Serves 6

    1 chicken, about 1.5kg
    1 cinnamon stick
    5 black peppercorns
    A pinch of saffron
    1 teaspoon salt
    1 bay leaf
    A 4cm piece of fresh ginger
    5 tablespoons good-quality mango chutney (I swear by Geeta's)
    50g ready-to-eat dried apricots, finely chopped
    2 tablespoons good curry powder
    2 teaspoons Worcestershire sauce

**200ml homemade mayonnaise (see *Perfect*
 for a recipe)**
200ml Greek yoghurt
A small bunch of fresh coriander, chopped
50g flaked almonds, toasted
Green salad and basmati rice, to serve

1. Put the chicken, breast side up, into a large pan with the cinnamon, peppercorns, saffron, salt, bay leaf and half the ginger. Fill with cold water until only the top of the breast is sticking out. Cover with a lid and bring to a simmer, then turn down the heat, so only the odd bubble can be seen. Cook gently for about 1½ hours, until the juices run clear. Take the chicken out of the pan and set aside to cool, then, when lukewarm, remove the meat in bite-sized pieces.

2. Peel and finely chop the remaining ginger. Put the chutney and chopped apricots into a large bowl. Toast the curry powder in a dry pan until aromatic, then stir in with the chopped ginger, followed by the Worcestershire sauce, mayonnaise and yoghurt. Season to taste.

3. Fold the cooled chicken through the dressing and refrigerate for at least a couple of hours before bringing to room temperature, folding in the coriander (reserving a couple of sprigs for garnish) and serving topped with the almonds and coriander sprigs, preferably with a green salad and basmati rice.

Perfect
Chicken and
Smoked Sausage Gumbo

I have to admit, this is a recipe that caused me sleepless nights, because gumbo is as sacred to Louisiana natives as pizza is to Neapolitans – everyone's mama makes the best version. I, as is probably obvious, am not from Louisiana (although I have been there and eaten a fair amount of gumbo) – so what hope did I have?

Quite a lot, it seems – because, according to Howard Mitcham, author of *Creole Gumbo and All That Jazz*, gumbo is 'an improvisational thing, like early jazz. You just take off with whatever tune is handy and then you travel . . . A Creole cook can take a handful of chicken wings or a turkey carcass or a piece of sausage or a few shrimp or crabs and whip up a gumbo.' Now, I may not be a Creole cook, but that's an idea I can run with.

Handily, then, the meat itself is relatively unimportant to the gumbo aficionado – I've gone with chicken and smoked sausage (Polish kabanos are the closest I could find to the authentic andouille), but you could stick in whatever you have handy, from rabbit to raccoon.

What matters more is the thickener: according to Sara Roahen, Louisianan cooks classify their gumbos by their choice of roux, okra or filé (the last is a powder made from ground sassafras leaves, which is unsurprisingly hard to track down in the UK, though it is sometimes available online).

I find the roux, which, unlike the classical French version, needs to be cooked until it's a deep, dark brown (nerve-racking indeed, given how quickly it burns), yields the best results — a thick gravy with a smoky, slightly bitter flavour — although there's no need to cook it for hours as many recipes suggest. Start with hot oil, as *Cook's Illustrated* advises, and you can be done in 20 minutes with no real loss of quality. (Oil is actually the best fat to use here: butter and lard are both too rich.)

Although okra usually has an either-or relationship with roux, I like the flavour and texture it gives the gumbo, so I'm going to add it as well. If you do come across some, filé should be kept as an optional extra to add at table: the gloopy, swampy taste doesn't suit everyone.

Personally, I like my gumbo thin enough to serve in a bowl, rather than on a plate — and the necessary liquid should come from chicken stock, water being too austere, and tomatoes too domineering. Although many recipes add the liquid to the roux hot, I find this makes it hard to mix the two — *Cooks Illustrated* explains that 'By adding cooler stock, the roux and the stock have time to blend thoroughly before the whole mixture comes up to temperature and the starch gelatinises, resulting in the smooth consistency we were seeking.' Cold stock it is.

The Cajun holy trinity — green pepper, onion and celery — is, of course, a must here, but otherwise, I've kept the flavourings pretty simple. Bay leaves and Tabasco, the latter a cunning suggestion by

Gwen McKee, author of *The Little Gumbo Book*, add depth and piquancy – but that spectacular roux will do most of the work in the flavour department.

This is a surprisingly easy recipe to master, but a good glass of bourbon by the stove should go some way to steady the nerves. After that, you can pretty much leave your gumbo to do its own sweet thing while you kick back and laissez les bons temps rouler.

Serves 4

> 4 chicken legs
> Cayenne pepper
> 100g flour
> 1 onion, finely chopped
> 1 green pepper, finely chopped
> 1 rib of celery, finely chopped
> 1 litre chicken stock, at room temperature
> 100ml oil
> 1 bay leaf
> 200g okra, chopped
> 200g smoked sausage, e.g. kabanos, thinly sliced
> ½ teaspoon Tabasco, according to taste
> Rice, to serve
> Filé powder, to serve (optional)

1. Take the skin off the chicken if necessary, and dust the pieces with salt, black pepper and cayenne. Leave to sit for at least half an hour (you can prepare the rest of the ingredients in the meantime).

2. Arrange the flour, onion, green pepper, celery and stock within easy reach of the stove. Heat the oil in a large, heavy-based pot (not non-stick!) over a medium-high heat and brown the chicken well, working in batches if necessary. Set aside.

3. Turn the heat down slightly and scrape any crusty bits off the bottom of the pan, then carefully stir in the flour. Stir it over a medium-low heat until it's a deep, rich brown colour, about the shade of melted milk chocolate. (If you are very brave and a fan of bitter flavours, you can take it to dark chocolate.) Do not so much as contemplate leaving the stove for even a second while making the roux.

4. Tip the onion, green pepper and celery into the pan and cook, stirring, for a few minutes until softened. Gradually stir in the stock, little by little, to make a smooth sauce, scraping the bottom of the pot as you do so.

5. Return the chicken to the pot, add the bay leaf and bring to a simmer. Reduce the heat, cover and leave to simmer for an hour and a half.

6. Add the okra and sausage to the pot, stir, then replace the lid and simmer for a further 45 minutes.

7. Remove the chicken (keeping the pot on the heat) and, when cool enough to handle, strip the meat from the bones and put it back into the pot, along with the Tabasco sauce. Season to taste.

8. Either serve immediately, with long-grain rice and filé powder (if using) on the side, or allow the gumbo to sit for a day, then reheat to serve.

Perfect
Thai Green Curry

*L*ike many things, Thai green curry has mellowed over the years, evolving into a sugary, creamy comfort food in the hands of cooks in thrall to British tastebuds — your local takeaway may indeed do one to blow your head off, but close your eyes, and the average ready-meal version could almost double as dessert. The only solution, if you don't happen to have a good Thai restaurant nearby, is to make your own.

This may require a little forethought, and a visit to a decent South-East Asian supermarket, because as Thai cookery teacher Kasma Loha-unchit admits, 'unless you have all of the fresh herbs and spices required to make authentic and traditional Thai curry pastes, you're better off using commercial curry pastes than trying to make do with ill-advised substitutes'. (Use 2 tablespoons of a good ready-made paste in the recipe below if this applies to you.)

You'll need Thai bird's-eye chillies, of course, which are fairly widely available (they're the little vicious ones), and shrimp paste and fish sauce to supply the salty element, sugar and coconut cream for sweetness, and — and this is where things get tricky — aromatics like fresh turmeric, kaffir lime zest or leaves and galangal. All are easily found online (it's illegal to import fresh kaffir limes into this country, but the leaves and zest are sold frozen or pickled), or in South-East Asian supermarkets if you happen to have one handy.

Using a pestle and mortar may seem like an unnecessary faff (and it is a faff), but the great David Thompson, the first Thai chef to win a Michelin star, is an advocate, and as Rosemary Brissenden explains in *South East Asian Food*, 'an electric blade will always chop rather than pound, no matter how finely it does so. Even though you may end up with very small particles in your paste, the flavours will remain "chopped" and separate rather than merged.' For a perfect curry, you need to put in the sweat and tears, I'm afraid.

Cooking the paste in coconut cream, rather than frying it first and then adding the liquids, is the proper way to do things — a split sauce, generally regarded as a Bad Thing by western cooks, is actually the sign of an authentic Thai curry.

My curry, which is strongly influenced by Thompson's recipe, uses more chilli, lemongrass and shrimp paste than you might think strictly wise, but give it a whirl, and you'll remember why you fell in love with Thai food in the first place.

Serves 2 (but easily doubled)

For the paste

20 green bird's-eye chillies
1 tablespoon chopped galangal
3 tablespoons chopped lemongrass
1 teaspoon makrut (aka kaffir) lime zest, or 2 teaspoons finely minced makrut lime leaves
1 teaspoon chopped coriander root, or 10 teaspoons pounded coriander stems
1 teaspoon chopped red turmeric

2 tablespoons chopped shallots
2 tablespoons chopped garlic
1 teaspoon shrimp paste
Ground white pepper and salt

For the curry
5 tablespoons coconut cream
1 teaspoon fish sauce
½ teaspoon palm sugar
180ml chicken or vegetable stock
180g chopped chicken (or seafood,
    pork or tofu if you prefer, but I like chicken)
100g pea aubergines or chopped purple aubergines
2 makrut lime leaves, shredded
3 red chillies, deseeded and finely sliced
A handful of Thai basil leaves

1. Use a large pestle and mortar to pound the paste ingredients in
   the order listed, making sure each is well incorporated before
   adding the next. (You can use a food processor if you must, but
   you won't get quite such good results.)
2. Heat the coconut cream in a small saucepan, and bring to the
   boil. Once it's reduced and begun to split, add 4 tablespoons of
   your curry paste and stir continuously until you can smell the
   spices — taste to see whether they're cooked.
3. Add the fish sauce and sugar to taste (you may want a little more
   of either), then pour in the stock and bring back to the boil.
   Add the meat, seafood or tofu, and the aubergines. Turn down
   the heat and simmer until cooked through (chicken will
   obviously take longer than seafood or tofu), then stir in the lime
   leaves, red chillies and basil leaves.

4. Taste, add a little more coconut cream if it's too spicy, or some more fish sauce or sugar if you think it needs it, and serve with jasmine rice.

Perfect
Pulled Pork

*I*n the US, barbecue suggests long, slow cooking, patiently allowing the smoke to do its work while you sink a few beers and set the world to rights. In this country, it means burning meat in the rain.

You could never cook pulled pork on a British grill – it takes hours of loving devotion to get meat this tender. Ideally, of course, you'd dig a barbecue pit for your piece of hog, but in the absence of available spots in my garden, I've chosen to stick with my trusty oven. If real, living, breathing Americans reckon decent pulled pork can be made without ever lighting a match, then who am I to quibble?

The traditional cut for pulled pork everywhere but eastern North Carolina, where they barbecue the whole hog, is Boston butt, or the top of the shoulder. Neil Rankin, chef at my local BBQ joint, the Smokehouse, tells me to ask for 'bone-in neck end, with a good layer of fat on top'. This is one you'll have to go to a butcher for.

Myths swirl around barbecue like wreaths of smoke – brining does not make your meat any juicier, as far as I can tell, and curing it in salt and sugar before cooking just makes it stringy. In fact, in terms of flavour, you can make pretty decent pulled pork with just pork, as Rankin suggests, adding spices and sauces to taste once it's done, but I like the smokiness of burnt sugar, so I add half the rub before putting the meat in the oven, and half when it comes out.

If you're to pull the meat apart with your fingers, you need to cook it low and slow — but doing this robs it of the burnt, savoury flavours which make roasted meat so delicious. As a compromise between taste and texture, I decide to give it an initial blast of heat to caramelize the outside, then turn the oven right down, before whacking it back up again for a final crisping. Resting the meat in a tent of foil so it gently steams as it cools, as *Guardian* reader and barbecue enthusiast Jonathan Dale suggests, gives it a final prod in the tenderness department.

You can add any old sauce you want once it's done, but I'm a purist — the same salt and sugar I use for the rub, with a little smoked paprika for spice and smoke, and, the secret ingredient, liquid smoke. Imported from the States and easily obtainable on the internet, it's optional if you're worried about carcinogens (in which case, also stay away from barbecues), but it does give a satisfyingly charred tanginess at a lot less cost to the garden than digging your own pit. And I firmly believe this is the best recipe you're going to get without doing so. Serve stuffed into soft white rolls. Disposable bibs entirely at your discretion.

Serves 6

1.6kg shoulder of pork from the neck end, bone in
2 tablespoons salt
2 tablespoons dark muscovado sugar
1 tablespoon smoked paprika
2 teaspoons liquid smoke (optional)

1. Preheat the oven to 220°C/fan 200°C/gas 7. Line a roasting tin with two sheets of foil large enough to eventually fold over the

top of the pork, then pat the meat dry with kitchen paper and put it in the tin. Mix the salt, sugar and paprika and rub about half of this mixture into the meat.

2. Cook the pork, uncovered, in the hot oven for about 40 minutes, until well browned, then take out and turn down the heat to 140°C/fan 125°C/gas 1. Pour the liquid smoke over the meat if using, then fold the foil securely over the top to make a sealed parcel. Return to the oven and cook for about 6–7 hours, until the internal temperature measures 89°C and, more importantly, it's soft enough to spoon. Pour off the juices and reserve for later.

3. Turn the heat back up to 220°C/fan 200°C/gas 7 and cook the pork, uncovered, for 10 minutes, until crisp. Remove, cover with a tent of foil, and leave to rest for 30 minutes.

4. Use two forks or your fingers to pull the meat into shreds, cutting up any crackling too, and then add a sprinkle of the remaining seasoning, plus any meat juices from the tin, and stir in.

5. If possible, leave to soak for 24 hours before reheating in a warm oven to serve. Or just eat immediately.

Perfect
Baked Ham

*T*his recipe was originally created for Christmas, but having made it in midsummer, if you can bear to have the oven on, it makes a winning cold centrepiece for lunch or dinner. It also makes superlative sandwiches. In short, there's no need to wait until that last Advent chocolate has been eaten: this truly is a ham for all seasons.

Those who are of an obsessively DIY bent might want to cure the pork themselves — all it takes is a big bowl of brine and a few days' notice — but if you leave everything until the last minute, like me, then a piece of ready-cured meat, known as a gammon (unless you're cooking the whole leg, in which case, confusingly, it's a ham from the get-go), is what you're after. I find unsmoked versions are best, so the flavour of the meat itself comes through: modern gammon tends to be less salty than its ancestors so you rarely need to soak it, but do check the packaging or ask your butcher, just in case.

Because gammon is cured, but not cooked, it's generally poached or baked before the final glaze is added. Having tried both methods, including a recipe which involves baking it in a rack above a pan of stock, I found that the former is a more effective way of infusing flavour into the meat.

You can use just about any liquid you fancy for this purpose, from cider to mulled wine to Coca-Cola (courtesy of Nigella Lawson), but I've gone for a treacly, spicy mixture inspired by Jane Grigson's Bradenham ham recipe, which makes me think of festive gingerbread and other similarly happy memories. It also has the benefit of giving the ham a rather striking black rim, which should draw admiring glances its way.

Once poached, the ham is crowned with its ceremonial glaze – a stiffish paste is required if it's to develop a crunchy crust, which means it needs to have a dry base. Toffeeish brown sugar and hot English mustard powder do the trick, with a little orange zest as a nod to the traditional marmalade ham (marmalade itself threatens the structural integrity of the crust) and a drop of spicy ginger wine, just to make it loose enough to spread.

A final sprinkling of extra sugar, as suggested by Delia Smith, gives a nice even caramelization – and of course, you can't have a ham without cloves. They just look so wonderfully Dickensian. With a big baked ham on the table, what could be wrong with the world?

Serves 8

> 1 boneless gammon joint, about 2kg
> 3 tablespoons molasses or black treacle
> 4 teaspoons cloves
> A pinch of mace
> 1 bay leaf
> 1 teaspoon allspice
> 1 tablespoon black peppercorns
> Peel of ½ an orange, cut into thin strips

For the glaze

5 tablespoons dark brown sugar,
plus extra to sprinkle
1½ tablespoons mustard powder
Finely grated zest of ½ an orange
20ml ginger wine

1. Place the ham in a stockpot or large saucepan, and cover with cold water. Bring slowly to a simmer, skimming off any scum, then add the molasses, 1 teaspoon of cloves, the mace, bay leaf, allspice, peppercorns and peel and simmer very gently for about an hour and a half, until the internal temperature of the ham reaches 68°C.

2. Preheat the oven to 220°C/fan 200°C/gas 7. Lift the ham out of the liquid (which can be used to make really brilliant baked beans), allow it to cool slightly, then use a sharp knife to carefully cut off the skin, leaving as much fat beneath as possible. Score the fat in a diamond pattern, and stud the intersections with cloves. Place the ham in a foil-lined roasting tray.

3. Mix together the glaze ingredients to make a thick paste, and brush this all over the scored fat. Bake the ham in the hot oven for about 25 minutes, basting twice during this time, and adding a sprinkle more sugar each time, until the top is nicely caramelized and bubbling. Allow to cool completely before serving.

Perfect
Barbecue Ribs

*T*here can be few more primal pleasures than teasing juicy, tender meat from its accompanying bone, getting up close and personal with your dinner (anyone who tackles ribs with a knife and fork is not to be trusted) and then licking your fingers afterwards. Meat from near the bone tends to be tastier, and marbled with fat, making it wonderfully succulent in the right hands — just make sure that every rib you have is worth the effort.

Although they're more fiddly than the larger spare rib, I think baby back, or loin rack ribs have more flavour — and, because they're smaller, you can cook a whole rack of them, which always looks impressive. And although we might think of them as a barbecue classic, unless you have a proper American pit or kettle, an oven is better than the average British barbie.

However, you can get the barbie out at the end, if you like: although you need to cook the ribs on a fairly low heat to keep the moisture in (Harold McGee suggests a temperature of between 95 and 80°C for 6–8 hours, but, ever impatient, I settle on a more efficient, but still gentle 170°C/fan 150°C/gas 3), I'm sold on the caramelized, slightly crisp crust on Nigella Lawson's 'finger lickin' ribs', which are cooked at 200°C. To achieve the same effect, I finish them off on a hot grill or griddle pan, as suggested by *Leiths Meat Bible*.

Some older recipes simmer the ribs in water first, presumably to start breaking down the chewy connective tissue (sorry) which holds them together, but with baby backs, I find this actually makes them tougher than their roasted counterparts. More important is a step many recipes neglect to mention: stripping off the translucent membrane from the back of the ribs. If you buy them from the butcher, they may have already done this for you – and if not, they will, it only takes a second.

I try Asian-style five-spice and soy sauce marinades, and fennel seed and brown sugar rubs and spicy barbecue sauces, but in the end find myself agreeing with McGee when he says that, although 'it can be fun to concoct rubs and mopping liquids and sauces with dozens of ingredients, the end result is usually an indistinct, generically fruity and spicy flavour'.

Instead, I've kept things simpler with a rather more British marinade: rich and savoury Marmite (though you could substitute soy sauce if you really hate the stuff), English mustard for heat, ketchup and muscovado sugar for fruity, treacly sweetness, and a little smoked paprika to add the merest hint of fire.

Just enough sticky flavour to lick from your fingers, while letting the meat itself do the talking. Sucking the bones clean is entirely up to you.

Serves 4

2 racks of baby back/loin ribs
1 tablespoon Marmite
1 tablespoon English mustard
1½ teaspoons smoked paprika
2 tablespoons tomato ketchup
2½ tablespoons dark muscovado sugar

1. If the ribs haven't been trimmed as described above, turn the racks curved side down, with the wider end facing you. You should see a translucent membrane covering the ribs: use a small knife to peel the edge of this away from the smaller end of the rack to form a tab. Grip this and pull it towards you, so the membrane comes away from the bones. Discard.

2. Mix together the remaining ingredients and rub about half of it into the ribs, making sure they're well coated. Put them into a shallow dish, cover and leave them in the fridge for 4 hours, turning once or twice to make sure they marinate evenly. Remove from the fridge an hour before you want to cook.

3. Preheat the oven to 170°C/fan 150°C/gas 3. Cover the dish tightly with foil and cook the ribs for about 2½ hours, until tender, basting them once or twice, and removing the foil for the last 15 minutes. The rack should be floppy once done.

4. Heat a barbecue or a griddle pan until hot, then brush the ribs with the remaining marinade and cook them until charred and caramelized. Serve immediately.

Perfect
Moussaka

I'd made many assumptions about moussaka, including that it was Greek, that it always contains lamb, and that it should be served hot, all systematically shot down by about five minutes of research. Although the name is actually Arabic, and it pops up in various forms from Egypt to Romania, I've stuck with the Greek version, simply because that's the one most familiar to Britons from a thousand Ionian holidays.

Talking to Greek cookery teacher Elisavet Sotiriadou, who modestly concedes she makes a moussaka nearly as good as her mother's, I discovered 'the mince used is veal, or pork and veal', although in the UK she goes for beef. Elizabeth David also suggests beef in *A Book of Mediterranean Food*, and Tessa Kiros a beef and pork mix in *Falling Cloudberries*, but, heathen that I am, I use just lamb: the sweet, robust flavour seems to work so much better with the spices than blander beef. (Hugh Fearnley-Whittingstall uses leftover roast lamb, finely chopped, which is a great idea if you happen to have drastically over-catered.)

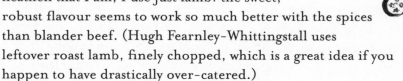

Tomato sauce is a must (indeed, the name moussaka apparently comes from the Arabic for to moisten, such is the importance of this ingredient) – in Greece, thin perasti (like the Italian passata) is traditional, but I can't help falling for the richer, more intensely flavoured tomato purée and red wine versions used in *The Prawn*

Cocktail Years, and by Hugh Fearnley-Whittingstall. Along with the traditional cinnamon, I'm adding oregano, for a touch of sun-baked herbaceousness, parsley and a generous amount of garlic.

It's aubergines that I think really set moussaka apart from the likes of lasagne or shepherd's pie, however: a layer of silky soft, wonderfully juicy and ever so slightly bitter purple slices, too often let down by too much grease. Salting them helps, as, according to Nigel Slater, it allows them to 'relax, allowing them to soak up less oil', but it's baking the slices rather than frying them which really makes the difference — and that way there's no need to pre-salt either, which speeds things up a bit. Thanks, Hugh.

My mum, whose excellent moussaka I rejected for so many years, finishes things off with a simple béchamel, but actually a thicker sauce, made with beaten eggs and seasoned with salty sheep's cheese, makes for a richer, more satisfying crown for this truly regal dish. Eat with plenty of rustic red wine, and holiday memories.

Serves 4, generously

4 tablespoons olive oil
1 large onion, finely chopped
4 cloves of garlic, finely chopped
1½ teaspoons ground cinnamon
1 teaspoon dried oregano
500g minced lamb
2 tablespoons tomato purée, mixed with 150ml water
150ml red wine
A small bunch of flat-leaf parsley, chopped
3 medium or 2 large aubergines, sliced

For the béchamel
500ml milk
60g butter
60g plain flour
50g kefalotyri or pecorino cheese, grated
2 eggs, beaten
Nutmeg, to grate

1. Put 2 tablespoons of olive oil into a large frying pan over a medium-high heat and cook the chopped onion until golden and soft. Add the garlic, cinnamon and oregano to the pan and cook for a further couple of minutes, then stir in the lamb.

2. Turn up the heat slightly, and brown the lamb well (by which I mean a deep brown), cooking until the mixture is quite dry. Stir in the tomato purée and wine, bring to a simmer, then turn the heat down low and cook for 30–40 minutes, until most of the liquid has evaporated. Season and stir in the chopped parsley.

3. Meanwhile, preheat the oven to 200°C/fan 180°C/gas 6. Cut the aubergines laterally into 0.5cm slices, and arrange in one layer on oiled baking sheets. Brush with a little olive oil and season with salt and pepper, then bake for about 25 minutes, until they're soft, golden and floppy (keep an eye on them towards the end, as smaller slices may char faster).

4. While they're cooking, make the béchamel. Bring the milk to just below the boil, and melt the butter in another, larger saucepan. Whisk the flour into the butter and cook for a couple of minutes until you lose that raw flour smell, then very gradually whisk in the hot milk until smooth. Simmer gently to make a thick sauce, then add the cheese, stirring it in until melted.

5. Remove the sauce from the heat and allow it to cool slightly, then beat in the eggs, season to taste and add slightly more

nutmeg than you might think wise (it's a strong flavour, but this dish can take it — use ½ teaspoon at least).

6. Line the base of an ovenproof dish with a third of the aubergines, and top with half the meat. Repeat these layers, finishing off with a layer of aubergine, then top with the sauce.

7. Bake at 200°C/fan 180°C/gas 6 for about 45 minutes, until well browned on top, and leave to cool for half an hour before serving.

CHAPTER 6

Vegetables, Nuts and Pulses

*I*t may say something about my tastes that half the recipes in this chapter involve potatoes – but I prefer to keep my greens blessedly simple. At least, that's my excuse.

On the subject of potatoes, for a country that eats so many of the things (by tonnage, the British are the biggest consumers in Europe), we're remarkably careless about them: how often have you struggled to find out what variety is inside that supermarket bag of 'white potatoes', or even where they come from?

The fact is that all potatoes were not made equal: most are better for some things than others – the firmer, waxy sort, with dense, often yellow flesh, hold their shape well during cooking, making them the superior choice for salads and dauphinoise. Floury potatoes, by contrast, yield to heat, making them the only option for fluffy mash and baked potatoes.

The most common waxy varieties in this country are probably Maris Peer, Desiree and the smaller Charlottes, while Maris Piper and King Edwards are ever-reliable floury sorts, but it's well worth giving more unusual names a try if you come across them.

You'll notice I always leave potato skins on where possible, both out of laziness and because that's where most of the flavour (and much of the fibre) seems to reside — even if you don't want the skins in the finished dish, it's worth cooking the potatoes in them where possible, and peeling them off afterwards.

Potato lecture over, I'd happily eat every single one of these recipes on its own with no further accompaniment, so please don't just regard this chapter as 'sides' — yes, a dal is nice with rice and curried vegetables, and aubergine parmigiana is lovely with roast lamb, but both are also great dishes in their own right, and really don't need to play second fiddle to anything.

Perfect
Gratin Dauphinoise

*N*amed after the ancient Alpine province, a gratin dauphinoise is the pinnacle of potato-based glamour. Put a bubbling dish of this on the table, and the meal becomes an occasion as far as I'm concerned.

But, for something so simple — really, it's little more than sliced potatoes, cooked in cream — dauphinoise is fraught with risk for the cook. Soggy spuds — or even worse, semi-raw in unappetizingly curdled cream or no cream at all, the liquid having evaporated into the ether — it's a surprisingly tough one to get right, as I can testify.

Oddly, most recipes seem to use fluffy potatoes such as Maris Piper, which have a tendency to collapse during cooking, making the dish stodgy. Elizabeth David and Raymond Blanc are both with me in preferring a waxier variety, like Charlottes or Maris Peers — much better at keeping their shape, and more importantly, their texture in the oven.

Whichever you happen to prefer, however, it's vital to slice them wafer thin, so they cook through — almost impossible to do with a knife, but the work of a few minutes with a mandoline. They're not expensive, especially in Oriental shops, but please be careful: I sacrificed the top of my finger to the perfect dauphinoise, so there's no need for you to do the same.

Cream is, regrettably, inevitable here – I found Richard Olney's milk and egg version too solid and heavy. That said, Michel Roux Jr's beautifully simple recipe, which just involves tossing the potatoes in double cream and shoving them in the oven, is too sticky and rich to eat in the requisite greedy portions. A mixture of milk and cream, as favoured by Blanc, Nick Nairn and Stevie Parle, gives a more homely, and quite possibly more digestible result.

Giving the potatoes a head start by par-boiling them in the sauce before baking, as Nairn suggests, proves wise insurance against crunchy disappointment, but there's no need to cook them until almost tender, or you risk making them mushy.

Par-boiling also has the benefit of thickening the sauce slightly, as the starch from the spuds leaches out into the liquid – Elizabeth David may be of the view that starch is a very bad thing for a dauphinoise (indeed, she rinses the potato slices before use), but on this occasion, she's wrong. There, I said it.

Nigel Slater writes that 'restraint with the garlic will be rewarded', but I'm of the opinion that potatoes and cream are a combination that can tend dangerously towards the bland – it may be more 'authentic' to rub the dish with a cut clove, but I'm going to crush two and add them to the sauce to give it a bit of Gallic poke.

I don't think infusing the cream with herbs, as Anthony Bourdain suggests, is necessary though – too many flavours can spoil such a simple dish, and a little pinch of sweet nutmeg is a much subtler seasoning. I must admit I do like Bourdain's anchovies though, which add a gorgeously savoury richness: if you're not averse, or afraid of the French, then please, give them a try.

Fish may not be on *Larousse Gastronomique*'s list of permissible additives, but cheese certainly is. They suggest two layers, one on the base, one on top, while Olney stirs his into the cream itself, but I've stuck to a modest amount on top: just enough to melt and brown, in contrast to the creamy starch beneath.

Serves 6

750g waxy potatoes
250ml double cream
100ml whole milk
2 small cloves of garlic, crushed
Nutmeg, to grate
Butter, to grease
50g Gruyère, grated

1. Peel the potatoes and cut them into very thin slices using a food processor or mandoline.
2. Pour the cream and milk into a large saucepan, add the garlic and a liberal grating of nutmeg, and bring just to the boil. Season and add the sliced potatoes, then reduce the heat and simmer them gently for about 10 minutes, until the slices have softened, but not cooked through.
3. Meanwhile, grease a gratin dish with butter, and heat the oven to 180°C/fan 160°C/gas 4.
4. Scoop the potatoes into the buttered dish and spread them out evenly. Pour over the milk and cream mixture, cover with foil and bake for 30 minutes.
5. Remove the foil, sprinkle the grated cheese on top, and bake the dauphinoise for a further 10–15 minutes, until the cheese has

melted into a golden, bubbling sea. Allow to cool slightly before serving.

TIP: Potatoes do not do well in plastic — like us it makes them sweat — so if you do buy them in big polythene bags, take them out as soon as you get home, and store them somewhere cool, dark and well ventilated. Buy them unwashed if possible, as they'll keep much better, and it's the work of a mere minute and a stout brush to clean them before cooking.

Perfect
Potato Salad

*B*ritish picnic foods tend to be hearty, in obedience to the prevailing climate — potato salad is perhaps the ultimate example, the word salad suggesting a seasonally light dish belied by the realities of starch and mayonnaise. Cold, but warming, it also happens to go very well with other classic picnic fare, like ham, or poached salmon.

The potatoes in this case must be waxy: floury versions crumble when I toss them with the dressing, leaving me with a potatoey mush. Plus, new potatoes are at their best in picnic season, so the more excuse to eat them the better.

Nigel Slater and I agree on the happy rusticity of unpeeled potatoes; it's not laziness, I promise, they add both texture and flavour to the dish. It also means you won't burn your fingers trying to peel them straight out of the pan, because you do need to introduce the dressing while they're still warm, or it'll just run off and be lost to the bottom of the bowl.

That dressing should be vinaigrette: Jane Grigson's white wine just isn't acidic enough to cut through the buttery blandness of good new potatoes. Adding a little mustard, as suggested by Simon Hopkinson and Lindsey Bareham in *The Prawn Cocktail Years*, gives it a nice little kick. You could just stop there, as they do, but I'm with Grigson in preferring to finish things off with homemade mayonnaise, which, I think, makes the difference between a good potato salad and a truly great one. You do also need the vinaigrette though, else the potatoes and mayonnaise remain two separate entities.

As Spry wisely advises, a decent potato salad 'should be garnished with some sharp ingredient such as capers, sliced gherkin or sliced pickled walnuts to relieve the somewhat cloying taste of potatoes'. Never one to stint, I've thrown in Signe Johansen's spring onions, capers and gherkins from *Scandilicious*, and Simon Hopkinson and Lindsey Bareham's chives, Sarah Raven's fresh herbs for freshness, and a good dollop of wholegrain mustard for texture and warmth. And that last is something you might well be needing if it's a proper British picnic.

Serves 4

600g waxy potatoes
½ teaspoon Dijon mustard
I tablespoon red wine vinegar
2 tablespoons vegetable oil
I tablespoon extra virgin olive oil
115ml good mayonnaise
I tablespoon wholegrain mustard
3 spring onions, thinly sliced
2 tablespoons capers, chopped
2 anchovies, finely chopped
A small bunch of chives, finely chopped
A handful of parsley, finely chopped
A handful of mint, finely chopped

1. Scrub the potatoes clean if necessary, then put them into a pan of well-salted water, bring to the boil and simmer for about 15 minutes, until tender.
2. While they're cooking, whisk together the Dijon mustard and vinegar with a pinch of salt, then slowly whisk in the oils to make a vinaigrette.
3. Drain the potatoes, and when just cool enough to handle, cut into halves, or quarters if large, and toss with the dressing, then leave to cool completely. (You can prepare the salad ahead up to this point.)
4. Stir the remaining ingredients into the mayonnaise, keeping back a little of each of the herbs for garnish. When the potatoes are at room temperature, drain off any remaining vinaigrette and toss them in the mayonnaise to coat. Garnish with herbs and serve.

Perfect
Rösti

*F*inding out anything to do with this Alpine favourite, from the
variety of potatoes to the cooking method, proved about as hard as
scaling the north face of the Eiger. In fact, all I could really establish
was that I was pronouncing it wrong: it's reursch-ti. So, in the
absence of definitive recipes, I went off piste and created a few of my
own based on the scant wisdom available.

Raw versus cooked potato seems to be the Swiss equivalent of cream
first or jam first on a scone: in Zürich, it seems they use raw
spuds, but the rest of the country boils them first, and very
sensible they are too — although the raw strands cook through,
they retain an unpleasantly crunchy texture and starchy
flavour. Even salting them to draw out moisture, as
some sages suggest, while making the outer layer
crisper, does nothing to improve the middle.

Some Swiss, apparently, will only use day-old boiled potatoes for
rösti: this is a little excessive, but they're certainly easier to grate and
shape once they've been chilled for a couple of hours. Peeling,
gratifyingly, is definitely not necessary: the skin adds flavour to the
dish.

Although I can't find a consensus on the correct texture of potato,
with Mark Hix and Jane Clarke going for floury and Valentine
Warner and Leiths suggesting waxy, I find the latter preferable:

strands of floury potato meld into a kind of mashed potato cake, while those cut from firmer varieties keep their shape during cooking, giving the finished rösti a crunchier, more interesting texture.

There's no need to add any fat to the cakes themselves: they should bind together nicely without it, but frying them in goose fat will ensure a crisp finish, while adding a little butter gives a rich flavour. Serve plain as a side dish, or add onion, bacon and Alpine cheese to make a complete meal of it. Or, of course, just top with a fried egg for a breakfast you could climb mountains on.

Serves 4 as a side dish, 2 as a main course

2 medium-sized waxy potatoes, unpeeled
1 tablespoon butter
1 tablespoon goose fat
   (or 2 tablespoons butter)

1. Put the potatoes into a pan of salted water, bring to the boil and simmer until just tender, but not soft. Allow to cool, then chill for at least a couple of hours before continuing.
2. Coarsely grate the cold potatoes and season well. Heat half the fat (equal parts butter and goose fat, if using) in a small, heavy-based frying pan over a medium-high heat until it sizzles, then tip in the grated potato. Leave to cook undisturbed for a couple of minutes, then use a spatula to shape it into a flat cake, pressing down on the strands as lightly as possible. Cook for a couple of minutes, then gently shake the pan to loosen the potato from the base.

3. Cook the cake for about 10 minutes, until golden and crisp on the bottom and sides, then place a plate larger than the pan on top of the pan and carefully, holding the pan with a tea towel, invert it so the cake sits, cooked side up, on the plate.

4. Add the remaining fat to the pan and, when sizzling, gently slide the potato cake back into the pan to brown the other side. Cook for another 10 minutes, then serve.

Perfect
Aubergine Parmigiana

*I*talian comfort food of the first order, these days there's no real
need to salt aubergines to draw out their bitterness (modern
varieties have had it bred out of them) but I think the practice is still
popular amongst recipe writers because it improves the flavour
immeasurably. The slight salinity that lingers, even after rinsing,
seasons the parmigiana from the inside out.

Peeling the aubergines, as some recipes suggest, is
quite pointless: indeed, the skins offer a pleasing
contrast in texture in a dish which otherwise runs
the risk of verging on the mushy.

Traditionally, the slices (it's easier to build if you cut
long strips, rather than rounds) are fried in generous
quantities of oil before baking, which makes the
whole dish quite ridiculously rich — oil actually spills out of Anna del
Conte's parmigiana as I slice into it. Though this has the benefit of
also leaving it meltingly tender, if you want to eat more than a sliver,
some compromise is needed.

Jamie Oliver chargrills his slices, which looks pretty, but leaves
the dish sadly dry, and *New York Times* writer Ed Schneider bakes
them first, but the best result, surprisingly, comes from Jane
Grigson's blanched aubergines. Used in combination with the
fried variety, they yield a parmigiana that's soft, but not too oily.

I have to disagree with Grigson's caution against colouring the aubergines in the pan, however: they look more attractive in gold, and the slightly caramelized flavour is more interesting too. Breadcrumbs should remain on top, where they can crisp up in the oven.

In an ideal world, of course, we'd be making this dish with obscenely ripe tomatoes, but in this country it's much safer to stick with the tinned variety. If you've got great fresh tomatoes, then enjoy them in a salad instead.

Parmesan is, as Jane Grigson observes, 'the soul' of the dish, but I like the milky blandness of mozzarella in parmigiana too — lifting a slab, stringy with melted cheese, is a pleasure quite beyond measure. No need to splash out though: good buffalo stuff is too wet, and the sharp flavour is lost in the oven: ordinary, rubbery cheese, of the kind used to top pizzas, is actually preferable.

One last thing: if it's cold outside, by all means tuck in right away, but in more clement weather, heed Ed Schneider's advice when he says that the key to parmigiana, 'as to many other Italian things, is not to serve it hot, though it's hard to wait sometimes'. Let it rest for a few minutes — it'll be even more delicious.

Serves 4–6 (main course/side dish)

> **1.5kg aubergines**
> **Fine salt**
> **2 tablespoons olive oil**
> **3 cloves of garlic, crushed**
> **800g good tinned tomatoes**

150ml red wine
A pinch of sugar
½ teaspoon dried oregano
Oil, to fry
200g mozzarella, thinly sliced
125g Parmesan, grated
50g breadcrumbs
A handful of basil leaves

1. Cut the aubergines lengthways into 5mm thick slices, sprinkle lightly with salt and leave in a colander to drain for half an hour.

2. Meanwhile, heat the olive oil in a medium pan over a medium-high heat and add the crushed garlic. Fry for a minute, stirring, then pour in the tinned tomatoes and wine. Bring this to the boil, mashing the tomatoes roughly as you do, then turn down the heat slightly. Add a pinch of sugar, some salt and pepper and the oregano, and simmer the sauce gently for 45 minutes, stirring occasionally. Purée with a hand blender until smooth, and taste for seasoning.

3. Preheat the oven to 200°C/fan 180°C/gas 6. Put a large pan of water on to boil if you feel like being relatively healthy. Rinse the aubergines well to get rid of the salt, and dry each slice thoroughly with kitchen paper. Pour enough oil into a frying pan to coat the bottom and put this on a high heat.

4. Fry half (healthy) or all (not), the aubergine slices in this pan until golden brown on both sides, working in batches. Put the cooked slices on paper towel to drain. Blanch the other half, for the more virtuous version, in the boiling water for 2 minutes, then drain well and pat dry with more paper.

5. Lightly grease a baking dish with oil and spread the bottom with a thin layer of tomato sauce, followed by a single layer of

aubergines (packing them tightly, and mixing blanched and fried versions together), a layer of mozzarella and a layer of Parmesan, seasoning all but the Parmesan. Add another layer of aubergines, followed by tomato sauce, the cheeses and seasoning. Repeat this order until you've used up all the aubergine, finishing the dish with a layer of sauce (NB: You may not need all the sauce) — but keep a little Parmesan back for the top.

6. Toss the breadcrumbs with a little olive oil and the remaining Parmesan and sprinkle on top, then bake for about 30 minutes, until the top is bubbling and browned. Allow to cool slightly, and sprinkle with torn basil just before serving.

Perfect
Dal

Sometimes – often at dinner parties when conversation flags – I'm asked if I have a 'signature dish'. Truly, *Masterchef* has a lot to answer for. Sometimes I say my brownies (recipe in *Perfect*), which I really, without wishing to seem boastful, believe to be the best in the world. Sometimes I say garlic bread (page 71), because it's the only reason certain people come to my parties. But, if I'm being truthful, I say dal.

Signature may be the wrong word, because it's rarely the kind of thing I make for guests, but, comforting and requiring little in the way of shopping, it's a Sunday night staple in my house. I'm not alone: Madhur Jaffrey writes evocatively of the 'deep satisfaction' of the dish in her *Curry Bible*, describing dal as 'the core of [an Indian] meal'.

Technically dal means a split pulse, but the word has come to describe all dried peas and beans, as well as dishes in which they're the main ingredient. This allows for a dizzying array of options, but the one I cook the most often is mung dal, according to Madhur the most digestible, eaten 'with equal relish by toothless toddlers, husky farmers and effete urban snobs'.

You don't need to soak the dal before cooking – this was traditionally done to save fuel, but I think you get a better result from long slow cooking, as advocated by Jaffrey herself. The aim is to break it down into a silky soup, and this requires patience.

Although some western recipes cook the dal in stock, this is completely unnecessary: not only does a good dal contain quite enough spice as it is, but the contrast between these spices and the creamy blandness of the pulses is a key part of the dish's charm.

The secret of a great dal is the finishing tarka (sometimes called the baghaar or chownk): a mixture of sizzling spices folded through the creamy pulses just before serving. Thinly sliced shallots, as recommended by *Riverford Farm Cook Book*, supply sweetness, Madhur Jaffrey's cumin seeds spice, and mustard seeds and chilli flakes colour and heat, all fried in rich ghee, although oil would no doubt be the healthier option. Some recipes also add a squeeze of lemon juice for freshness, but I find sharpness unwelcome in my comfort blanket dish of choice.

The consistency is up to you, it can be as soupy or as thick as you like – indeed dals are endlessly versatile, taking just about any spice you'll throw at them. Cooked gently and patiently, until creamy, and with a sizzling, aromatic garnish, it's the dish that never disappoints.

Serves 4

400g mung dal (skinned yellow split mung beans)
4 cloves of garlic, peeled and crushed
A 4cm piece of fresh ginger, peeled and cut into 4
1 tablespoon turmeric
4 small green chillies, 2 finely chopped, 2 left whole
2 tablespoons ghee or groundnut oil

2 shallots, finely sliced
1 tablespoon cumin seeds
1 teaspoon mustard seeds
1 teaspoon crushed chilli
Fresh coriander, chopped, to serve

1. Wash the dal in cold water until the water runs clear, then drain and put into a large saucepan. Cover with 2 litres of cold water, bring to the boil and use a slotted spoon to skim off any scum that rises to the top.
2. Add the garlic, ginger, turmeric and chopped chillies to the pan along with a pinch of salt, then turn down the heat, partially cover, and simmer the dal very gently for about 1½ hours, stirring occasionally, until it's soft and creamy in texture.
3. Add boiling water if you prefer a soupy dal, or reduce it further by turning up the heat if you'd like it to be thicker (bear in mind it'll reduce slightly during the final simmer, so don't make it too dry at this point), season to taste, then add the whole chillies and simmer very gently for 15 minutes.
4. Meanwhile, heat the ghee or oil in a frying pan over a medium-high heat and fry the shallots until golden and beginning to crisp. Add the dried spices and cook for a couple of minutes, stirring regularly, until you hear the mustard seeds beginning to pop.
5. Stir the tarka, oil and all, into the dal, and top with chopped coriander. Serve with plain rice or flatbreads.

TIP: An old wives' tale suggests salting any pulses during cooking will make them tough — it doesn't seem to, but with any such lengthy simmering, it's better to add most of the salt at the end, or you risk misjudging the amount and spoiling the end result.

Perfect
Nut Roast

*T*hough veggies may have reason to be grateful for Yotam
Ottolenghi, that's no reason to neglect the classics — this is one of
those vegetarian options that they'll have to fight the omnivores for.
I know: I put it on the table with a roast chicken, and the bird lost.

I think the mistake many nut roast recipes make is to forget just
how energy dense the main ingredient is — unless you
lighten the load with some sort of carbohydrate,
you'll end up with something so dry and heavy you'd
be better off selling it in bars to mountaineers.

Breadcrumbs are the most popular choice, used
by the likes of Rose Elliot and Mary Berry, but they can make for
rather a bland dish — instead, I've bound my roast with fluffy mashed
parsnips, which lend a festive flavour for a dish that, after all, should
be the centrepiece of the meal, adding just a handful of wholemeal
breadcrumbs for lightness.

The flavours are all deliberately chosen to work well with all the
traditional trimmings of a roast — so no Mediterranean aubergine
(Mary Berry), or goat's cheese (Annie Bell) here. Instead
mushrooms act as the savoury element, while chestnuts work well
with the sweetness of the parsnips, and the sage and onion are a nod
to the classic roast stuffing.

As this feels like a very wintery dish to me, I've also added crumbled Stilton for richness, although you could substitute any full-flavoured vegetarian-friendly cheese — or, indeed, if you'd prefer, a teaspoon of Marmite instead, a tip I picked up from a friendly vegetarian on Twitter.

Tasting good, though important, isn't quite enough for a ceremonial dish like a roast — a boring brown loaf lacks the visual impact of a bronzed bird, or a rare joint of beef, so I've wrapped it in blanched cabbage leaves to add a little colour to the table. Good with cranberry sauce or redcurrant jelly — and, of course, bread sauce and the inevitable roast potatoes. Cooked in olive oil, naturally.

Serves 6 (with accompaniments)

2 large parsnips
Oil, to grease
1 small Savoy cabbage, 4–6 outer leaves only
150g hazelnuts
40g butter
1 red onion, finely chopped
150g chestnut mushrooms, finely chopped
100g cooked chestnuts, roughly chopped
100g Stilton, crumbled (or other vegetarian-friendly cheese of your choice)
100g brown breadcrumbs
2 tablespoons chopped fresh sage
1 free-range egg, beaten

1. Peel the parsnips, cut them into quarters (or halves if small) and cook in boiling, salted water until tender. Drain thoroughly, then mash until smooth.

2. Meanwhile, grease a loaf tin approximately 20cm x 10cm x 7cm with oil, then line it with foil, and grease this generously too. Blanch 6 Savoy cabbage leaves in boiling, salted water for 2 minutes until just softened: you'll need enough to line the tin with overlapping leaves, but exactly how many depends on the size of your cabbage, so make sure you have enough before you tip away the water. Once softened, immediately plunge the leaves into iced water to cool, which will keep them a nice, vibrant green colour.

3. Toast the hazelnuts in a dry frying pan over a high heat until starting to colour, then scoop out and set aside. Turn the heat down to medium, add the butter and chopped onion and cook for 5 minutes, then add the chopped mushrooms and cook for about another 7 minutes, until the mixture is thoroughly softened.

4. Roughly chop the hazelnuts and put them into a large bowl with the chopped chestnuts, crumbled Stilton, breadcrumbs and chopped sage. Add the mashed parsnip, onions and mushrooms, followed by the beaten egg. Season and stir together well so everything is thoroughly combined. Preheat the oven to 200°C/ fan 180°C/gas 6.

5. Pat the cabbage leaves dry and use to line the prepared tin, leaving any excess leaf hanging over the sides. Spoon in the mixture, pressing it down well, and fold any overhanging cabbage back over the top to cover. Cover the tin tightly with foil and bake for 45 minutes. (Alternatively, you can keep it in the fridge for a day or so at this point before baking.)

6. Remove the foil from the top, put the loaf back into the oven for

another 15 minutes, until the top is golden, then remove and allow to cool slightly.

7. Put a large serving plate over the top of the tin. Holding the tin securely with oven gloves, turn the plate over so the loaf inverts on to it. Carefully peel off the foil and cut the loaf into slices to serve.

CHAPTER 7

Rice, Noodles and Pasta

*T*hree of my favourite things; I'm a complete carbohydrate junkie. Forget chocolate — I'm rarely happier than when contemplating a big bowl of silky pasta, some soupy noodles or enough fluffy rice to bury my head in.

These tend to be good value meals, designed to bulk out pricier ingredients like seafood, but it's still worth paying a little extra for the main attraction. Value pastas are actually pretty rubbish value in that, though the ingredients are the same (though the quality of the flour may vary), the manufacturing process isn't.

Better-quality pastas are made in bronze dies, giving any sauce a rough, textured surface to cling on to — and also making them more interesting in the mouth. Cheaper brands use easy-clean dies, which produce a smooth, boring result. It may sound silly, but trust me, it makes a difference.

And don't make the mistake of thinking that fresh pasta is always the best option when you can afford it — all the recipes in this chapter are better with the dried variety (fresh tends to suit richer cheese or meat sauces, or filled pastas like ravioli).

The same goes for rice; it's easy to taste the difference between aromatic basmati, or jasmine rice, and bog-standard long-grain, and no use at all using any of the above for paella, or indeed risotto, because they behave in completely different ways when cooked.

If you eat a lot of any of these carbs, they keep so well that it's worth buying in bulk — rice and noodles can be purchased in large quantities at Asian supermarkets, and multipacks of pasta are available online. Even with postage, you'll save money on the supermarket price, which will, of course, leave you more cash to spend on the toppings.

Perfect
Paella

*P*aella is one of those dishes which is a victim of its own popularity —
a little too tasty, and a little too easygoing for its own good, it's
bravely put up with every indignity the modern world can throw at it,
from 'quick-cook rice' to Thai green curry fusion versions.

The Spaniards themselves can't agree upon the best thing
to put in a paella, whether chicken, or rabbit or snails
— indeed, according to Valencian chef Llorenç
Millo, 'paella has as many recipes as there are
villages, and nearly as many as there are cooks'.

Actually, the garnishes are all but irrelevant — as Colman Andrews
explains, 'paella is above all a rice dish — and it is ultimately good
rice, not good seafood (or whatever) that makes a paella great'. So,
just how do you cook that rice?

First off, it needs to be a short-grained variety, which absorbs
liquid easily and doesn't dry out — and stirring is absolutely
forbidden. With a paella, unlike a risotto, the aim is to keep the
grains separate, rather than beating them into creamy submission.
Alberto Herráiz, author of the book *Paella*, and thus, one suspects,
something of an authority, claims that Japanese sushi rice, or
Italian risotto rice, will do as well as Spanish bomba (often sold
under its geographic indication, Calasparra), and indeed, Arborio
works just fine.

Whatever the variety, the rice should be cooked in stock — jazzing up a bought version with shellfish heads, as Herráiz suggests, is a nice touch, giving a greater depth of flavour with very little more work.

The aromatic sofrito — gently sautéd onions, garlic and tomato — is a cornerstone of many Spanish classics and paella is no exception. You can spend an hour simmering it, but I find José Pizarro's version, made in the pan itself before adding the rice, gives as good a result in half the time — especially with tinned tomatoes, which are more reliable than the fresh sort in this country.

The seafood is largely a matter of choice: firm white fish, like monkfish, work best, and I like the smooth chewiness of squid and the sweetness of prawns and mussels, but feel free to experiment, both here and with the vegetables. My broad beans are a nod to the fresh white lima beans that would traditionally be included in its homeland, but peas would work just as well if you prefer. Copious amounts of olive oil are, however, non-negotiable.

You also, ideally, need a wide flat paella pan to achieve the proper contrast between the crunchy caramelized crust on the bottom, and the moist, fluffy top layer — but there's no truth whatsoever in the old lore that a good paella can only be prepared by a man, in the open air, at midday — 'preferably under the shade of an old vine or fig tree'. Although, if you happen to have one knocking around . . .

Serves 2—4, depending on hunger

4 raw, unshelled tiger prawns
90ml olive oil
3 cloves of garlic, finely chopped
500ml good-quality fish stock
150g sustainable monkfish, cut into chunks
I onion, finely diced
I teaspoon smoked paprika
200g chopped tomatoes
50ml dry white wine
150g baby squid, cut into rings
150g broad beans
200g Calasparra or other short-grain rice
A pinch of saffron, soaked in I tablespoon hot water
150g mussels, scrubbed
A handful of flat-leaf parsley, roughly chopped, to garnish
½ a lemon, cut into wedges

1. Remove the shells from the prawns and, keeping the shells, put the meat aside for later. Heat I tablespoon of olive oil in a wide pan and sauté a third of the garlic over a medium heat for a couple of minutes. Add the prawn shells and fry, stirring to break them up, for about 3 minutes, until pink. Pour in the stock and leave to simmer gently for 30 minutes, then strain, discarding the shells, season to taste and keep warm.
2. Heat the remaining oil in a 26cm paella or other wide, thin-based pan and add the chunks of monkfish. Sauté for 5 minutes, until slightly browned, then take out of the pan and set aside.
3. Add the onion and remaining garlic to the pan and cook until softened, then stir in the paprika and cook for a further minute.

Add the tomatoes and wine, turn up the heat and simmer for 10 minutes. Add the squid and beans, and fry for 30 seconds.

4. Tip the rice into the pan and stir to coat with the liquid already there, then arrange it into an even layer. Pour in 400ml of the warm stock and the saffron and its soaking water. Simmer vigorously, without stirring, for 10 minutes, then arrange the monkfish, mussels and prawns on the top of the dish, pushing them well into the rice but not otherwise disturbing it.

5. Cook for about 8 minutes – if the dish starts to looks very dry before the rice has finished cooking, add the rest of the stock, bearing in mind paella shouldn't be at all soupy.

6. Take the pan off the heat, cover with foil and allow to rest for 10 minutes. Garnish with flat-leaf parsley and wedges of lemon to serve.

Perfect
Egg-fried Rice

According to Ken Hom, no one actually eats the fried rice at a Chinese banquet — it's served late, to allow guests to appreciate their host's generosity in encouraging them to fill up on meat and fish first. Should anyone ever invite me to such a bash, I'll be sure to save space, however, because, simple as it may be, there's little I enjoy more than a bowl of egg-fried rice. Even pickled sea cucumber.

It's actually a surprisingly difficult dish to get right, however. First of all, you need cold rice. Merely room temperature rice will give a mushy result, and hot rice will, as Delia explains, leave you with a sticky mess. Whatever you happen to have left over will be fine, but jasmine is ideal — its slightly glutinous nature will keep it moist in the heat of the wok, which would kill a more delicate long-grain like basmati.

Fried rice will happily absorb most other leftovers you happen to have lying around, but egg should be mandatory, adding a delicious richness to the dish. Hom's method of adding beaten egg to the rice, then stirring it all together, gives a better result than scrambling the eggs separately and mixing them in once cooked, as Ching-He Huang, Rose Prince and Allegra McEvedy suggest. Their recipes have too many large, dry flakes of egg for my liking, while Hom's rice is moist and richly golden all the way through.

McEvedy does offer some good advice on the heat front, however — it should be stir-fried over a high flame, until the rice 'smells good and is beginning to get nice little brown crunchy bits', and, I think, in a neutral oil. Many recipes add a little sesame oil, but I find the nutty flavour completely overpowering — add it, along with soy sauce, at the table if you like.

Garlic has no place here as far as I'm concerned, but the fresh, green flavour of a few finely chopped spring onions cuts through the richness of the eggy rice nicely. Add peas or pork or prawns if you must, but this is all I need for a solitary banquet.

Serves 2, generously

3 tablespoons groundnut oil
500g cooked jasmine rice,
    at fridge temperature (about 175g raw rice)
2 eggs, beaten with ½ teaspoon salt
2 spring onions, finely chopped

1. Heat the oil in a wok or large frying pan over a high heat until it begins to smoke, then add the rice. Working quickly, spread out the rice so it heats evenly, then toss it until every grain is well coated with oil.
2. Pour in the eggs while stirring furiously, so most of the egg is absorbed into the rice. Continue to stir-fry for a couple of minutes until some grains have just begun to caramelize and turn golden.
3. Sprinkle with the chopped spring onions and serve immediately.

Perfect
Pilaf

*T*here's only one thing you need to know about this ancient Middle Eastern rice dish — every grain must remain separate. Thirteenth-century Arabic texts explain that they should resemble plump peppercorns: master that, and you've cracked every single one of its thousands of variations, from Uzbek plovs to Indian pilaus. This basic version should set you on the right path.

Basmati rice is the only choice — its delicate flavour really shines in such a plain setting. You can use the brown variety if you're feeling virtuous, but I wouldn't bother: it takes ages to cook, and the chewiness seems to clash with the simple elegance of the dish. Soaking reduces the cooking time slightly if you're in a hurry, and rinsing it first, to wash off surface starch, will help avoid any stickiness.

Because I like the rice to be the star, I cook my pilaf in water, like Elizabeth David and Anissa Helou, but you could use chicken or vegetable stock if you prefer a fuller flavour. I'm also ditching the onions used by Gordon Ramsay and Tamasin Day-Lewis; their melting softness seems at odds with the fluffy texture of the grains, and without it, you can taste the delicate spices: sweet cinnamon and fragrant cardamom, as well as the aromatic lemon zest inspired by Anissa Helou's recipe, and saffron for colour and fragrance.

Elizabeth David suggests cooking the pilaf in dripping, which is not at all my idea of a fragrant fat — oil is better, but it seems more like a pure lubricant, whereas butter adds a gorgeous rich flavour to the dish.

Pilafs are traditionally boiled then steamed — and the only way to achieve the desired effect of crunchy bottom and fluffy top is indeed to par-boil the rice and then steam it in butter, as Sally Butcher and Anissa Helou suggest, poking air holes with a wooden spoon to allow the steam to escape. And then, well, good things come to those who wait.

Serves 4

300g white basmati rice
A generous knob of butter
3 cardamom pods, crushed
1 cinnamon stick
A pinch of saffron
2 strips of lemon zest

1. Rinse the rice well in cold water, and tip it into a large saucepan of boiling, liberally salted water. Stir once, bring back to the boil, and simmer for 7 minutes.
2. Drain the rice thoroughly, and season to taste. Melt the butter in a large, clean pan over a medium heat, then add the spices and lemon zest. Cook for a minute, stirring so they don't burn, then add 2 tablespoons of water and a layer of rice to the pan, making sure it covers the base completely.
3. Heap the rest of the rice on top in layers, but don't push it down

or you'll crush it. Make 5 air holes in the surface of the rice with the handle of a wooden spoon or similar, then wrap the lid in a clean tea towel and cover. Leave to cook undisturbed over a very low heat for 30 minutes.

4. Fill the sink 5cm full of cold water. When the rice is ready, and leaving the lid on, plunge the pan into the water and allow to sit for a minute, then turn the pilaf on to a serving platter.

The best bit

The tastiest bit of any pilaf, is, of course, the caramelized crust that forms on the bottom of the pan — known as tah-dig, literally the bottom of the pot, it's fought over in Middle Eastern households and is often prized as a dish in its own right. Some recipes add extra ingredients to help it along (egg is a favourite), but there's no need: just cook the rice gently, and then, in a great tip from Sally Butcher, Persian queen of Peckham, dunk the bottom of the dish in cold water to dislodge the tah-dig in one gorgeous golden piece. It's rice, yes, but not as you know it.

Perfect
Pad Thai

*B*rilliantly quick to make, as a visit to any night market will
demonstrate — but that doesn't make it easy. This must be one of the
most difficult recipes I've ever tried to perfect. Fortunately, I've
made the mistakes so you don't have to.

Experts use a large, flat pan specially designed for the purpose,
as the greater surface area encourages evaporation. For
amateurs, however, a wok is a better bet, allowing you to
keep the noodles off the heat while you cook the other
ingredients in the base.

One piece of advice everyone, expert or not, should heed,
however, is Pim Techamuanvivit's warning that you must never try to
cook more than two portions of pad thai at a time — it's tricky
enough to cook everything at the same time as it is, without adding
overcrowding to your problems.

Getting your rice stick noodles to the right texture — cooked, but
still elastic and chewy — is the secret here. They'll try and clump
together whatever you do, but softening them in cold water will at
least give you a bit of a head start — they should be pliable enough
for you to wind them round your finger. Keep them moving in
the wok, make sure they don't dry out — and keep your fingers
crossed.

The best way to ensure they don't dry out is to add liquid — the most common pad thai sauce is a mixture of tamarind,* fish sauce and palm sugar, prepared ahead of time so you don't ruin the dish while you fiddle around trying to achieve the perfect balance in the wok. Heating it helps to dissolve the sugar, and also gives you more of an idea of what it will taste like in the finished dish.

With the sauce and noodles sorted, the dish is done — protein and garnishes are essentially up to you, but prawns, both fresh and dried, eggs and tofu are the most popular options. (Please don't be tempted to skip the dried shrimp unless you really can't find them: they add a pleasing savoury note.)

Chinese chives and beansprouts contribute crunch, and preserved radish and peanuts a lovely salty kick — there are so many different flavours and textures in this dish that every bite should be a different experience.

Serves 2

120g 2–3mm wide flat rice sticks
60ml fish sauce
60ml tamarind water (you can use tamarind concentrate, thinned with a little water)
60g palm sugar
A pinch of chilli powder, to taste
80ml groundnut or vegetable oil
2 cloves of garlic, finely chopped
100g extra-firm tofu, chopped into small cubes

---

* For a brief guide to Thai basics, see page 95.

8 large raw prawns
2 large eggs, ready cracked
25g preserved salted radish, chopped
1 tablespoon small dried shrimp
100g beansprouts
4 stalks of Chinese chives, chopped (or spring onions)
50g roasted peanuts, roughly chopped
Lime wedges, chilli flakes, fish sauce and sugar, to garnish

1. Soak the rice sticks in cold water for about 30 minutes until pliable but still chewy (you should be able to wind them round a finger). Drain thoroughly and place near the hob.

2. Meanwhile, to make the sauce, put the fish sauce, tamarind water and palm sugar into a small pan. Heat gently, stirring to dissolve the sugar, then taste – add more of any of the ingredients as you wish, so it feels balanced to you. Season with chilli powder to taste and set aside near the hob.

3. Arrange the remaining ingredients within easy reach of the hob in the order they'll be used (as above). Take a deep breath: everything from this point on must be done quickly.

4. Put a wok on a high heat and add half the oil. Add the garlic, stir-fry for a couple of seconds, then add the drained noodles and a splash of water. Stir-fry until they're beginning to dry out, then pour in the sauce. Fry until they're almost soft enough to eat (they should still be slightly chewy).

5. Push the noodles to the side of the wok and add the remaining oil. Fry the tofu and prawns until the prawns are pink and the tofu is beginning to colour, then push them to the side and add the eggs. Pierce the yolks and leave until they're just starting to set on the bottom, then scramble.

6. Quickly stir all these ingredients through the noodles, and add

the radish, dried shrimp, beansprouts, chives and peanuts. Stir-fry vigorously until well combined, then serve with the garnishes for people to add as they wish.

TIP: Please heed my instructions and set everything out neatly by the hob before lighting the gas. Otherwise, you've got no hope.

Perfect
Spaghetti alle Vongole

*I*f ever a dish makes me think of summer holidays, it's this — fresh,
but rich in flavour, spiked with spice and studded with plump,
briny clams, it's as perfect for banishing winter blues as it is for
lunch at an Adriatic café in July. And it's simple, by God it's
simple.

Vongole recipes divide into two main camps: those with tomatoes,
and those ('bianco') without. Jamie prefers it with, Nigella
would have it without for her last meal. I'm not keen
on the tinned tomato sauce of Elizabeth
David's 1954 recipe, but I have to
concede that Gwyneth Paltrow's use of
cherry tomatoes nearly wins me over — but
in the end I decide that it's at the expense
of the clams themselves. Bianco for me.

Fresh chilli is a must: the flavour is much sharper and keener than
the dried sort, and a copious amount of garlic adds its own heat.
Things you don't need in a vongole include Gwynnie's fennel seeds,
anchovies and basil (parsley works far better), the River Café's
porcini mushrooms and oregano, or David's onions — the simpler
the better here.

That said, I will be stealing a tip the River Café ladies picked up at a
seaside restaurant near Rome, and adding butter as well as olive oil:

it may be unorthodox, but it gives the dish a richer, more satisfying flavour, without distracting from the few other ingredients. A spritz of lemon juice finishes things off nicely.

If you're going to buy fresh clams, don't smother them with other flavours — enjoy their salty sweetness au naturel, with perhaps a cold glass of Vermentino for good measure.

Serves 4

500g small fresh clams (palourdes or
    carpetshell are ideal — tinned clams are not)
350g dried spaghetti
30g butter
2 tablespoons extra virgin olive oil
3 fat cloves of garlic, finely chopped
½ a medium-hot red chilli, finely chopped
100ml dry white wine
A small bunch of flat-leaf parsley,
    roughly chopped
Zest of ½ a lemon and a spritz of juice

1. Rinse the clams in cold running water, and scrub if necessary, then tip them into a large bowl and cover with cold water. Salt generously and leave them undisturbed for a couple of hours. Drain and rinse well in a colander to remove any grit or sand.
2. Bring a large pan of salted water to the boil and cook the spaghetti for a couple of minutes under the recommended time on the packet, until approaching al dente.
3. Meanwhile, put half the butter and all the olive oil into a large

pan over a medium heat and, once the butter has melted, cook the garlic and chilli for a couple of minutes, making sure the garlic doesn't burn.

4. Add the drained clams to the pan, and turn up the heat. Pour in the wine, bring it to the boil, cover the pan and leave it closed for a couple of minutes: most of the clams should have opened. If not, give it another minute or so, then discard any that are still closed. Pick a few of the rest out of their shells if you like, for variety.

5. Drain the spaghetti and add it to the pan along with the remaining butter. Toss well to coat and leave to cook for a minute, then stir through the chopped parsley, lemon zest and juice. Season to taste and serve.

Happy as a clam?
Clams, like many shellfish, are sold live. Check them just before cooking, and throw away any that are open, and don't close when tapped, or any with damaged shells. Rinse the rest in running water to get rid of any grit before use.

Perfect
Spaghetti Carbonara

*F*ew dishes make me happier than spaghetti carbonara — rich with eggs, savoury with bacon, and festooned with salty cheese.

It's a dish with an interesting history: although almost everyone agrees that it probably originated in the Roman region, the supposed creators range from Apennine charcoal burners (carbonai) to the American GIs who asked local street vendors to prepare their bacon and egg rations for them over their charcoal braziers. Most plausible, in my opinion, is the theory that the name simply refers to the copious amounts of black pepper the dish is usually seasoned with — like tiny specks of charcoal, but infinitely tastier.

The spaghetti is there for good reason. One of the principal pleasures of this dish is slurping up the egg-slick strands, which is impossible with anything other than long pasta.

Cream and butter, purists claim, are recent additions to the recipe — introduced by restaurants because they're easier to control, and somewhat safer than a sauce of barely set egg. That said, they have some heavyweights on their side: Hopkinson and Bareham, and Nigella Lawson, use double cream, Ursula Ferrigno crème fraîche, and the River Café and Anna del Conte butter. All, in my opinion, are mistaken: cream dilutes the delicate flavour of the egg yolk, and the richness of the butter competes with the richness of the pork fat. There's no need for such an excess of sauce in any case; there should be just enough there to coat the pasta and no more.

It's the egg yolk that adds the flavour, but using just the yolk, as the River Café and Simon and Lindsey suggest, makes the dish rather cloying, and exhibits a tendency to clump together amongst the strands of pasta. Whole eggs, as used by Nigella, Elizabeth David, *The Silver Spoon* and Ursula Ferrigno, give a looser sauce – but, as this is a dish you don't eat every day, I've sneaked in one extra yolk for extra eggy richness.

Back bacon, as favoured by my dad, won't cut the mustard here: you need pancetta, or a good dry-cured slab of streaky, cut into chunky little cubes, and cooked, as Nigella suggests, until 'crispy but not crunchy'. Make sure it's unsmoked, or you'll be faced with an umami overload – because this isn't a dish where you can get away with a delicate sprinkle of Parmesan. No, cheese plays a major part – preferably a half and half mix of salty Parmesan and the slightly fresher, more lactic pecorino romano, a salty ewe's milk cheese popular in central Italy.

Garlic, in subtle quantities, is a welcome addition, though I'd whip it out before adding the other ingredients, or it can dominate. You don't need parsley if you've got enough pepper, but I do love Nigella's final grating of nutmeg, which, although it will no doubt make Romans throw up their hands in horror, always pairs beautifully with egg.

The devil, when cooking carbonara, is in the detail – namely how to add raw eggs to a hot pan of pasta without ending up with egg-fried spaghetti. I'd advise the briefest of encounters between eggs and heat, so they thicken to a creamy consistency, without solidifying.

The secret is to work quickly, tossing the cooked pasta in the oily pancetta until every strand is greased, then remove from the heat, toss briefly with the eggs and cheese — with a little cooking water just to loosen — and serve immediately. There's an art to it, but, like art in general, once you get it, it's a thing of rare beauty.

Serves 2

1 tablespoon olive oil
1 clove of garlic, sliced
75g pancetta, cubed
250g dried spaghetti
2 eggs and 1 egg yolk
25g pecorino romano, finely grated
25g Parmesan, finely grated
Freshly ground black pepper
Nutmeg, optional

1. Put two bowls into a low oven to keep warm, or boil a kettle and half fill them with hot water. Heat the oil in a large frying pan on a medium heat, then add the sliced garlic and cook, stirring, until well-coloured but not burnt. Remove from the pan with a slotted spoon and discard. Add the pancetta to the garlicky oil and cook until translucent and golden, but not brown.

2. Meanwhile, cook the spaghetti in a large pan of boiling, salted water until al dente. Beat together the eggs and the extra yolk, then stir in the pecorino and most of the Parmesan, reserving a

little as a garnish. Grind in plenty of black pepper and set the mixture next to the hob.

3. Scoop out a small cupful of the pasta cooking water and set aside next to the hob, then drain the pasta thoroughly. Tip it into the frying pan and toss vigorously so it's well coated with the pancetta fat.

4. Remove the pan from the heat and tip in the egg mixture, tossing the pasta furiously, then, once it's begun to thicken, add a dash of cooking water to loosen the sauce.

5. Toss again, and divide it between the warm bowls, finishing off with a light grating of nutmeg, if using, more black pepper and a little more Parmesan. Eat immediately.

Perfect
Crab Linguine

*S*paghetti alle vongole's richer, more indulgent cousin, and made with spider crab in its homeland, this is a lovely fate for a native brown crab – zesty and intensely seafoody, it's one of the nicest things you can do to a crustacean, bar eating it with mayonnaise and brown bread on a Cornish rock.

Most recipes miss a trick by using only the white meat – in fact, as anyone who's ever dressed one knows, most of the flavour resides in the less pretty brown stuff. The version from Brixham's Old Market House restaurant, which stirs brown meat into the sauce, is a revelation to me, giving the whole dish a rich, deeply crustaceous character. The fluffier, sweeter white meat can be tossed through the pasta just before serving, like a kind of pescatorial Parmesan.

As so often with pasta, garlic works better than spring onions or Tom Aikens' shallots – finely chopped it melts into the sauce, lending it a slight heat as well as its distinctive pungent flavour. That's all it needs – anything else, from the River Café's shaved fennel to Aikens' cherry tomatoes, risks distracting from the crab.

Spice-wise, fresh chilli adds a fruity kick, Angela Hartnett's lemon zest a welcome bitterness and the River Café's fennel seeds an aromatic sweetness – all set off nicely with peppery flat-leaf parsley.

Aikens makes a proper crab stock for his recipe, but I think the brown meat gives you a far greater concentration of crustacean flavour for a lot less work, and there's no need for the Old Market House's cream here either. Instead, Angela Hartnett's lemon juice adds a tangy freshness which makes a lovely contrast to the rich crabmeat — all you need is a final flourish of extra virgin olive oil, and you could be back on that Neapolitan terrace in the spring sunshine . . .

Serves 4

400g dried linguine
1 tablespoon olive oil
2 cloves of garlic, finely chopped
1 red chilli, deseeded and finely chopped
1 teaspoon fennel seeds, crushed
1 lemon
200g brown crabmeat
200g white crabmeat
A small bunch of flat-leaf parsley, roughly chopped
Extra virgin olive oil, to finish

1. Bring a large pan of generously salted water to the boil and cook the pasta until al dente.
2. Meanwhile, heat the oil in a frying pan over a medium-low heat and cook the garlic, chilli and fennel seeds for a couple of minutes until soft, but not coloured.
3. Add the zest of half the lemon and the juice of all of it to the pan, then stir in the brown crabmeat.
4. Drain the pasta well, reserving a few spoonfuls of the cooking

water, and toss it with the sauce, along with the white crabmeat and chopped parsley. Add the reserved cooking water, a little at a time, if the dish seems dry.

5. Season to taste, and divide between bowls. Drizzle each bowl with extra virgin olive oil, and serve immediately.

Perfect
Macaroni Cheese

I must confess, I've come to macaroni cheese pretty late in life. Despite it containing two of my favourite ingredients, namely cheese and pasta, I just didn't get it. And then — then, well, I just did.

That's not to say I've embraced the outrageously rich, cheesy versions that seem to have become popular recently — although I try recipes using double cream, and Parmesan (that from Mrs Beeton, no less!), garlic (I'm looking at you, Jamie Oliver) and Lancashire cheese, in the end, I keep coming back to Tom Norrington-Davies' simple version, with its plain white sauce and modest Cheddar content. Creamy, rather than oppressively rich, and savoury, not cheesy, it's almost the dictionary definition of nursery food.

That said, Parmesan is rather nice on top, along with Martha Stewart's crunchy golden breadcrumbs, which offer a welcome contrast in texture, while a few caramelized tomatoes add a touch of sweetness. English mustard powder, a less acidic version of the mustard used in many recipes, supplies a subtle heat without any accompanying sourness.

Giving credence to every cliché going about Victorian cooking, Mrs Beeton boils the pasta for 1½ to 1¾ hours until 'quite tender' — I only managed an hour before it started to disintegrate, so perhaps stoves were less efficient in those days. More helpful is Martha's tip about rinsing the pasta before adding to the dish, so it doesn't clump together in a gluey mess.

Simon Hopkinson and Lindsey Bareham suggest using penne instead, on the grounds that 'the cheese sauce is better able to flow inside this larger-sized pasta' but I disagree — it's the small size of macaroni, perfect for scooping up in greedy spoonfuls, which sets the dish apart from a pasta bake in my opinion. I quite like their leeks though — softened in a little butter, they're a useful optional extra, especially if you're serving this as a stand-alone supper.

Otherwise, however, this is a dish that epitomizes modest simplicity — to add strong flavours, or fancy ingredients is to miss the point. It should be subtle, creamy and soft; perfect for eating on the sofa in your pyjamas.

Serves 2

200g macaroni
35g butter, plus extra for greasing
25g plain flour
450ml whole milk
A grating of nutmeg
½ teaspoon English mustard powder
50g mature Cheddar, grated
1 slice of white bread, made into crumbs
1 tablespoon grated Parmesan
2 tomatoes, halved

1. Bring a large pan of salted water to the boil, tip in the pasta, stir and cook until tender. Drain well and rinse under cold running water.

2. Meanwhile, melt 25g of the butter in a pan, and, once it's melted, stir in the flour to make a paste. Cook, stirring, for a couple of minutes, then gradually whisk in the milk until it becomes a smooth sauce. Simmer this, stirring all the time, for a few minutes until it thickens, then add a grating of nutmeg, the mustard powder and grated cheese and stir until smooth. Take off the heat, and season to taste.

3. Preheat the grill. Grease a baking dish with butter, then tip the drained pasta into the cheese sauce and pour it all into the baking dish. (You can make it ahead up to this point, in which case you'll need to reheat it in the oven until warm through before going on to step 4.)

4. Melt the remaining butter and mix it with the breadcrumbs and the Parmesan. Spread the mixture over the top of the pasta, then arrange the tomatoes, cut side up, on top.

5. Grill for about 10 minutes, until the top is golden and the tomatoes charred. Allow to stand for 5 minutes before serving.

CHAPTER 8

Puddings

*A*nd I mean puddings, rather than desserts. If you want to end the meal elegantly, turn to the tarte au citron on page 314. If, however, you're craving something sticky, or oozy, or even wobbly, then read on.

That's not to say none of the recipes in this chapter are suitable for what's still rather quaintly known as 'entertaining': a simple panna cotta or a magnificent trifle can both be dressed to impress, but, like the humbler bread and butter pudding, or rhubarb fool, they're both fundamentally satisfying desserts.

In other words, they encourage you to make a bit of a pig of yourself — much as I love tarte au citron, a single rich, citrussy sliver is enough. With trifle, however, I could happily eat the entire bowl, and one day, I fully intend to.

Many of these are dishes that must be prepared ahead of time, which makes them absolutely perfect candidates for guests, when you're loath to leave the conversation and start faffing about in the kitchen. Panna cotta, rhubarb fool, trifle all fit the bill — even the crèmes brûlées just need finishing off with a blowtorch.

But you don't need a tableful of people to make any of them: a homemade pudding once a week is an easy way to lift the spirits, because who could fail to be cheered by the sight of a sticky syrup sponge and a jug of yellow custard, or even a simple ice cream sundae with chocolate sauce in front of the Saturday film? This is the kind of food that makes me happy, and I hope it does the same for you.

Perfect
Bread and Butter Pudding

*T*he British equivalent of the Italian panzanella salad (page 112), or the Arabic fattoush, this is a way of using up stale bread that's good enough to merit letting bread stale for. Blandly milky, comfortingly stodgy and modestly spiced, it's a childhood favourite that still delivers.

It does, however, require patience: there's no point making it with fresh bread, it just goes soggy, which is not the idea at all. Otherwise, you can use just about any plain or sweet loaf you happen to have hanging around – potato and thyme might be a bad idea, but white bloomers, old panettone or even chewy sourdough all yield pleasing, if very different results.

You also need to give the ingredients time to get to know one another – leaving the bread to soak in the custard gives a softer, more yielding texture, although I like to add a second layer of bread and custard just before baking to give the pudding a crisp top, like Delia's version.

Thankfully there's no need to spend hours caressing the custard as it infinitesimally thickens over a candle flame – the thinner the sauce, the better it will be absorbed by the bread, so you can just mix the ingredients together and pour them on without further ado. Baking the pudding in a bain-marie, as suggested by *Leiths Cookery Bible*, moderates the temperature, giving the finished dish a smoother, silkier texture which contrasts beautifully with the crunchy, caramelized top.

Because this is such a plain pudding, I don't think soaking the dried fruit in booze first is gilding the lily – it's an idea I nicked from the nineteenth-century cookery writer Eliza Acton, and she doesn't seem to have been a woman given to needless extravagance. Hot toddy and hot-ish pudding in one quivering, creamy mouthful; come on, 3 tablespoons of brandy is hardly going to break the bank.

Do heed the instruction to leave it to cool slightly before tucking in – like many milk-and-egg-based dishes, the flavour develops as the temperature comes down.

Serves 4

50g currants, raisins or sultanas,
   or a mixture (optional)
3 tablespoons brandy (optional)
200ml whole milk
100ml double cream
I vanilla pod, halved
Zest of ½ a lemon
75g slightly salted butter
8 slices of slightly stale good white bread,
   fruit bread or panettone
3 eggs
2 tablespoons caster sugar
I tablespoon demerara sugar
Nutmeg, to grate

1. If using panettone or any other sort of fruit bread, feel free to skip this step. Otherwise, put the dried fruit into a small cup or jar, pour over the brandy, cover tightly and leave to plump up overnight.
2. When you're ready to start making the pudding, pour the milk and cream into a small pan and add the vanilla pod. Bring gently to a simmer, then turn off the heat, add the lemon zest and leave to cool.
3. Meanwhile, butter both the bread and your baking dish and cut the bread into triangles. Arrange half these triangles in overlapping rows inside. Beat the eggs together with the caster sugar until well combined, then remove the vanilla pod from the pan before beating the milk and the cream into the egg mixture. Pour a little more than half this custard over the bread, scatter with the soaked fruit if using, and leave to sit for 20 minutes.
4. Preheat the oven to 200°C/fan 180°C/gas 6. Use the remaining bread to make a top layer in the baking dish and drizzle over the rest of the custard. Dot the top with the rest of the butter, scatter with demerara sugar and grate a little nutmeg over the top.
5. Place the baking dish in a slightly larger roasting tin, and fill this up to halfway with cold water, to make a bain-marie.
6. Bake for 35–45 minutes, until golden brown on top. Allow to stand for 10 minutes before serving.

Perfect
Chocolate Fondants

*T*he downfall of many a *Masterchef* hopeful, this little pudding has developed a fearsome, and quite undeserved, reputation in recent years. The issue is the fondant aspect, here indicating a melting middle rather than anything to do with French fancies, or violet creams. To achieve that perfect gooey interior, concealed within a fluffy shell, you need to get your timing dead on. Crack that, and you've cracked the secret of the fondant.

That said, this is a pudding with an air of dark sophistication about it; you don't want it to smack too much of the childish chocolate cake, so starting with a sponge mixture, as Nigella Lawson does for her saucy-sounding molten chocolate babycakes, is a mistake.

Getting too fancy is dangerous too: Raymond Blanc's meringue-like version ends up tough and dry, and John Torode's complicated recipe has me more stressed than a finalist on his television show.

This is a recipe where the best method is the simplest: beat together the eggs and yolks (for extra richness) with sugar to make the fondant light and fluffy, as suggested by Tamasin Day-Lewis, then fold in melted butter and chocolate, along with a little cocoa powder to give it a more intense flavour, and a negligible amount of flour.

The difficult part comes in the cooking — so, if you're relying on these to impress (and the recipe is easily scaled up), please, please check the timings in your oven first. A dry run of a chocolate pudding is never unwelcome, and that way, if your oven thermometer runs slightly hotter or colder than mine, you won't end up with a molten brown disaster on your hands on the night. (If that does happen, spoon them into bowls and top with ice cream — I guarantee no one will complain.)

Lining the moulds with cocoa powder, as Gordon Ramsay suggests, not only looks pretty but will help you turn the fondants out if you're feeling brave — if you have a crisis of confidence, serve them in the moulds with a blob of crème fraîche on top instead.

Makes 2

60g unsalted butter, cut into dice,
    plus extra to grease
1 tablespoon cocoa powder
60g dark chocolate, broken into pieces
1 egg and 1 egg yolk
60g caster sugar
1 tablespoon plain flour

1. Preheat the oven to 200°C/fan 180°C/gas 6 if baking the fondants immediately, and put a baking tray on the middle shelf. Boil the kettle for your bain-marie. Grease the inside of two small ramekins or pudding moulds with butter, then put the cocoa into one and turn it until the inside is well coated,

holding it over the second mould to catch any escaping powder. Once coated, tip the remaining cocoa into the second mould and repeat.

2. Pour the boiling water into a small pan and put the butter and chocolate pieces in a heatproof bowl set over, but not touching, the simmering water. Stir occasionally until both butter and chocolate have melted. Allow to cool slightly.

3. Whisk together the egg, yolk, sugar and a pinch of salt until pale and fluffy. Gently and slowly fold in the melted chocolate and butter, followed by the flour.

4. Spoon the mixture into the prepared moulds, stopping just short of the top — at this point the moulds can be refrigerated until needed, or even frozen for up to a month, as the puddings need to be served straight from the oven.

5. Put the fondants on the hot baking tray and bake for 12 minutes (14 if from cold, 16 if frozen), until the tops are set and beginning to come away from the sides of the moulds. Leave to rest for 30 seconds, then serve in the ramekins or loosen the edges and turn out on to plates if you're feeling confident — they're great with clotted cream or plain ice cream.

Perfect
Chocolate Sauce

Not strictly a pudding, you might well say — but add a few scoops of ice cream and you've got yourself a bona fide treat. It may not be as trendy as salted caramel sauce, or as sophisticated as a campari syrup, but, with the notable exception of tinned ravioli, what tasted good when you were eight still tends to taste good today, and this is one versatile recipe to have up your sleeve.

Although cocoa powder is often a useful ingredient when cooking with chocolate, adding flavour without weight, it's too intense and bitter for a chocolate sauce — this isn't a sophisticated condiment. That said, you need good-quality dark chocolate, or the end result will be far too sweet to pour over ice cream.

Chocolate sauce recipes seem to fall into two distinct camps: the syrupy kind, good for drizzling, but too sugary to eat on their own, and the richer, creamier sort, which could almost stand alone as a pudding if you were feeling very, very greedy. I've tried various recipes for the former, including Robin and Caroline Weir's water-and-golden-syrup-based number, and David Lebovitz's corn syrup version, but they're too sickly for my taste.

Far better are those recipes which, like Nigel Slater, Bill Granger, and Simon Hopkinson and Lindsey Bareham, use cream — it seems to temper the bittersweet intensity of the chocolate, making the whole thing mild enough to eat by the spoonful.

Whipping cream gives the lightest result; double makes the sauce too rich and cloying, and in fact I've ended up using rather less than most of the other recipes in any case. The sauce is principally designed to be served with ice cream, rather than on its own, and it shouldn't steal its thunder.

Though I'm not sold on the very sweet versions, adding no extra sugar whatsoever, as is not uncommon in cream-based sauces, makes things a wee bit dour. A little golden syrup, as in Alice Hart's recipe, supplies a toffeeish sweetness and a hint of glorious stickiness too, and it's balanced by a pinch of sea salt, though you can add whatever flavourings you like; I've included a few suggestions to get you started below.

Makes enough for 4 sundaes

150g plain chocolate, broken into small pieces
50ml whipping cream
2 tablespoons golden syrup
A knob of butter
A pinch of sea salt

1. Put the chocolate pieces and cream into a small, heavy-based pan over a low heat. Heat, stirring occasionally to help things along, until the chocolate has melted smoothly into the cream.
2. Stir in the syrup, followed by the butter and salt, and you should

have a beautifully glossy sauce. Keep warm until ready to serve, or just eat straight from the pan.

A few flavour suggestions, to be stirred in at step 2
- Grated zest of ½ an orange (organic ones are best, as they aren't waxed)
- 1½ tablespoons strong black coffee
- ½ teaspoon almond essence (you may need to add more depending on the strength of the brand you buy)
- ¼ teaspoon peppermint essence (ditto)
- A pinch of cinnamon and a pinch of chilli powder, if you're feeling a bit Mexican
- ½ teaspoon rose water

Chocolate sauce is good with . . .
- American pancakes (page 20)
- Panna cotta (page 264)
- Ice cream (add some chopped nuts and fruit and you've got yourself a sundae)
- Ripe bananas
- Fridge-cold orange segments
- Profiteroles
- Poached pears
- Churros (Spanish doughnuts)
- Roughly broken digestive biscuits and vanilla ice cream

Perfect
Crème Brûlée

There was a time when I couldn't see this on a menu without ordering it — I love all things custardy, and once you add a crisp crust of caramelized sugar, well, it's pretty much a perfect dessert. Too many disappointments — soft, sticky tops, grainy or over-eggy disasters beneath — have made me wary, however; a mediocre crème brûlée is still better than most other things in life, but it's so simple to make a great one that why waste the calories?

I try various custard recipes; Mary Berry's single cream is a little bit thin, and Heston Blumenthal's egg yolk and milk mixture is so rich I can hardly face going back for a second spoonful — possibly for the first time ever.

Double cream, as used by Claire Clark, Simon Hopkinson and Lindsey Bareham, gives the best result for a thick custard, although, as I prefer the light, creamy flavour of Mary's recipe, if not the thin texture, I'm going to copy her and use fewer yolks than the others.

Older crème brûlée recipes call for the cook to thicken the custard in the pan before baking, patiently stirring until it has an almost 'jelly-like consistency', which Hopkinson and Bareham claim gives the dessert a voluptuous texture, but, to be honest, I prefer the light wobbliness of the modern version.

It also has the benefit of being far quicker: all you have to do is stir hot cream into egg yolks and sugar, and bake it, which seems almost dangerously easy for a fanatic like myself. Once in the oven, Claire Clark's bain-marie helps keep the custard smooth and silky in the heat.

Mary's also got it right with the topping: demerara sugar may not melt into such a glossy, mirror-like shell, but the larger grains make it crunchier than caster sugar, and I love the toffee flavour it brings. Using a cook's blowtorch, if you have one, will melt the sugar faster than a grill, so the custard beneath stays cool and creamy.

Vanilla, is, of course, the classic flavouring, and the one I tend to stick with, though it's easy enough to ring the changes should you want to: jasmine tea, and lemon peel and orange flower water are two of the other options in the recipes I try, but just about anything goes. It's a bowl of custard — really, how wrong can you go?

Makes 2

> **300ml double cream**
> **1 vanilla pod**
> **3 egg yolks**
> **15g caster sugar**
> **1 tablespoon demerara sugar**

1. Preheat the oven to 170°C/fan 150°C/gas 3 and place two small ovenproof ramekins in a baking tin.
2. Pour the cream into a small, heavy-based pan and slit the vanilla pod in half lengthways. Scrape out the seeds and stir both the

pod and the seeds into the cream. Bring slowly to the boil over a medium-low heat.

3. Meanwhile, put the yolks and caster sugar into a medium-sized heatproof jug or bowl and whisk until just combined. When the cream comes to the boil, remove the vanilla pod, then pour the hot cream on to the egg yolk and sugar mixture, stirring constantly as you do so.

4. Pour the mixture into the two ramekins, then fill the tin with cold water until it comes two-thirds of the way up the sides of the ramekins. Bake for about 40 minutes, until the custard is set — it should only wobble faintly when shaken. Allow to cool, then cover and refrigerate until cold.

5. Cover the tops of the cold brûlées with demerara sugar, and use a blowtorch or hot grill to caramelize the tops — if using a grill, you may need to put them back in the fridge for half an hour before serving, to cool down again.

Perfect
Panna Cotta

As I once heard someone say to the half-Italian chef Angela Hartnett on television, panna cotta is just blancmange with a fancy accent. As is so often the case, however, it's smoother, richer, more elegant than its British counterpart — infinitely less suitable for pouring into a bunny mould and serving at a children's party perhaps, but rather more likely to impress at a dinner party.

Like blancmange, however, it's child's play to make: despite the name, there's next to no cooking involved. But, with a recipe this simple, there's also no room for error.

The most important ingredient, of course, is the cream — but using just double cream, as recommended by Ursula Ferrigno in her *Complete Italian Cookery Course*, makes the panna cotta so rich it's almost impossible to finish. Although the dish should be luxuriously creamy, this is too much.

Likewise, Locatelli's milk-only recipe feels just a little bit frugal and clean, like an Asian milk jelly. Yoghurt, as used by Nigel Slater and Irish chef Denis Cotter, makes the panna cotta taste, well, like yoghurt, and Angela Hartnett's long-life cream, intended to 'stabilize' the mixture, renders it sadly bland.

The Silver Spoon hedges its bets with a combination of milk and cream which I think produces the best results — definitely creamy, but stopping just short of sickly. However, to make the flavour a little more interesting, I've added tangy buttermilk to the mixture as well, to help balance the sweetness of the cream and sugar.

The other important issue is the set: a florid Las Vegas chef once told me a good panna cotta should jiggle 'like the breast of a beautiful lady': in other words, it should be wobbly, rather than rock hard, and (and here the analogy breaks down) melt in the mouth, rather than chewy. I think I've got the balance just right here.

These are plain panna cottas, which make a beautifully simple pudding with some sharp fresh fruit, or a compote, but I've listed some alternative flavouring ideas below. If you choose an alcohol-based one like rose water, however, wait until the mixture has cooled slightly, or it'll evaporate into the ether.

Serves 4

> **2 x 2g leaves of gelatine**
> **300ml double cream**
> **115g caster sugar**
> **100ml whole milk**
> **50ml buttermilk**
> **Vegetable oil, to grease**

1. Soak the gelatine leaves in cold water. While they're soaking, pour the cream into a small pan, add the sugar and heat gently,

stirring until the sugar has dissolved. Bring to a simmer, then take off the heat.

2. Squeeze out the gelatine thoroughly and stir it into the warm cream mixture until dissolved. Pour the mixture through a sieve into a clean bowl and stir in the milk and buttermilk. Taste for sweetness and add more sugar if necessary.

3. Grease the inside of four espresso cups or small ramekins and divide the mixture between them. Allow to cool, then cover and refrigerate for at least 4 hours or overnight, until set.

4. To turn out, dip the dishes very briefly into boiling water and invert on to plates, thumping the bottom to encourage them. Serve with berries or fruit compote.

Panna cotta flavour suggestions
- 2 teaspoons rose or orange blossom water (taste and add more if necessary – brands vary in strength) added at the end of step 2, once the mixture has cooled slightly
- 50ml neat elderflower cordial, added in step 1
- Seeds from ½ a vanilla pod, added to the cream and sugar in step 1
- A strip of unwaxed lemon zest, added to the cream in step 1, heated, then left to infuse off the heat for 15 minutes before removing. Bring the cream back to a simmer before step 2
- Crushed seeds of 2 cardamom pods, added as for lemon zest
- 1 cinnamon stick, added as for lemon zest
- 1 stalk of lemongrass, split, and 2 slices of ginger, added as for lemon zest

Perfect
Rhubarb Fool

*L*ike trifle, the very name of this wonderfully British pudding is a joy, almost a whimsy worthy of Carroll himself — Elizabeth David puts it very nicely when she writes that 'soft, pale, creamy, untroubled, the English fruit fool is the most frail and insubstantial of English summer dishes'. Although, that said, the name probably comes from the French word to press.

We're better at the kind of fruit that really shines in a fool, however: sweet-sour berries and currants, and, of course, bitter rhubarb.

The recipe here is for rhubarb, because its natural astringency makes it the most difficult fool to get right, but it's simple enough to adapt to more easygoing fruits: just simmer them gently, with sugar to taste, until they collapse, then use as below.

The important thing with rhubarb is not to add any liquid when cooking it (shame on you, Antony Worrall Thompson), or you'll dilute the flavour and make your fool runny. I don't think there's any need to waste power by baking it, as Simon Hopkinson does, when softening in a pan works just as well. Rowley Leigh suggests turning the heat up at the end to burn off any excess liquid, then draining the rhubarb before adding it to the fool — both excellent ideas that will help stop the syrup splitting the cream.

Neither do you need to purée it before use — once broken down, the strands will be easy to fold through the cream (the Nigel Slater school of half-hearted mixing, 'so the fruit forms pale pink streaks', is not for me; it may look pretty, but the distribution is very haphazard).

Nigel uses an almost 50:50 mix of cream and custard, which smacks too much of a compromise with that other great pudding, rhubarb and custard, for my liking — I prefer a blander base, for maximum contrast with the bittersweet fruit. Yoghurt is too sour on its own, but combined with cream, it lends the dish a delicate tanginess which feels appropriately summery.

Vanilla, ginger and orange are all popular flavourings for rhubarb fool, but I don't think it needs any extras. All I'm going to top it with, however, is fresh mint, to remind me of my grandmother's garden in midsummer — which is exactly where I'd like to be eating this fool.

Serves 4

450g rhubarb, roughly chopped
5 tablespoons golden caster sugar
300ml double cream
100ml Greek yoghurt
A small bunch of mint, leaves only

1. Put the chopped rhubarb into a pan with 4 tablespoons of sugar, put the lid on and heat gently until tender. Take the lid off and turn up the heat slightly to let some of the juice evaporate. Taste

and add more sugar if necessary, then drain the rhubarb well, reserving the juice. Leave to cool.

2. Pour the cream into a large bowl and whip until it forms soft peaks. Stir in the yoghurt, fold in the cooled rhubarb, making sure it's well distributed, and chill for at least an hour.

3. Serve the fool, preferably in glasses, with the reserved juice for people to pour over the top, and a few torn mint leaves atop each portion.

Perfect
Summer Pudding

Britain is a land of two seasons: the short dark days of bread and
butter pudding, and the lazy, light evenings of the summer variety.
The latter is brief, but glorious – a solid bread pudding doesn't
sound particularly suited to warmer weather, but, well chilled and
sodden with sharp, fruity juices, it's remarkably refreshing stuff,
especially when served with a dollop of cold, ivory cream.

I have no time for bad bread, and summer pudding is no
exception – Tom Norrington-Davies may believe
it's best made 'with the most plastic sliced bread
you can get your mitts on' but I can't put it
better than Nigel Slater: cheap bread 'turns slimy
rather than moist . . . it's like eating a soggy J-cloth'.

That said, you do need thin, homogeneous slices, rather than
something full of artisanal holes – go for a good soft white bloomer
or similar, and ask the baker or supermarket to slice it for you.

I've always considered blackcurrants the life and soul of summer
pudding, so I'm surprised by Elizabeth David's haughty claim that
the authentic recipe includes only redcurrants and raspberries.
Nigel Slater doesn't care – he adds blackcurrants for 'their glorious
colour and for the extra snap of tartness that they bring', but I find
myself won over by the gentler flavour of David's pudding,

unadulterated by the aggressive tang of Ribena. Somehow, blackcurrants seem too intense and in your face for such an old-fashioned pudding.

There doesn't seem to be much need to macerate the fruit overnight with sugar, as Jane Grigson suggests: they're not noticeably more juicy the next morning, but a couple of tablespoons of water helps the situation, despite David's insistence that no further lubrication is needed.

I also find the bread soaks up more juice if the fruit is added hot, as Ballymaloe recommends, while buttering the basin makes it much easier to unmould.

The flavours of summer pudding are so modest, so subtle that to add any other ingredients seems like a mistake. That said, a delicate hint of rose water, the scent of a British garden in summer, seems pleasingly apt; but if you don't have any in the house, feel free to leave it out. Serve with thick, cold cream.

Serves 6

Butter, to grease
½ a loaf of slightly stale, good-quality
   white bread, crusts removed
225g redcurrants
675g raspberries
2–3 tablespoons caster sugar
I teaspoon rose water

1. Grease a pudding basin or a deep, narrow bowl (about 1 litre capacity) with butter, then line it with bread, cutting the bread so it fits the basin snugly with no gaps. Cut a lid and set aside.
2. Put the fruit into a small pan with the sugar, 2 tablespoons of water and the rose water and heat very gently until just simmering – don't stir it unless absolutely necessary to avoid crushing the fruit. Taste and add more sugar, or indeed rose water if you think it needs it.
3. Pour the hot fruit and most of the syrup into the bread-lined basin and top with the lid of bread, keeping any excess syrup (or fruit) to serve it with. Put a small plate on top of the basin, pressing it into the bread lid, and weigh it down with a tin or similar.
4. When the pudding is cool, refrigerate overnight before turning out on to a serving dish and dousing with extra syrup (useful for covering any pale patches). Serve with plenty of cream.

Perfect
Syrup Sponge

*A*nyone who's ever passed through the British education system should be familiar with this dish in one form or another — simultaneously fluffy and outrageously sticky, it's a cold weather classic. With sugar, in the form of golden syrup (a great national institution if ever I saw one — the Scott Polar expedition travelled on the stuff, much good it did them), as the principal ingredient, it's not an everyday dish, but as a cheering treat on a cold day, it takes quite some beating.

Syrup sponge is sometimes known, oddly, as treacle sponge, but I only find one recipe using it — Delia Smith adds a tablespoon to her sponge mix, which gives it a gorgeous tan, but I'm not keen on the bittersweet flavour. Tamasin Day-Lewis stirs syrup into her sponge mix as well as using it as a topping, which I don't like either — although it tastes good, I think one of the joys of this pudding is the contrast between the gooey layer of sponge on top and the fluffy sponge beneath — which is why you have to be generous with the sticky stuff. If you add a little lemon juice to it, as Margaret Costa cunningly suggests, the syrup will dribble down the side of the sponge in a very satisfying way.

Steaming is, I'm afraid, a necessary evil: patience is a virtue, and none of the baked or microwaved versions I try hit the spot in quite the same way. If you don't have the time, make something else instead.

Mary Norwak and Tamasin Day-Lewis make their puddings with suet: although lovely and light, this lends them a slightly savoury flavour — I prefer the rich fluffiness of butter. There's no need for any extra raising agent, however: self-raising flour should be quite sufficient.

Neither, I think, does this pudding require any extra flavouring — ginger and vanilla are popular, and lemon zest adds a pleasant bitterness, but toffeeish syrup alone ought to be enough, along with a pinch of balancing salt. Fluffy sponge, sticky syrup: what more could you want, apart from a big jug of Bird's custard?

Serves 4—6

6 tablespoons (90ml) golden syrup
¼ of a lemon, juice only
150g softened butter, plus extra to grease
150g soft light brown sugar
A pinch of salt
2 eggs, beaten
150g self-raising flour
Milk

1. Butter an approximately 900ml pudding basin well, and spoon the golden syrup into the bottom (dipping your spoon in boiling water first will make this easier). Stir in the lemon juice and set aside.
2. Beat the butter and sugar together in a mixing bowl with a pinch of salt until fluffy, then gradually beat in the eggs, a little at a time, until well combined. Gently fold in the flour, followed by

enough milk to give a smooth dropping consistency (i.e. the mixture falls from a spoon easily), then transfer to the basin, stopping just short of the top in order to give the pudding room to rise as it cooks.

3. Cover the basin with a lid if it has one, or with a layer each of greaseproof paper and foil, pleating the centre of both in order to give the pudding room to rise, and securing these with string. Trim the excess from the sides if using the latter, then put the pudding into a steamer, or a large saucepan half full of water, and steam for 2 hours, topping up the water as necessary. It will evaporate surprisingly quickly, so don't forget about it.

4. Run a knife around the inside of the basin, and turn the pudding out on to a lipped plate, to accommodate the syrup. Serve immediately, with custard, cream or ice cream.

Perfect
Winter Trifle

*I*n my experience, people don't tend to be tepid for trifle. Either they love it — just the way their mum or their granny always made it — or they loathe it, and nothing will persuade them to give the dish a second chance. For me, it's the obvious choice to end my fantasy last meal: the other courses may change according to whim, but the trifle is not for turning. As you may have guessed, I adore the stuff.

There do seem to be as many variations on the theme as there are hundreds and thousands in a tub: this one is specifically designed for the winter, which means it doesn't contain the classic tinned raspberries which always put in an appearance in my ancestral version. The summer variation would use berries (these days, probably fresh, but macerated with a couple of spoonfuls of sugar for half an hour before use, to make them nice and juicy) instead of compote, sitting on top of boudoir biscuits soaked in medium-dry sherry, and topped with custard and cream as below, with crystallized rose petals replacing the pomegranate if I'm feeling fancy.

A successful trifle needs a solid foundation. Sarah Raven bakes a Madeira cake specifically for the occasion, and Nigella uses the same thing, but I find both disintegrate too quickly; although you want the base to soak up a goodly amount of booze and fruit juice, it should retain some texture of its own. In a summer trifle, this means sugar-coated boudoir biscuits alone, but here I've added almond-scented amaretti too: their sweet nuttiness works brilliantly with the winter fruit compote, and I like the defiant crunch they add to the base.

Sherry is an absolute must: no deviations on the theme allowed. I will generously allow you to use any fruit you like, however – frozen berries or jarred summer fruits are better than the fresh or tinned sort in winter – while gently suggesting that the compote below, full of warming spice, feels like by far the most satisfying choice for cold weather. Dried fruit always has a rather festive feel for me, and, even after soaking, retains a chewiness which ensures it won't dissolve into the background.

As I'm not using jelly (my mum never puts it into a trifle, and I won't countenance it either), a robust custard is required to take the strain of the upper layers. Bird's would be the nostalgic choice, but for a special occasion, Nigella's more luxurious cream and milk version seems appropriate; Helen Saberi's all-cream recipe is too rich for my taste (I like to eat trifle in quantity, as I may have mentioned), and Rose Prince's milk custard too thin.

On top, I've gone for a thick layer of whipped cream. A syllabub, frothy with wine and cream, is the more impressive, and traditional choice, but, though delicious in its own right, I think the flavours are lost here.

Flaked almonds add a little crunch, and pomegranate seeds a flash of seasonal colour; indeed, the jewel-like sparkle is entirely appropriate for such a regal dish.

Serves 6–8 (depending on enthusiasm for trifle)

For the fruit compote

**4 handfuls of dried fruit – I like a mix of figs,
    prunes and apricots**
½ a cinnamon stick
3 cloves
Zest and juice of 2 oranges

For the custard

300ml whole milk
300ml double cream
1 vanilla pod, slit in half and seeds scraped out
6 egg yolks
1 tablespoon cornflour
3 tablespoons caster sugar

Also

**1 packet of boudoir biscuits (also sold as
    lady fingers or savoiardi)**
1 packet of ratafia or amaretti biscuits
100ml sweet sherry
300ml double cream
15g flaked almonds, toasted
Seeds of ¼ of a pomegranate

1. Begin by making the compote. Put all the ingredients into a small pan and just cover with cold water. Heat gently until it comes to the boil, then simmer for about 15 minutes, until the fruit is plump and the surrounding liquid has become slightly syrupy. Allow to cool.
2. Meanwhile, make the custard. Stir together the milk and cream

in a thick-bottomed pan and add the vanilla pod and seeds. Heat gently until the mixture is just below a simmer, but do not allow it to boil. While it heats, beat the egg yolks and cornflour together in a large heatproof bowl and stir in the sugar.

3. Remove the vanilla pod from the hot milk mixture and pour this on to the yolks and sugar, stirring all the time.

4. Turn the heat down to medium-low, and pour the custard back into the same pan. Stirring steadily, cook the mixture until it coats the back of a wooden spoon – the longer you cook it, the thicker it will get. If it doesn't appear to be thickening at all after 10 minutes, you may have the heat slightly too low, but only turn it up a notch, or you'll spoil all your hard work. (Alternatively, if you're not feeling terribly brave, suspend a heatproof bowl over, but not touching a pan of simmering water, pour the yolk and milk mixture into that, pour the hot milk on to them, and proceed as above.) Bear in mind you'll be tied to the stove for at least 20 minutes, so put some good music on to keep yourself entertained. Once the custard has thickened, decant into a jug to cool, pressing some clingfilm on to the top to stop a skin forming.

5. Line the base of a glass trifle bowl with boudoir biscuits and, after picking out all the spices (3 cloves, remember!), spoon the cooled compote and its juices over the top. Scatter with amaretti and pour over the sherry with a liberal hand. Dollop the cooled custard on top, then cover with clingfilm and refrigerate until set.

6. Whip the cream in a large bowl to soft peaks, then spoon on top of the trifle and chill for at least 2 hours before serving.

7. Just before serving, arrange the almonds and pomegranate seeds on top of the cream – if you leave them there too long the seeds will bleed into the cream, and the nuts will go soggy. Take to the table with all due fanfare.

CHAPTER 9

Baking

*P*erhaps my favourite chapter in any cookbook – because, unless you're looking at this with wild eyes at 11 p.m. the night before a school cake sale or surprise birthday party, this is the kind of cooking that's pure pleasure. Let's be honest, no one needs a piece of chocolate cake, or a gingerbread man; the truly hungry would be better off turning to page 86 for a wholesome chicken soup, or cooking up the nice dal on page 215.

No, baking is all about indulgence – and thank God for that. We're bombarded with 'wicked' brownies and 'naughty' cream horns, and frankly I'm bored with it all: the recipes in this chapter aren't designed to be guiltily gorged on, but shared with friends and loved ones in joyous greed. And, OK, if there happens to be a slice left over afterwards . . . well, wasting food, there's a real sin if ever there was one.

It's a special sort of alchemy, to turn flour and sugar and butter and eggs and their ilk into something so happy – and whether you end up with a fancy tarte au citron or a homely ginger cake, when it comes out of the oven you're never sorry you bothered.

Although baking does demand a certain pedantry (leaving out half the eggs in a cake recipe because your boyfriend ate them for breakfast is likely to end in disaster), it also has one of the best effort to results ratio of any branch of cookery. There's very little in the way of finicky chopping or patient reducing, and, as long as you've followed the recipe, the results are guaranteed to please.

Equipment-wise, a good pair of scales is invaluable, and, if you bake a lot, an electric mixer of some kind – a stand one that sits on the counter is great, but if, like me, you have limited space, and an even more limited budget, it's helpful to know I get a lot more use out of my hand-held version. For about £25, you can take all the elbow grease out of the process and still have your cake and eat it.

A silicone spatula is useful for getting every last bit of mixture out of the bowl (though you can still save the last bit for licking), and a few variously sized mixing bowls, preferably stainless steel or ceramic, will also come in handy: pound shops are a good source of them, though, as with everything else in there, they generally cost more than the name suggests.

Measuring spoons, though not essential, are an inexpensive way of ensuring your teaspoon of baking powder really is 5ml, and I've recently discovered reusable baking mats, which make lining tins and trays much less of a faff.

Lastly, with all these recipes, check you've got roughly the right-sized tin before switching the oven on: there's little more frustrating than making the mixture, and then realizing you've got nowhere to put it, and your proud 7 inch cake will actually be more of a 9 inch pancake. I speak from experience.

Perfect
Banana Bread

Not really a bread, if I'm honest — more of a loaf-shaped cake, but the name lends it a spuriously wholesome air, allowing it to be included on breakfast menus in the States without a blush. And, like many cakes, it's not hard to see why it's so popular, the fruit lending a natural sweetness, and delectable gooeyness, to what's otherwise a fairly standard recipe.

Contrary to popular opinion, you don't need bananas so ripe they're almost black, although this is certainly a good way to use up fruit on its way out — the overripe versions are somewhat easier to mash, but surprisingly, they don't seem to give the cake a more intense banana flavour. However, if you are using really ripe specimens in the recipe below, you may want to reduce the amount of sugar slightly, depending on taste.

However ripe they are, there's no need to purée the bananas, as Charles Campion does in *Fifty Recipes to Stake Your Life On*: though it gives the whole loaf a great flavour, I miss the chunks of whole fruit that are such a highlight of the America's Test Kitchen version. A mixture of well-mashed (bananas aren't worth washing up a blender for) and coarsely chopped seems to offer the best of both worlds.

A little squidginess is good but I like my banana bread to have a certain fluffiness, so I use baking powder, like pastry chef Claire

Clark, whose cake is the lightest I try. If you'd prefer to keep it dairy free, as she does, you can use vegetable oil, but I'm a sucker for the richness and softness you can only get from butter.

The caramel flavour of light brown sugar, as used by the Hummingbird Bakery, goes wonderfully with the bananas (just think of banoffee pie), but I've left out their spices — after trying vanilla, cinnamon and ginger, I decided the sweet fruit needed no such help.

I have added walnuts, though: I love the contrast between the soft, sweet crumb and their slightly bitter crunchiness, but feel free to leave them out, or indeed substitute some other nut if you're not a fan.

Nigella Lawson also adds bourbon-soaked sultanas to her rather louche loaf, but, though delicious, I think my bread is moist enough not to require any extra juiciness. In any case, such outrageous decadence has no place in a good, wholesome bread, as I'm sure you'll agree.

Makes 1 x 21cm loaf

350g ripe bananas (peeled weight)
180g plain flour, plus extra for the tin
2½ teaspoons baking powder
4 tablespoons melted butter,
    slightly cooled, plus extra to grease
160g soft light brown sugar
2 eggs, beaten
50g walnuts, roughly chopped

1. Preheat the oven to 190°C/fan 170°C/gas 5. Put two-thirds of the peeled bananas into a bowl and mash them with a fork or potato masher until smooth. Roughly mash the remainder, and stir in gently.
2. Sift the flour and baking powder into a bowl with a generous pinch of salt, and grease and lightly flour a 21cm loaf tin.
3. Put the sugar, eggs and melted butter into a large mixing bowl and use an electric mixer or a whisk to beat them together until the mix is pale and slightly increased in volume. Gently fold in the banana and the dry ingredients until there are no more streaks of flour, then fold in the walnuts and make sure they're evenly distributed.
4. Spoon the mixture into the tin and bake it for about an hour, until a skewer inserted into the middle comes out clean. Allow to cool in the tin for 10 minutes before turning out on to a wire rack to cool completely.

Perfect
Carrot Cake

*F*or many years in this country, carrot cake was seen as the teatime choice of the sandal-wearing *Guardian*-ista – until its American cousin came visiting. Then the humble health food suddenly super-sized, with a topping of sugary cream cheese icing – and, surprise surprise, went mainstream.

Carrot cake actually has quite a long history here: Britons have been using such root vegetables as a canny substitute for pricier imported dried fruits and sugars since the Middle Ages, and the idea was revived by the wartime Ministry of Food.

A recipe with such a past is never going to be neat and tidy, and indeed I try two very unusual carrot cakes in my quest for perfection. Nigella Lawson's version, which originated in the Venetian Jewish community, is made with ground almonds, eggs, olive oil and pine nuts. It's flat as a pancake, but deliciously moist and nutty – not quite what I'm after here, but as it's both gluten and lactose free, it's a good one to remember. Jane Grigson, meanwhile, offers a fatless sponge that's light as a cloud – even the carrots are finely shredded – but far too delicate for my liking.

As a nod to its hippy heritage, I've decided to make my more conventional carrot cake with wholemeal flour, like Delia Smith and Claire Clark – theirs are heavier than those made with white flour, but they have a defiantly wholesome texture which seems apt. Carrot cake, like muesli, shouldn't melt in the mouth.

I've rejected white sugar for the same reason; Geraldene Holt's unrefined light sugar gives the cake a lovely toffee flavour, without taking over like Delia's dark muscovado. Holt's butter also gets the thumbs up: although it may have been the enemy back in the marge-happy 1970s, it's definitely the wholesome choice nowadays, and more importantly, it gives the cake a wonderful richness.

I've loaded the cake with dried fruit and nuts — pecans are my nod to its popularity in the States, but you could substitute walnuts if you wanted to keep things British. Sweet spices go brilliantly with carrot, as does Holt's orange zest, though her coriander seems a step too far. Save that for the soup.

If you're determined to be healthy, you can leave the cake at that, but I've warmed to the cream cheese icing over the years. I've gone for a very classic version — no butter, as used by Claire Clark, or mascarpone, like Nigel Slater's recipe — and in strictly restrained quantities. Lemon zest adds a little freshness, but here, less is definitely more. This is a cake, after all, that's good enough to eat on its own.

Makes 1 x 18—20cm cake

150g butter, melted, plus extra for greasing
150g soft light brown sugar
3 eggs
200g self-raising wholemeal flour
I teaspoon bicarbonate of soda

½ teaspoon salt

1 teaspoon ground cinnamon

½ teaspoon grated nutmeg

Zest of 1 orange

100g sultanas or raisins

200g carrots, peeled and grated

100g pecans, toasted and roughly chopped,
   plus extra to decorate

For the icing

150g full-fat cream cheese

50g soft light brown sugar

Zest of ½ a lemon and a squeeze of juice

1. Preheat the oven to 200°C/fan 180°C/gas 6, and grease and line
   the bases of two 18–20cm sandwich tins with butter.
2. Put the melted butter, sugar and eggs into a large mixing bowl
   and whisk well, preferably with an electric mixer, until the
   ingredients are thoroughly combined and the mixture has almost
   doubled in volume.
3. Sift together the flour, bicarb, salt and spices and fold these very
   gently into the liquid mixture, being careful to knock as little air
   out as possible as you do so. Fold in the remaining ingredients
   with similar care, and divide the mixture between the tins. Bake
   these for about 30 minutes, until a skewer inserted into the
   middle comes out clean. Allow to cool in the tins.
4. Meanwhile, beat together the ingredients for the icing and chill
   to make it easier to spread. When the cakes are cool enough to
   ice (ideally, room temperature), remove from the tins, and top
   one with half the icing, and then the other cake. Ice the top of
   the upper cake, and decorate with the remaining pecans.

Perfect
Chocolate Cake

I never, ever order chocolate cake. Not because I don't like chocolate (well, duh), but because, unless it's the kind you get for dessert, a cake only in name, and so rich you can only pick at teeny-tiny morsels with a fork, they always disappoint. They may look the part, all dark and crumbly, but they rarely deliver on flavour — they're always too, well, cakey. This one, I'm pleased to say, will not let you down. It's moist yet fluffy, and packs a proper cocoa punch.

Most recipes I try actually use cocoa, rather than chocolate — as with brownies, this supplies all the flavour of chocolate with none of the fat, so it doesn't weigh the cake down. The exceptions are Margot Henderson's steamed chocolate cake in *You're All Invited*, which uses melted chocolate for a ridiculously rich result, and Florence White's Really Delicious Chocolate Cake from the 1920s, which calls for me to grate the chocolate into the mixture. Not an experience my knuckles would care to repeat, and thank goodness I won't have to; it creates a strange mottled effect, although I do like the interesting pockets of melted chocolate it creates.

I love the intense flavour of Henderson's version, but because I'm after a lighter cake I've used a mixture of melted chocolate and cocoa, with a few chocolate chips thrown in as a nod to White.

I've also chosen, like White, to use butter rather than the oil favoured by Nigella Lawson, because I prefer the flavour. A little milk makes the crumb even softer, like a favourite blanket.

Dense, flourless chocolate cakes, good as they are, are outside my remit here (and ground almonds supply too much of a marzipan flavour for my liking), and where there's flour, there must be a raising agent — simple baking powder suffices.

As usual, I've chosen the caramel flavour of light muscovado over boring white or bitter dark sugar; it works particularly well here, adding an extra layer of flavour which is the only extra I'm allowing: vanilla extract, coffee and cinnamon are all a distraction from the main attraction as far as I'm concerned.

That said, there's certainly room for some icing. Making the cake into a sandwich allows for a double whammy of excitement — London baker Lily Vanilli's simple cocoa buttercream supplies the perfect gilding, topped with Annie Bell's crushed Oreos. Though we make some fabulous chocolate biscuits in this country, the slightly bitter cocoa crunch of these American imports makes them the only option, I'm afraid.

Light enough to eat for tea, rich enough to serve for dessert, I really believe this is the ultimate chocolate cake. I'm excessively pleased with it.

Makes 1 x 20cm cake

250g butter, at room temperature, plus extra to grease
250g light muscovado sugar
½ teaspoon salt
100g cocoa powder
250g plain flour
2 teaspoons baking powder
3 large eggs
50g dark chocolate, melted and allowed to cool slightly
250ml milk
50g chocolate chips

For the buttercream
140g butter, softened
50g cocoa powder
200g icing sugar
A pinch of salt
2 tablespoons milk

To garnish
5 Oreo cookies

1. Grease and line the bases of two 20cm springform cake tins with butter and greaseproof paper. Preheat the oven to 200°C/ fan 180°C/gas 6. Use a hand or stand mixer, or a wooden spoon, to cream together the butter and sugar with ½ teaspoon of salt until light and fluffy.
2. Sift together the cocoa, flour and baking powder until well combined. Beat the eggs into the butter mixture one at a time, then fold in half the flour mixture, followed by the melted

chocolate. Fold in the rest of the flour mixture, followed by just enough milk to give the batter a soft dropping consistency (so it falls off a spoon easily), and finally the chocolate chips. Divide equally between the two tins and bake for about 25–30 minutes, until firm in the centre.

3. Allow the cakes to cool completely on a wire rack, then make the buttercream. Beat the butter in a mixer, or with a wooden spoon, until fluffy, then sift in the cocoa, icing sugar and salt and, if necessary, a little milk to loosen the mixture.

4. Put one of the cakes on a serving plate and spread a third of the icing on top of it, spreading it more thickly around the edge. Place the second cake on top, then spread the rest of the icing over the whole thing, smoothing the sides with a palette knife.

5. Blitz the biscuits to a fine crumb in a food processor, and sprinkle them over the cake.

Perfect
Chocolate Chip Cookies

*J*ust before writing this recipe, I heard on the radio that the British are one of the world's biggest spenders when it comes to biscuits. This made me pretty proud, I can tell you – we've created some fine examples in our time, but even I have to admit that our supremacy on the teatime seas is seriously challenged by the American chocolate chip cookie.

It's that combination of crunch and chew, dough and chocolate that makes them so damn addictive – and a good CCC ought to be a bit chewy. British imitations often give them the texture of shortbread: another fine biscuit, but quite beside the point here.

The original Toll House cookie, invented in Whitman, Massachusetts, in the 1930s, is incredibly buttery and sweet, with a crisp, sugary shell – addictive, but too one-dimensional to be quite perfect. I do approve of their choice of sweeteners though: a mix of granulated sugar for crunch, and light brown sugar for flavour.

Chewiness is a virtue, then, but you want a bit of crunch too, which is why I've plumped for plain flour instead of the strong bread flour recommended by Marcus Wareing and American culinary celebrity Alton Brown, which gives a tougher, puffier result. I've deployed bicarbonate of soda for the same reason: Wareing's baking powder makes the cookies too cakey.

Fat-wise, butter is an essential: my old school friend Alex's mum Charlotte (a real live American) has an incredible recipe using margarine, which gives a crisp, moist result but, in a side-by-side tasting, I miss the richness of the butter.

In the pioneer spirit, you can chuck in just about anything you like along with the chocolate (having experimented with dark and milk, I've chosen the bitterness of the former to contrast with the sweetness of the cookie itself, but would note that a mixture is preferred by a discerning younger audience) — nuts would be nice, dried fruit if you must, even spices if you're feeling exotic. Chopping your own chocolate may seem like a faff, but it gives a more interesting result than evenly-sized chips.

Resting the dough before baking may seem like an odd idea for a biscuit, but in fact, although it's not mentioned in many modern versions of the recipe, the 1953 *Little Toll House Cook Book* notes that, at the inn, they refrigerated the dough overnight.

Baking batches at 12, 24, 36 and 48 hours reveals they're at their best between 12 and 24 hours: still doughy in the middle, but dry and crunchy without. But if you really must have cookies immediately, all is not lost — these may get better with time, but bear in mind they're starting from delicious.

Makes 15

120g salted butter, at room temperature
75g light brown sugar
75g granulated sugar

½ teaspoon vanilla extract
1 egg, beaten
240g plain flour
½ teaspoon bicarbonate of soda
170g dark chocolate, roughly chopped
Sea salt flakes (optional – but if not,
    add a pinch of fine salt to the dough along with the sugars)

1. Using a wooden spoon, or (and even better) a food mixer, beat together the butter and both sugars until just combined. Add the vanilla extract, then the egg, and beat in well.
2. Sift the flour and bicarbonate of soda into the bowl, and stir in until it just comes together into a dough. Mix in the chocolate pieces until evenly distributed, then, if you've got time, chill the mixture overnight, or for up to 72 hours.
3. Preheat the oven to 200°C/fan 180°C/gas 6. Line two baking trays with greaseproof paper, and divide the mixture into golf-ball sized spheres, spacing them well apart on the tray, so they don't melt into each other as they cook. Bake the cookies for about 15 minutes, until golden, but not browned.
4. Sprinkle them lightly with sea salt, if using, and allow to cool on the tray for a couple of minutes, before moving to a wire rack to cool completely – or alternatively, sampling immediately.

Perfect
Chocolate Macarons

I'd like to be as anti macaron as I am contra cupcake – in the last couple of years, they've gone from a rarefied Parisian treat to a supermarket standard. But the thing is, unlike the giant fairy cake, they're more than just a pretty face: that rainbow-bright shell shatters to reveal a soft, deliciously nutty interior and a silky ganache filling – no wonder they've become so popular.

These are chocolate versions, but once you've nailed the technique, the recipe is easily adaptable to give you a whole colour spectrum of sugary delight. And you will master it, I promise. Practice makes perfect.

Oddly, given the precision involved in baking, there are two distinct methods of macaron making: one, favoured by Ladurée and pastry chef Claire Clark, uses a French meringue, beating together egg white and caster sugar until stiff before folding in the ground almonds, sugar and flavourings.

The other, deployed by mavericks such as Pierre Hermé ('the Picasso of pastry' according to *Vogue*), is based on an Italian meringue, which means adding the sugar to the whisking whites in a molten stream – the stress of juggling hot syrup and cleaning solidified sugar from my mixer steers me in favour of the French version, which also has the benefit of being lighter and less intensely sweet.

All sorts of tricks are used to ensure the egg whites remain stable and billow obligingly into a meringue – cream of tartar, powdered egg whites, ageing them for a week before use – but given a pinch of salt will do the same job while actually enhancing the finished flavour, I've gone for that instead.

Granulated sugar, as used by pastry chef and writer David Lebovitz, adds a pleasing crunch, but if, like me, you struggle to achieve a smooth texture as it is, then you'll find caster more forgiving.

Lebovitz also contests the idea that resting your macarons before baking forms a skin which, according to Australian pâtissier Adriano Zumbo's book, 'lifts as the macaron cooks, creating a "foot" at the base'. The foot (a term that always reminds me of molluscs) is the little frill at the base of each shell, highly prized by macaron aficionados for reasons unknown to me – but it can't be denied that, after half an hour, the tops are flatter and the feet below more even.

I do take Lebovitz's advice and whiz my ground almonds in a food processor to grind them yet more finely, however: the macaron is an unforgiving mistress, and any lumps will be sadly obvious in the finished batch.

The chocolate flavour here comes from cocoa powder: Hermé uses melted chocolate, but this makes them too sickly for my liking – the biscuit itself should be light and sugary, with all the richness coming from the ganache itself. I've gone for a whipping cream version loosely based on Zumbo's filling, and with no added sugar, so it contrasts nicely with the macaron shell.

One last thing: although it's understandably tempting to eat them all right away, macarons are one of those things which actually improve with age: after a few hours the ganache begins to melt into the shell, making them moister and even more delicious. Your call.

Makes about 10

65g ground almonds
85g icing sugar
25g cocoa powder
75g egg whites (about 2)
A pinch of salt
60g caster sugar

For the ganache
100g whipping cream
100g dark chocolate, chopped
20g butter, cut into small pieces
A pinch of sea salt

1. Start by making the ganache. Heat the cream in a small pan until it's just coming to the boil, then remove from the heat and add the chopped chocolate. Leave it to melt for a couple of minutes, then stir furiously until you have a smooth chocolate cream. Gradually beat in the pieces of butter and finish with a pinch of salt. Pour into a shallow dish and leave in a cool place to set.

2. To make the macarons, you'll first need to make a template. Cut two pieces of baking paper to fit your baking trays. Find a glass, pastry cutter or other round object about 3.5cm in diameter and draw round it as many times as you can fit on one of the pieces

of baking paper using a dark, waterproof pen, spacing the circles about 2cm apart. Either repeat with the second piece, or trace the second set from the first. Prepare a piping bag with a 1cm nozzle, or cut the end off a disposable one so you have a hole about 1cm in diameter.

3. Whiz the ground almonds in a food processor or spice grinder for a couple of minutes until powdered, then sift these, the icing sugar and cocoa into a bowl. Repeat so they're really well mixed.

4. Put the egg whites and a pinch of salt into a stand mixer and begin whisking at speed (alternatively use a hand or electric hand-held whisk). As soon as the whites begin to hold their shape, whisk in the caster sugar, and continue whisking at high speed until you have a stiff meringue — you should be able to hold the bowl upside down without them falling on your head.

5. Fold the almond and cocoa mixture into the whites, then beat the mixture vigorously until it's loose enough to fall off the spatula: if it's too thick, it will be hard to pipe. Don't worry about beating the air out of it: you don't want too much trapped in the shells anyway.

6. Spoon the mixture into the prepared piping bag and carefully pipe it on to the baking paper circles. Pick each baking tray up and drop it on to the work surface a couple of times to knock the air out, then leave it to rest for about 30 minutes, until the macarons feel dry to the touch: they shouldn't be sticky. In the meantime, preheat the oven to 200°C/fan 180°C/gas 6.

7. Bake the macarons for about 17 minutes, until firm, opening the oven door briefly a couple of times during this time to let out any gathering steam. Once you're sure they're cooked, slide the baking paper off the tray immediately to stop the macarons cooking and transfer to a flat cold surface to cool completely.

8. Carefully peel the macarons off the paper: if they're cooked,

they should come away easily. Match up fairly equally-sized macarons, and then, using a small palette knife or spoon, sandwich them together with ganache.

9. Refrigerate for 24 hours if possible, then serve at room temperature.

Perfect
Jam Doughnuts

*H*ow I love doughnuts. Not just any old doughnuts, mind — not
fancy St John Bakery custard versions, or cakey Krispy Kremes,
or the sugar-dusted beignets hawked so loudly on every French
beach; my affections are reserved for the slightly greasy golden lumps
found in the more traditional bakery, oozing with sticky pink
jam . . . but not too much of it. Just a modest spoonful in every
one, a sweet surprise hidden amongst that rich and savoury yeasty
dough (looking for the jam entry hole before starting is, of course,
cheating).

Having tested a number of recipes, I decide that I want the substance
of my doughnuts to have quite a plain, savoury flavour
— the Fabulous Baker Brothers give a recipe in
their book which contains 6 egg yolks, which
makes their version meltingly rich, while Richard
Bertinet makes a brioche-style dough which I find
similarly sickly. Paul Hollywood, who made his first
batch at the age of eleven, clearly knows his stuff,
however: his recipe is featherlight, and pleasingly
plain.

I've adapted it to use strong white flour, to give the doughnuts a
fluffier texture, and reduced the amount of sugar yet further to suit
my taste (remember, you'll be rolling them in sugar before serving,
so you won't be short-changed). To make the mixing process easier,

I've taken a tip from a 1914 recipe by one Florence Jack, and melted the butter in the warm milk, and to aid shaping, I've kept them modestly small, like Richard Bertinet's beignets — you can always have a couple, after all.

Sadly the baked doughnut recipe I find on one US blog ends up more like doughballs: deep-frying is the only way to doughnut perfection, so make sure you have a few people round before cooking these, because they don't keep well — fry, scoff, and repent at leisure.

Makes 6

> 210g strong white flour, plus extra to dust
> 7g dried yeast
> ½ teaspoon salt
> 15g caster sugar, plus extra to dust
> 20g unsalted butter, at room temperature, chopped, plus extra to grease
> 65ml whole milk, warmed
> 45ml warm water
> 1 egg, beaten
> 2 litres vegetable or sunflower oil, to cook
> 6 teaspoons raspberry or strawberry jam

1. Mix the flour, yeast, salt and sugar in a large bowl. Put the butter into a separate bowl with the warm milk and water, and stir together to melt. Pour this into the mixing bowl, along with the egg, and stir until it all comes together into a dough: it should be firm, but soft.

2. Tip the dough on to a lightly floured surface, or into a mixer fitted with a dough hook, and knead until smooth and elastic, which should take about 10 minutes. Put it into a lightly greased bowl, cover with a damp tea towel or a shower cap, and leave in a warm place for about an hour, until it has doubled in size.

3. Divide the dough into 6 balls of about 80g each. To shape, fold each edge tightly into the centre in turn, turning the ball as you go, then turn the ball over and put it on a lightly floured baking tray or board, spacing the balls well apart. Cover and leave to rise again for 45 minutes.

4. Heat the oil in a large pan or deep-fat fryer to 160°C. Add half the doughnuts and cook for about 3 minutes on each side, until golden, turning carefully with a slotted spoon, then remove, blot with kitchen paper and sprinkle with caster sugar to coat. Repeat with the other half.

5. Allow them to cool slightly, then make a small hole in the side of each doughnut, and use a piping bag to inject a generous splodge of jam. Eat immediately, while they're still warm and crisp.

Perfect
Ginger Cake

Sweet and fiery, Asian ginger has been warming our northern cockles for centuries — indeed, the *Oxford Companion to Food* claims that in the late Middle Ages, it was almost as common as pepper. Our taste for spicy ginger biscuits and cakes is perhaps the last remnant of this national passion — and while I regret I've never tasted a gingery, garlicky medieval stew, I suspect it wouldn't be half as comforting as a sticky loaf on a wintery tea table. Why, it's almost medicinal in our climate.

The ginger flavour should be pungent enough to clear the sinuses — David Lebovitz's fresh root is just too delicate, and even Delia's fine version, which uses both fresh and dried ginger, is a little underpowered. That said, a Ripon ginger cake using just the ground sort, taken from Florence White's 1932 collection, *Good Things in England*, seems a bit one-dimensional. The solution seems to be to do as Geraldene Holt does in her magnificent book *Cakes*, and use fresh, dried and (her contribution) candied, all in quantity. The last adds a satisfyingly crunchy texture, the root contributes zing, while the ground is responsible for supplying heat. Together they give a pleasingly rounded, wonderfully fiery gingeriness.

That's not enough for many of these recipes, however: Holt adds cinnamon, David Herbert mixed spice, and Lebovitz a medieval-sounding mixture of cloves, cinnamon and black pepper. Like the ground almonds and dried fruit Delia uses, or the mixed peel Herbert goes for, they're just a distraction from the main attraction — who needs raisins when you've got candied ginger?

Icing is always welcome, however, elevating this from an everyday cake (I do like the idea of an everyday cake, and wish I had the metabolism to accommodate one) to something rather more special. A mere ginger syrup, like Herbert's, is too boring. Delia goes for a lemon icing, which, though the tanginess goes well with the ginger, doesn't quite fit with my cake — instead I've gone for a ginger version, spiced with ginger wine, and stuck a slug in the cake mix as well, for good measure. Better to be safe than sorry.

Makes 1 x 23cm loaf

100g butter, plus extra to grease
100g dark muscovado sugar
175g self-raising flour
4 teaspoons ground ginger
175g golden syrup
3 tablespoons ginger wine
2 free-range eggs, beaten
A walnut-sized piece of fresh ginger,
    peeled and finely grated
150g candied ginger, finely chopped
75g icing sugar
1 piece of stem ginger, to decorate

1. Preheat the oven to 180°C/fan 160°C/gas 4, and grease and line a 23cm loaf tin with butter. Use an electric mixer or a wooden spoon to cream together the butter and sugar in a mixing bowl with a pinch of salt until fluffy. Sift together the flour and ground ginger and set aside.

2. Pour the golden syrup (the easiest way to handle the syrup is with a spoon dipped in boiling water and a silicone spatula) and 1 tablespoon of ginger wine into the mixture and stir to combine.

3. Gradually beat the eggs into the mixture, then slowly fold in the sifted flour. Finally, stir through the fresh and candied ginger, making sure they're evenly distributed, and spoon into the prepared tin.

4. Level the top with a spatula and bake the cake for about 50–60 minutes, until a skewer inserted into the centre comes out clean.

5. Allow the cake to cool in the tin. When it's at room temperature, make the icing by mixing together the icing sugar and remaining ginger wine until smooth, and drizzle this over the top of the cake (it will be quite liquid, but will set as it cools). Slice the stem ginger thinly and arrange down the centre of the cake as decoration.

TIP: If ginger wine isn't already sitting in pride of place in the wine rack I urge you to invest: it's pretty cheap, keeps for ages, and comes in useful for all sorts of things, including whisky macs for clearing colds.

Perfect
Gingerbread Biscuits (and men, and women, and children, dinosaurs and assorted animals)

*I*f any recipe sums up the joy of cooking with, and for, children, it's this one — everyone remembers the slightly cannibalistic joy of biting off a fat little leg, or tenderly saving the head until last (just so the poor fellow had time to really appreciate his predicament), and the beauty of these robust biscuits is that they're very easy to shape into whatever takes your fancy. Policeman, princess, pirate: all you need is the right cutter, and some artistic flair with the icing.

Medieval gingerbread was made from stale bread, and sweetened with honey and spices, making it more like a sticky flapjack than anything we'd recognize today — and Mrs Beeton's Victorian version is heavy on the treacle and cayenne pepper, giving it a rather dour, serious flavour. Even the famous Grasmere gingerbread isn't fit for shaping — made with oatmeal, the dough is so crumbly we end up with quite a few stray limbs.

I turn to the Germans, kings of festive lebkuchen biscuits, for help — after all, their version is so solid you can build houses out of them.

James Beard's recipe involves heating honey, sugar, water and butter together before mixing in flour, bicarbonate of soda and spices to make a tacky dough that's easy to roll out and shape. So far, so promising, but the flavour just isn't right: it tastes of Christmas markets and glühwein, not picnics and currant eyes.

In the end, I decide to adapt a recipe from Leiths Cookery School, which uses baking powder for a slightly lighter texture — I find the flavour of the original too meek and mild, so I've swapped the caster sugar for the caramelly soft brown sort, and increased the levels of spice, so they have a definite kick.

And, because you can never have enough ginger in a ginger biscuit, I've added the crystallized sort for a more interesting texture: admittedly, it will give your little people a rather pock-marked complexion, but that's nothing a little icing can't conceal. (It also strikes me that such a warty appearance might be a positive boon to a gingerbread stegosaurus or similar.)

I've also provided a recipe for a simple white icing, in case you just want to make pretty shapes, rather than people or animals — they do make good decorations, so follow the instructions for poking a hole in each for hanging if that's their destiny.

Makes about 30 small biscuits or about 20 gingerbread people

340g plain flour
½ teaspoon baking powder
½ teaspoon salt
1½ teaspoons grated nutmeg

1½ teaspoons ground cloves

2 teaspoons ground cinnamon

3 teaspoons ground ginger

225g unsalted butter, softened, plus extra to grease

340g soft brown sugar

1 egg, beaten

75g crystallized ginger, finely chopped

Currants (optional)

225g icing sugar (optional)

Hundreds and thousands (optional)

1. Sift the flour, baking powder, salt and spices together into a mixing bowl.

2. Beat together the butter and sugar with a hand mixer or wooden spoon until fluffy, and then add the egg very gradually, so the mixture doesn't curdle.

3. Stir this into the flour to make a dough, then mix in the crystallized ginger, making sure it's evenly distributed throughout.

4. Put the dough between two sheets of clingfilm and roll it out to the thickness of a £1 coin. Chill for half an hour. Preheat the oven to 200°C/fan 180°C/gas 6, and grease and line two baking trays.

5. Cut out the biscuits to your preferred shape, and arrange, well spaced out, on the lined trays. If you're going to add currant eyes and buttons, do so now, poking them firmly into the dough.

6. Bake for about 10 minutes, then, if you're going to hang them, poke a hole in each straight from the oven (a skewer is the best thing to use) and leave to cool completely on a wire rack before threading a ribbon through.

7. Decorate with writing icing, or, if you prefer, sift the icing sugar, then mix to a stiff consistency with boiling water (add it gradually, because you'll need less than you think). Brush the icing over the cooled biscuits, and decorate with hundreds and thousands while still wet.

Perfect
Lemon Drizzle Cake

Drizzle isn't often good news – not on the weather forecast, not on a menu when followed by the words 'balsamic vinegar', and definitely not where the hot water's concerned, but with this cake it makes an honourable exception. Drizzle here means sticky and citrussy and deliciously moist – a deluge would be too much, a sprinkle too little. Here, a drizzle is just right.

The cake itself is a classic Victoria sponge: solid enough to stand up to the drizzle, light and fluffy enough to invite a second slice. Extra indulgence is unnecessary: Raymond Blanc uses double cream and eggs, for example, but this just makes his cake dense and heavy in comparison. I do like the way Nigel Slater's sweet ground almonds point up the sharpness of the lemon, however, as well as creating a more interesting texture.

Blanc does redeem himself slightly by adding lemon zest to the batter – if you stick it in early, before you cream the butter and sugar together, you'll release the citrus oils as you work, creating, as Tonia George explains, 'a much more lemony sponge'. That said, you can overdo it: adding lemon juice at this point, like Gary Rhodes, just makes the cake sour (and Blanc's rum, meanwhile, just gets lost. A rare occasion when booze in a cake is a bad idea).

More important than the cake, of course, is the drizzle. I had to disqualify Blanc from the contest at this point, because he uses a lemon-flavoured icing which has no hope of sinking into the sponge. Slater squeezes over some lemon juice, which makes things a little austere for my taste — better is Gary Rhodes' golden syrup and lemon juice combination, which reminds me pleasantly of a steamed pudding, but best of all is the granulated sugar used by Geraldene Holt and Tonia George. It creates a crust so robust it's almost crunchy: a lovely contrast to the soft, fluffy cake beneath.

Adding the syrup while the cake's still warm will help the absorption process, as will poking a few discreet holes in the top — don't worry if there seems to be more liquid than the cake could possibly hold, because by some wondrous miracle, it always disappears.

You can have too much of a good thing, though: George sandwiches her cake with lemon curd and mascarpone too. Sharp and rich, it steals the cake's thunder utterly — this should be a simple sticky pleasure, not a rococo masterpiece of icings and fillings.

Makes 1 cake

175g butter, softened, plus extra to grease
175g caster sugar
2 unwaxed lemons
3 eggs, beaten
100g self-raising flour
75g ground almonds
A little milk
100g demerara sugar

1. Preheat the oven to 200°C/fan 180°C/gas 6, and grease and line a 900g loaf tin with butter and greaseproof paper.

2. Use an electric mixer or a wooden spoon to beat together the butter, caster sugar and the finely grated zest of 1 lemon until well combined, light and fluffy. Add a pinch of salt and the eggs, the latter one at a time, beating until each is thoroughly absorbed before adding the next.

3. Sift the flour over the top and fold in, followed by the ground almonds. Add just enough milk to take the mixture to a dropping consistency (so that it falls easily off the spoon), then spoon it into the prepared tin and smooth out the top. Bake for about 50–55 minutes, until a skewer comes out of the middle dry (a few crumbs clinging to it are fine).

4. While the cake's still hot from the oven, mix together the remaining lemon zest, the juice of both lemons and the demerara sugar, then poke holes all over the top and pour over the drizzle, waiting for the cake to absorb one lot before adding the next.

5. Allow to cool in the tin before turning out.

Perfect
Tarte au Citron

I make no apologies for the name – this isn't some homely thing, generously filled with sticky lemon curd, but a proper piece of Parisian pâtisserie, with all the airs and graces that suggests. Crisp, wafer thin pastry filled with a wobbly, delicate yellow custard, it's a restaurant classic that's surprisingly easy to recreate at home.

The Roux brothers are said to have popularized the dish in this country, but I find their version, as passed to Marco Pierre White, slightly disappointing: the richness of the lemon custard filling, with its egg yolks, sugar and double cream, seems to mute the pure, sharp flavour of the fruit itself.

Jane Grigson gives a recipe in her *Fruit Book* supplied by the local doctor in the Loire village where she and her husband owned a 'cave-cottage', with an unusual fluffy, ground almond filling. The sweetness of the nuts works well with the sour fruit, but it has a bit too much of a whiff of the Bakewell about it for me.

The 10-minute tart from American blog Smitten Kitchen, which blitzes a whole lemon with butter, sugar, eggs and cornflour, meanwhile, is just a disappointment: bitter, with an off-puttingly floury texture, the lesson I take away is that this isn't a recipe you can rush.

Much more to my taste is the lemon curd used by macaron man

Pierre Hermé, made by rubbing together sugar and zest into an unusually fragrant pile of yellow snow, then adding eggs and lemon juice and cooking the lot slowly over a pan of simmering water until it's as thick as Bird's custard. He then beats in a ridiculous amount of butter, but the results are well worth it: silky smooth, and intensely, shockingly citric, it's the kind of dessert best served in elegant slivers. All I had to do to make it perfect was to tone down the sugar slightly, to further accentuate the lemon flavour.

Making your own pastry is a worthwhile enterprise here: you need a crisp, delicate pâte sucrée rather than a bog-standard crumbly shortcrust for this most refined of desserts, and that's not easy to buy in. It's pretty easy to make though — and perfectly complemented by Grigson's topping of candied lemon slices, which are both utterly delicious, and make the tart look even prettier on the table. Almost too good to eat — but not quite.

Serves 8

For the pastry
180g plain flour
90g caster sugar
90g unsalted butter, diced,
    plus extra to grease
3 egg yolks and 1 egg white

For the filling
6 unwaxed lemons
275g caster sugar
4 eggs, beaten
300g unsalted butter, diced

1. Start by making the pastry. Put the flour, sugar and a pinch of salt into a food processor and pulse briefly to mix. Add the diced butter and continue to pulse until well combined.

2. With the motor still running, add the egg yolks, and continue to pulse until the mixture comes together into a dough. Remove from the machine, shape into a disc, wrap in clingfilm or baking paper and chill for about an hour, until it's pliable but not sticky to the touch.

3. Grease a 22cm fluted tart tin. Roll out the pastry on a lightly floured surface until it's about 5mm thick, and use to line the tin. Chill until firm, meanwhile preheating the oven to 190°C/fan 170°C/gas 5, then line with greaseproof paper and baking beans, and blind bake for about 15 minutes, until the edges are golden. Remove the paper and beans and brush the base with egg white. Return to the oven for another 8 minutes, then remove and set aside to cool.

4. Bring a small pan of water to the boil. Meanwhile, finely zest 5 of the lemons into a heatproof bowl which will sit over, but not touching the water, then add 225g of caster sugar and rub the two together with your fingers: you should be able to smell the zest.

5. Stir the eggs and the juice of 3½ lemons into the sugar, then put the bowl over the pan. Heat, whisking gently but continuously, until the mixture thickens to the consistency of lemon curd: this should take about 20 minutes.

6. Take off the heat, leaving the pan of water where it is, and allow the filling to cool for 10 minutes, then stir in the diced butter and either whiz with a hand blender, or beat with a wooden spoon, until completely smooth. Spoon into the tart case, flatten the top and allow to cool completely.

7. Meanwhile, cut the remaining unzested lemon into delicate slices and remove any pips. Soften them in the pan of simmering

water for 10 minutes. At the same time, put the remaining 50g of sugar into a wide pan with 50ml of water, stir to dissolve, then bring to the boil. Add the drained lemon slices and simmer them for 10 minutes, then remove with a slotted spoon and arrange on top of the cooled tart. Brush the slices with more syrup, and chill to set before serving.

Perfect
Bakewell Tart

A fittingly solid doorstop to a chapter on baking, this modest Derbyshire creation has excited its fair share of controversy — in Bakewell itself, it's known as a pudding, but truth be told, as Alan Davidson's *Oxford Companion to Food* observes, 'it's more of a tart', wherever it's baked.

More interesting than this linguistic squabbling I think is the fact that, although the first recorded recipe dates from 1836, its medieval precursors came in two forms, both custard and almond flavoured, and until the mid-twentieth century it was the former that was usually served up as a Bakewell tart or pudding. Nowadays, however, the frangipane is a deal breaker: and I like to think I've created a good one.

My frangipane, like those in Annie Bell and Lily Vanilli's recipes, is made in much the same way as any cake, by creaming together ingredients — I find this gives a much fluffier result than Tamasin Day-Lewis' version with hot butter. Bell also adds baking powder for an even lighter texture, which I really like, especially with Lily Vanilli's lemon zest, which stops the filling from being overpoweringly sweet.

I've not added an extra layer of marzipan, as Bell does — very much almond overkill for me — but instead of the bog-standard jam, I've followed Vanilli's example and made a compote. This sounds very fussy, but actually allows you to create a slightly sharp, emphatically fruity contrast to the sweet topping. (If you're not convinced, I'd urge you to go for a seedy, low-sugar raspberry number instead of ordinary jam: it's a better match for the almonds than strawberry, or even apricot, which I also try.)

The pastry is almost always shortcrust these days: puff is more traditional, but it's far too flimsy for frangipane. You could add ground almonds to the dough, as Bell does, but I prefer the more savoury plain version deployed by Day-Lewis, blind baked, as Lily Vanilli suggests, so it's extra crunchy. (Vanilli makes individual cupcake sized tarts which are a great idea for a picnic – topped with an almond buttercream and a cherry, they're pretty as a picture.)

I've also gone for the traditional toasted almond topping, to add an extra crunch to every mouthful of your tart. Or pudding, if you prefer – whatever you call it, it will still be delicious.

Makes 1 x 23cm tart

For the pastry
140g plain flour, plus extra to sprinkle
A pinch of salt
85g cold butter, plus extra to grease
Ice-cold water

For the frangipane
110g butter
110g caster sugar
2 eggs, beaten
110g ground almonds
25g plain flour
½ teaspoon baking powder
Zest of ½ a lemon

For the compote (or use 100g low-sugar raspberry jam)
250g raspberries (fresh or frozen)
25–35g caster sugar, depending on
    sweetness of tooth
Juice of ½ a lemon

25g flaked almonds, to top

1. First make the pastry by combining the flour and salt in a mixing bowl, then grating in the cold butter. Rub the strands of butter into the flour, then stir in only as much cold water as you need to bring it together into a firm dough; it shouldn't be sticky. Alternatively use a food processor to do all this. Shape the pastry into a disc, wrap in clingfilm or baking paper and chill for at least an hour.

2. Preheat the oven to 210°C/fan 190°C/gas 6 and grease a 23cm tart tin. Roll out the pastry on a lightly floured surface until it's large enough to line the tin, and about 5mm thick. Use to line the tin, then line the pastry with baking paper and top with baking beans or dried pulses. Blind bake for about 15 minutes, until golden.

3. Meanwhile, make the compote, if using, by putting the berries into a small pan with the sugar and lemon juice, stirring to dissolve the sugar, and bringing to the boil. Turn down the heat slightly and simmer for about 12 minutes, stirring occasionally, until the mixture has thickened. Allow to cool slightly.

4. For the frangipane, beat together the butter and sugar in a mixing bowl with a stand/hand mixer or a wooden spoon until fluffy, then gradually beat in the eggs. Gently fold in the remaining ingredients.

5. Remove the paper and beans from the pastry case, and return to

the oven for about 4 minutes, until the top is beginning to colour.

6. Spread the compote, or jam, over the base and spoon the frangipane over the top. Smooth out with a spatula and bake the tart for about 20 minutes, then arrange the almonds on top and bake for another 5–10 minutes, until the frangipane is golden and well risen. Serve warm (but not hot), or at room temperature, with cream.

CHAPTER 10

Drinks

When it comes to drinks, I'm fairly conservative – a gin and tonic is about as exotic as I get at home, though if someone else offers to knock me up a nice old-fashioned before dinner, I rarely refuse. Much as I like the idea of making cocktails at home, the effort and mess involved often takes the shine off the glamour, and somehow an elegant Martini always tastes better perched on a bar stool than slumped on the sofa. With drinks, I find, the context is all-important.

That said, even if you're as lazy as me, there are a few drinks that are handy to have in your repertoire. A fiery bloody Mary is a must at any good brunch, and a large pan of mulled wine is the key to a merry Christmas party. Fresh lemonade is a summer essential and the making of a proper picnic, and hot chocolate – well, I probably don't need to explain to you that it's the absolute best thing to curl up with on a cold winter's evening, or to cheer up a weeping friend or child. All these things are much, much better made from scratch, and none of them require a muddler, or a swizzle stick, or even Tom Cruise in a slick of hair gel.

Perfect
Bloody Mary

*I*n my experience, the idea of drinking at breakfast time is often more glamorous than the reality. The bloody Mary is the honourable exception; conversely it seems to have an almost rejuvenating effect before the sun hits the yardarm. Perhaps it's the kick of spice, or the wholesome taste of the tomato juice, but after a pitcher, I feel ready to seize the day — as long as that day doesn't involve work.

Even the simplest of bloody Marys, the aeroplane version, seasoned hastily and almost always inadequately before the trolley moves on, can satisfy, but to really appreciate the beauty of this classic cocktail, it's worth putting in a bit of effort.

The most important element, and I can hardly stress this enough, is the tomato juice. Given it makes up the bulk of the drink, it's amazing how many people think they can get away with a watery, value product. Spend a bit more on thick, quality stuff, and infuse it with spice ahead of time, so the flavours have time to really blend. Margot Henderson leaves it in the fridge for a week, but I find her version slightly overpowering at breakfast time; half an hour will do just fine, though if you have longer, a few hours won't hurt. (Who thinks of making a bloody Mary a week in advance anyway?)

Vodka is the demon drink of choice; some use gin, which strictly makes it into a red snapper, and, in my opinion, doesn't work as well with the other ingredients — vodka's clean flavour is far preferable.

I have borrowed an idea from a gin recipe, though: Hawksmoor infuse their spirit with horseradish, which mellows that root a little, lending the finished drink a peppery kick without the usual harshness that comes from grating it in fresh.

You could leave it at that, alcohol-wise, but many years ago, I had an excellent bloody Mary in a bar in Bristol. When we questioned the barman, he revealed his secret ingredient with an almost apologetic flourish: sweet, sticky Bristol cream sherry. Indeed, drinks writer Victoria Moore claims that, for her, 'It's the sherry that really makes [the drink], bridging the gulf between the hot but clean spirit and the fruity tomatoes.' Lindsey Bareham rinses the glass with bone-dry fino, but I prefer the fuller flavour of Victoria's amontillado, or indeed, a drop of rich cream sherry for old times' sake.

The basic spices are non-negotiable: Worcestershire sauce, hot sauce (generally Tabasco), lemon juice, salt and pepper. Having mucked around with, and been disappointed by various frills and furbelows, the only one I'll make room in my glass for is celery salt: the intense savoury flavour works well with the sweet sherry and fruity tomato juice.

A stick of the fresh stuff makes a picturesque stirrer, but adding the leaves to the drink itself, as April Bloomfield suggests, just turns it into a tangled mess of soggy vegetation.

As bloody Mary is an American drink, many recipes go heavy on the ice, which is, in my opinion, a mistake — given this is a drink to be sipped, rather than glugged, the meltwater will have an unpleasant diluting effect.

Shaking it over ice is an even worse idea — in fact shaking tomato juice at all makes it weirdly fluffy and foamy, so this is a drink that must be stirred. To ensure maximum invigoration, instead make sure all the ingredients are thoroughly chilled before you embark on the project.

Serves 8, with horseradish vodka left over

5cm piece of fresh horseradish, peeled
300ml vodka
1 litre good tomato juice
2 teaspoons Tabasco
2 teaspoons Worcestershire sauce
1 teaspoon celery salt
1 lemon, cut into wedges
2 tablespoons amontillado or
    cream sherry (cream is sweeter)
Celery, to serve (optional)

1. Chop the horseradish into small chunks and push them into the bottle of vodka. Seal and leave to infuse for 24 hours, then strain and discard the bits of horseradish.
2. To assemble the drink, stir together the tomato juice, Tabasco, Worcestershire sauce and celery salt and lightly squeeze each lemon wedge into the jug, leaving some juice in each. Season the mixture well with black pepper, and check the seasoning and spice level for your taste, adjusting if necessary.

3. Drop the lemon wedges into the jug and stir everything together well. Cover and chill for at least 30 minutes – longer won't hurt.

4. Pour 300ml of vodka (the rest will keep until next time) and the sherry into the jug and stir in with a celery stick. Seize the day and serve immediately.

Perfect
Hot Chocolate

I tend to cook for pleasure, rather than medicinal purposes, but there are a handful of recipes in this book which fall into both camps, and if tom yum is there to clear your head, and chicken soup will soothe the soul, then hot chocolate is the one to warm your heart — a warm, comforting mug of milky nostalgia.

When I was little, I drank Cadbury's hot chocolate like grown-ups drank tea, but these days it's more of a treat, reserved for snow and really bad days, when nothing hits the the spot like a cocoa rush. And if you're going to indulge, then you may as well make it worthwhile: the powdered version only cuts the mustard for defrosting purposes halfway up a mountain.

For all my pleasant childhood memories, I find an all milk-chocolate drink too blandly creamy these days; I want to taste that bitter, earthy cocoa, though not quite as strongly as Nigel Slater does: he recommends using 'the most bitter chocolate you can find' and sweetening it to taste, but my 100% pure Venezuelan cacao proves more than a match for demerara. It's the kind of thing you could drink in elegant espresso-sized portions after dinner, but it's not what I'd describe as comforting.

A mixture of milk and dark seems the best bet. The combination is richer than a drink made with only dark chocolate, but still retains that slightly savoury cocoa edge. There's no need to use cocoa powder too, as Jamie suggests: it only adds more bitterness.

As an occasional treat, I think hot chocolate deserves something a little more luxurious than Jamie's semi-skimmed milk too, but *Good Food* magazine's double cream makes it more like a dessert than a drink. I've used whole milk, mixed with just enough single cream to make it silky smooth — because, after all, you want to finish the whole mug, if not go back for seconds.

You don't need any extra flavourings, really — if you do, then you haven't added enough chocolate — but a pinch of salt is mandatory to enhance the cocoa, and I've also allowed myself a little spice, in deference to the finest hot chocolate I've ever tasted, in Mexico's Oaxaca market. A hint of cinnamon works a surprisingly subtle magic here; you can also add chilli, nutmeg or vanilla if you fancy it, but personally I don't like to interfere too much with that all-important chocolate.

And, if things are really bad, you could always add something a little stronger, for extra fortification. Because, when the going gets tough, hot chocolate will always be there for you. Can you say the same for your skinny latte?

Serves 2

450ml whole milk
70g 70% cocoa chocolate,
    finely chopped or grated
30g good-quality milk chocolate,
    finely chopped or grated
75ml single cream
Scant ¼ teaspoon ground cinnamon
A pinch of sea salt

1. Warm about a third of the milk in a pan over a medium-low heat and add the chopped chocolate. Allow to soften for a minute or so, then stir until it's all melted into the milk. Whisk in the remaining milk and the cream.

2. Heat the mixture gently until it's hot, but not boiling, then add the cinnamon and a pinch of salt. Taste, adjust the seasoning if necessary (more cinnamon, perhaps, more milk, even more chocolate if you'd prefer it stronger), and pour into mugs to serve. For a frothy finish, whisk vigorously just before pouring.

Perfect
Lemonade

Lemonade has to be the most refreshing drink on earth — not the aggressively sugary, over-carbonated stuff in plastic bottles, but the real thing, tangy with citrus, and bursting with the zesty, bittersour flavour of the fruit itself. For some reason, it's extortionately expensive to buy, but really very reasonably priced to make yourself, which is fortunate, because people tend to put away quite a bit on a warm afternoon.

To get the most out of the fruit, you need to use it whole, rather than just squeezing out the juice. One way to do this is to infuse the water with the zest, as Delia Smith and Jane Grigson suggest, but this involves leaving it, in Smith's case overnight, and sometimes, when you're thirsty, you just can't wait that long.

Much quicker and easier to do as Gary Rhodes suggests, and whiz up some of the fruit, peel, seeds and all, in a blender, then strain it before serving. I find his recipe far too bitter, however, so I've reduced the ratio of whole fruit to juice for a more easy-drinking result.

A pinch of salt may seem a bit of a bizarre addition, but in fact, after trying blogger Mamta Gupta's recipe for a classic Indian nimbu pani, I realize it gives the drink extra refreshing qualities — she claims that 'salt and sugar together help to replace the lost electrolytes in the intense heat of India', although I'm not quite sure how many of these you lose on a sunny day in Surbiton, so if you don't fancy it, leave it out.

A few slices of cucumber and a sprig of mint — the flavours of a British garden in summer — allowed, if time permits, to infuse the lemonade, add the final touch. A tot of ice-cold gin is entirely optional.

Makes 600ml

NB: If you prefer a sparkling lemonade, add only 250ml of cold water to the blender and top up the jug with cold soda water just before serving.

> **2½ unwaxed lemons**
> **50g white caster sugar**
> **A pinch of salt (optional)**
> **570ml cold water**
> **¼ of a cucumber, sliced**
> **A small bunch of mint, leaves only**

1. Chop 1 lemon into chunks and put it into a food processor or blender, together with any juices from the chopping board and the juice of the remaining 1½ lemons, the sugar, the salt if using and a little of the water. Whiz it all to a purée, then stir in the remaining water. Taste and add a little more sugar if necessary: it's easiest to mix this in while it's still in the blender.
2. Pour the lemonade into a jug, add the sliced cucumber and a couple of sprigs of mint, then cover and chill until ready to serve.
3. Serve over plenty of ice, with a fresh slice of cucumber and a fresh sprig of mint for each glass.

Perfect
Mulled Wine

I reckon a drink that started life as a way for blingy medieval sorts to show off their wealth and spice cupboard deserves a little fanfare. That said, the mishmash of spice in a recipe from a late fourteenth-century cookbook is rather unpleasant — it tastes more like something you might use to ward off the plague than the ingredients for a fun evening in the long gallery.

Although it would be a crime to pop really good wine on the hob, don't be tempted to just buy the cheapest plonk you can find: some bargain-basement bottles are better than others, and a bad wine will be even worse warmed up. Instead, find something you'd be happy to drink all evening at a party, preferably quite fruity, and definitely unoaked.

Delia's classic recipe, flavoured with a clove-studded orange and various other spices, is an old favourite of mine, and a good last-minute standby, but if you're planning ahead, you can't beat Jamie Oliver's mulled wine base. Making a spice-infused syrup may sound like a lot of unnecessary work during Christmas party season, but it means the flavours really have a chance to get friendly. In place of Jamie's vanilla (too sickly) I've added zesty cardamom pods, in a nod to the dish's medieval roots.

Making it in advance is a must because, as Jamie points out, 'the syrup needs to be quite hot, and if you do this with both bottles of wine in there you'll burn off the alcohol' — which is certainly not what you want. Ideally, one idle autumn weekend make a big batch of syrup, and dispense it throughout the festive season in the manner of a proper paragon of domesticity.

Some people like to sneakily 'turbo-charge' their mulled wine. Believe me, this is a bad idea. Dale DeGroff's Scandinavian glög recipe contains generous amounts of vodka, and tastes so alcoholic I can imagine having one glass on Christmas Eve, then waking up on Boxing Day and wondering where all the presents have gone.

That said, you can rarely go wrong by adding a glug of my favourite ginger wine (also useful for the ginger cake on page 304), which gives the whole thing a festive kick of spice, though you could also substitute a pinch of ground ginger if you don't happen to have a bottle kicking around (shame on you).

Serve with a dose of Christmas cheer and you'll find it rapidly thaws the heart of even the sourest of Scrooges.

Makes about 12 servings

2 unwaxed oranges (you'll only need 1
  to make the syrup in advance)
1 lemon, peel only
150g caster sugar
5 cloves, plus extra for garnish
5 cardamom pods, bruised
1 cinnamon stick
A pinch of freshly grated nutmeg

2 bottles of fruity, unoaked red wine (you'll only need ½ a bottle if you're making the syrup in advance)
150ml ginger wine (not necessary for making the syrup in advance)

1. Cut the peel from 1 of the oranges in thin strips, and put into a large saucepan along with its juice, the lemon peel, sugar and spices. Pour in just enough wine to cover the sugar, and heat gently, stirring occasionally, until the sugar has dissolved.
2. Once it has, you can turn the heat up a bit, bring the mixture to the boil and cook for 5–8 minutes, until it bubbles down into a thick syrup. (Once cooled, this can be stored in clean bottles or jars for several months: to use, start the recipe at step 3.)
3. Stud the second orange with 6 vertical lines of cloves, then cut between these to make segments you can use as a garnish.
4. Pour the remaining wine into the pan with the warm syrup, and add the ginger wine. Stir well, gently heat through until hot but not bubbling, and serve with the orange segments as a garnish.

Bibliography

Acton, Eliza, *Modern Cookery for Private Families* (Southover Press, 1993; first published 1845)

Acton, Johnny, and Sandler, Nick, *Preserved* (Kyle Cathie, 2009)

Aikens, Tom, *Fish* (Ebury, 2008)

Allen, Darina, *Darina Allen's Ballymaloe Cookery Course* (Kyle Cathie, 2007)

Andrews, Colman, *Catalan Cuisine* (Grub Street, 1997)

Bareham, Lindsey, *The Big Red Book of Tomatoes* (Grub Street, 2011)

Bareham, Lindsey, *A Celebration of Soup* (Penguin, 2001)

Bayless, Rick, *Mexican Kitchen* (Absolute Press, 2007)

Bazzurro, Francesca, and Lowe, Jason, *The Silver Spoon* (Phaidon, 2005)

Beard, James, *New Fish Cookery* (Little, Brown, 1994)

Beeton, Isabella, *Mrs Beeton's Book of Household Management* (Oxford University Press, 2000; first published 1861)

Bell, Annie, *Baking Bible* (Kyle Books, 2012)

Bell, Annie, *Gorgeous Christmas* (Kyle Cathie, 2009)

Berry, Mary, *Mary Berry's Christmas Collection* (Headline, 2006)

Bertinet, Richard, *Crust: Bread to Get Your Teeth Into* (Kyle Cathie, 2007)

Bertinet, Richard, *Dough: Simple Contemporary Bread* (Kyle Cathie, 2008)

Bertinet, Richard, *Pastry* (Ebury Press, 2012)

Blanc, Raymond, *Foolproof French Cookery* (BBC Books, 2002)

Bloomfield, April, *A Girl and Her Pig* (Canongate, 2012)

Blumenthal, Heston, *In Search of Total Perfection* (Bloomsbury, 2009)

Bompas, Harry, and Parr, Sam, *Feasting with Bompas and Parr* (Pavilion, 2012)

Boulestin, Marcel, *What Shall We Have Today?* (Heinemann, 1931)

Bourdain, Anthony, *Anthony Bourdain's Les Halles Cookbook* (Bloomsbury, 2004)

Brissenden, Rosemary, *South East Asian Food* (Penguin, 1996)

Butcher, Sally, *Veggiestan* (Pavilion, 2011)

Campion, Charles, *Fifty Recipes to Stake Your Life On* (Timewell Press, 2004)

Child, Julia, Bertholle, Louisette, and Beck, Simone, *Mastering the Art of French Cooking* (Penguin, 2009)

Clark, Claire, *Indulge* (Absolute Press, 2010)

Clark, Samuel, and Clark, Samantha, *Moro* (Ebury Press, 2001)

The Cook's Illustrated Cookbook (Cook's Illustrated, 2011)

Colwin, Laurie, *Home Cooking: A Writer in the Kitchen* (Fig Tree, 2012)

Conte, Anna del, *Amaretto, Apple Cake and Artichokes: The Best of Anna del Conte* (Vintage, 2006)

Corbin, Pam, *Preserves: River Cottage Handbook No. 2* (Bloomsbury, 2008)

Cornwall Federation of Women's Institutes, *Cornish Recipes: Ancient and Modern* (A. W. Jordan, Truro, 1930)

Costa, Margaret, *Four Seasons Cookery Book* (Grub Street, 2008)

Cotter, Denis, *Wild Garlic, Gooseberries and Me* (Collins, 2007)

David, Elizabeth, *A Book of Mediterranean Food* (Penguin, 1998)

David, Elizabeth, *English Bread and Yeast Cookery* (Grub Street, 2010)

David, Elizabeth, *French Country Cookery* (Penguin, 1996)

David, Elizabeth, *French Provincial Cooking* (Grub Street, 2007)

David, Elizabeth, *Italian Food* (Penguin, 1998)

David, Elizabeth, *Summer Cooking* (Grub Street, 1999)

Davidson, Alan (ed.), *The Oxford Companion to Food* (Oxford University Press, 1999)

Day-Lewis, Tamasin, *All You Can Eat* (Weidenfeld & Nicolson, 2008)

DeGroff, Dale, *The Craft of the Cocktail* (Proof Publishing, 2003)

Dods, Meg, *The Cook and Housewife's Manual* (Rosters, 1988; originally published 1829)

Elliot, Rose, *The 30-Minute Vegetarian* (Collins, 2012)

Elliot, Rose, *A Vegetarian Christmas* (Thorsons, 2000)

Fearnley-Whittingstall, Hugh, *The River Cottage Meat Book* (Hodder & Stoughton, 2004)

Fearnley-Whittingstall, Hugh, and Fisher, Nick, *The River Cottage Fish Book* (Bloomsbury, 2007)

Ferrigno, Ursula, *Complete Italian Cookery Course* (Mitchell Beazley, 2006)

Francatelli, Charles E., *A Plain Cookery Book for the Working Classes* (History Press, 2010)

Goldstein, Darra, *A Taste of Russia* (Sphere, 1987)

Gott, Huw, Beckett, Will, Turner, Richard, and Lepard, Dan, *Hawksmoor at Home* (Preface, 2011)

Granger, Bill, *Every Day* (Murdoch, 2006)

Gray, Rose, and Rogers, Ruth, *The River Café Classic Italian Cookbook* (Michael Joseph, 2009)

Grigson, Jane, *English Food* (Penguin, 1998)

Grigson, Jane, *Jane Grigson's Fruit Book* (Penguin, 2000)

Grigson, Jane, *Jane Grigson's Vegetable Book* (Penguin, 1998)

Hart, Alice, *Friends at My Table* (Quadrille, 2012)

Hartley, Dorothy, *Good Food in England* (Piatkus, 2009)

Hartnett, Angela, *Angela Hartnett's Cucina: Three Generations of Italian Family Cooking* (Ebury Press, 2007)

Hazan, Marcella, *The Essentials of Classic Italian Cooking* (Macmillan, 1980)

Helou, Anissa, *Lebanese Cuisine* (Grub Street, 1994)

Helou, Anissa, *Modern Mezze* (Quadrille, 2007)

Henderson, Margot, *You're All Invited* (Fig Tree, 2012)

Herbert, Henry and Tom, *The Fabulous Baker Brothers* (Headline, 2013)

Hermé, Pierre, *Macarons* (Grub Street, 2011)

Herráiz, Alberto, *Paella* (Phaidon, 2011)

Hilferty, Trish, *Lobster and Chips* (Absolute Press, 2005)

Hix, Mark, *British Regional Food* (Quadrille, 2008)

Holt, Geraldene, *Geraldene Holt's Cake Stall* (Prospect Books, 2011)

Hom, Ken, *Complete Chinese Cookbook* (BBC Books, 2011)

Hopkinson, Simon, *The Good Cook* (BBC Books, 2011)

Hopkinson, Simon, and Bareham, Lindsey, *The Prawn Cocktail Years* (Michael Joseph, 2006)

Hopkinson, Simon, and Bareham, Lindsey, *Roast Chicken and Other Stories* (Ebury Press, 1999)

Huang, Ching-He, *Chinese Food Made Easy* (HarperCollins, 2008)

Jaffrey, Madhur, *Madhur Jaffrey's Ultimate Curry Bible* (Ebury, 2003)

Keller, Thomas, and Rouxel, Sebastien, *Bouchon Bakery* (Artisan, 2012)

Kiros, Tessa, *Falling Cloudberries* (Murdoch, 2004)

Jackson, C. J., and Waldegrave, Caroline, *Leiths Fish Bible* (Bloomsbury, 2005)

Johansen, Signe, *Scandilicious* (Saltyard, 2011)

Jones, Lily, *Lily Vanilli's Sweet Tooth* (Canongate, 2012)

Lambert Ortiz, Elisabeth, *Complete Book of Mexican Cooking* (Grub Street, 1998)

Larousse Gastronomique (Hamlyn, 2009)

Lawrence, Sue, *A Cook's Tour of Scotland* (Headline, 2006)

Lawrence, Sue, *Scots Cooking* (Headline, 2000)

Lawson, Nigella, *Feast* (Chatto & Windus, 2004)

Lawson, Nigella, *How to be a Domestic Goddess* (Chatto & Windus, 2003)

Leith, Prue, and Waldegrave, Caroline, *Leiths Cookery Bible* (Bloomsbury, 2003)

Locatelli, Giorgio, *Made in Italy* (Fourth Estate, 2008)

McGee, Harold, *The Curious Cook* (HarperCollins, 1992)

McGee, Harold, *McGee on Food and Cooking* (Hodder & Stoughton, 2004)

McKee, Gwen, and Davidson, Tupper, *The Little Gumbo Book* (Quail Ridge Press, 1986)

McLagan, Jennifer, *Cooking on the Bone* (Grub Street, 2008)

Malouf, Tarek, *The Hummingbird Bakery Cookbook* (Ryland, Peters & Small, 2009)

Mariani, John, *The Dictionary of American Food and Drink* (Ticknor & Fields, 1983)

Miers, Thomasina, *Mexican Food Made Simple* (Hodder & Stoughton, 2010)

Mitcham, Howard, *Creole Gumbo and All That Jazz* (Addison-Wesley, 1978)

Moore, Victoria, *How to Drink* (Granta, 2009)

Morales, Martin, *Ceviche: Peruvian Kitchen* (Weidenfeld & Nicolson, 2013)

Nairn, Nick, *The Nick Nairn Cook School Cookbook* (Cassell Illustrated, 2008)

Norrington-Davies, Tom, *Just Like Mother Used to Make* (Cassell Illustrated, 2004)

Norwak, Mary, *English Puddings, Sweet and Savoury* (Grub Street, 2009)

Oliver, Jamie, *Jamie's America* (Michael Joseph, 2009)

Oliver, Jamie, *Jamie's Italy* (Michael Joseph, 2005)

Olney, Richard, *The French Menu Cookbook* (Collins, 2010)

Ortes, Simone and Inés, *1080 Recipes* (Phaidon, 2007)

Ottolenghi, Yotam, and Tamini, Sami, *Ottolenghi: The Cookbook* (Ebury Press, 2008)

Ottolenghi, Yotam, and Tamini, Sami, *Plenty* (Ebury Press, 2010)

Paltrow, Gwyneth, *My Father's Daughter* (Grand Central Publishing, 2011)

Pizarro, José, *José Pizarro's Spanish Flavours* (Kyle Books, 2012)

Prince, Rose, *The New English Kitchen* (Fourth Estate, 2005)

Prince, Thane, *Jams and Chutneys: Preserving the Harvest* (Dorling Kindersley, 2008)

Raven, Sarah, *Sarah Raven's Garden Cookbook* (Bloomsbury, 2007)

Roahen, Sara, *Gumbo Tales: Finding My Place at the New Orleans Table* (Norton, 2008)

Rhodes, Gary, *New British Classics* (BBC Books, 1999)

Rhodes, Gary, *Rhodes Around Britain* (BBC Books, 1994)

Roden, Claudia, *Arabesque* (Michael Joseph, 2005)

Roden, Claudia, *The Book of Jewish Food* (Viking, 1997)

Rombauer, Irma S., *The Joy of Cooking* (Simon & Schuster, 1999)

Roux, Michel, *Pastry: Savoury and Sweet* (Quadrille, 2008)

Roux, Michel Jr, and Cazals, Jean, *Le Gavroche Cookbook* (Cassell, 2001)

Saberi, Helen, *Trifle* (Prospect Books, 2009)

Slater, Nigel, *Appetite* (Fourth Estate, 2000)

Slater, Nigel, *Real Cooking* (Michael Joseph, 1997)

Slater, Nigel, *Real Food* (Fourth Estate, 2009)

Slater, Nigel, *Tender, Vols. I & II* (Fourth Estate, 2009–10)

Smith, Delia, *Complete Cookery Course* (BBC Books, 1992)

Spaull, Susan, and Burrell, Fiona, *Leiths Baking Bible* (Bloomsbury, 2006)

Spaull, Susan, and Clark, Max, *Leiths Meat Bible* (Bloomsbury, 2010)

Spry, Constance, and Hume, Rosemary, *The Constance Spry Cookery Book* (Grub Street, 2004)

Stein, Rick, *English Seafood Cookery* (Penguin, 1988)

Steingarten, Jeffrey, *It Must Have Been Something I Ate* (Headline, 2003)

This, Hervé, *Kitchen Mysteries: Revealing the Science of Cooking* (Columbia University Press, 2007)

Thompson, David, *Thai Street Food* (Conran, 2010)

Tonks, Mitch, *Fish Easy* (Pavilion, 2012)

Warde, Fran, and Wilson, Tim, *Ginger Pig Meat Book* (Mitchell Beazley, 2011)

Wareing, Marcus, *How to Make the Perfect* (Dorling Kindersley, 2007)

Warner, Valentine, *The Good Table* (Mitchell Beazley, 2011)

Watson, Guy, and Baxter, Jane, *Riverford Farm Cook Book* (Fourth Estate, 2008)

Weir, Robin and Caroline, *Ice Creams, Sorbets and Gelati* (Grub Street, 2010)

White, Florence, *Good Things in England* (Persephone Books, 1999)

Willinsky, Helen, *Jerk: Barbecue from Jamaica* (Ten Speed Press, 2007)

Wilson, Bee, *Consider the Fork: A History of How We Cook and Eat* (Penguin, 2013)

Wilson, C. Anne, *Food and Drink in Britain: From the Stone Age to Recent Times* (Penguin, 1976)

Wolfert, Paula, *Mediterranean Cooking* (HarperCollins, 1996)

Zumbo, Adriano, *Zumbo: Adriano Zumbo's Fantastical Kitchen of Other-worldly Delights* (Murdoch, 2011)

Websites

bbc.co.uk/food
bbcgoodfood.com
theboywhobakes.co.uk
britishlarder.co.uk
chezpim.com
dailymail.co.uk
davidlebovitz.com
deliaonline.com
deliciousmagazine.co.uk
foodnetwork.com
ft.com
theguardian.com
independent.co.uk
jamesbeard.org
jamieoliver.com
mamtaskitchen.com
marthastewart.com
meemalee.com
nigella.com
nytimes.com
oldmarkethousebrixham.co.uk
thepioneerwoman.com
porridgelady.com
racheleats.wordpress.com
saveur.com
shesimmers.com
smittenkitchen.com
telegraph.co.uk
waitrose.com

Acknowledgements

Much gratitude is due to everyone at the *Guardian* for their support, but in particular to my editor Susan Smillie, without whom there would be no *Perfect*. No one else could make me see the vaguely funny side of all this washing up.

Enormous thanks also to Juliet Annan and Sophie Missing at Fig Tree for their enthusiasm, for producing such a beautiful book, and for laughing at – most of – my jokes, to Gill Heeley for the excellent illustrations, and to Annie Lee for saving me from myself on numerous occasions, again.

I'm truly grateful to Sarah Ballard and Zoe Ross at United Agents for all their advice, encouragement and support over the last twelve months – and especially for their kind patience.

This book has been a good three years in the making; thank you to all my recipe testers and long-suffering housemates over that time: Anna and Jot; Alex, James, Lucinda and Kelda; my family (always to be relied upon to give an honest verdict on jam doughnuts); and, latterly, Richard and the ever-discerning Wilf the dog. You can have whatever you want for dinner darling, as long as it's dal.

Most of all, thank you to all the *Guardian* readers whose thoughts, advice, and occasionally constructive criticism, make the column what it is. This book wouldn't have happened without you.

Index

(Perfect recipes in bold)

meatballs 157–9

Médecin, Jacques, salade Niçoise
    105

Miers, Thomasina, salsa 64, 65

Millo, Llorenç, paella 224

mise en place xii

Mitcham, Howard, chicken and smoked
    sausage gumbo 178

Moore, Victoria, bloody Mary 325

Morales, Martin 121–2

moussaka 195–8

muffins: **blueberry muffins 27–9**

mulled wine 333–5

mung dal: **dal 215–17**

Myers, Dave, steak and ale pie 143

Nairn, Nick
    cullen skink 90, 91
    gratin dauphinoise 202

New York Times
    calamari 118
    tomato soup 98

non-stick cookware xvii

Nordstrom, tomato soup 98, 99

Norrington-Davies, Tom
    macaroni cheese 247
    Scotch eggs 49, 50
    steak and ale pie 143
    summer pudding 270

Norwak, Mary, syrup sponge 274

nut roast 218–21

oatmeal, porridge 3–6

Old Bay, crabcakes 130

Old Market House, crab linguine 244,
    245

Oliver, Jamie
    aubergine parmigiana 211
    bacon sandwich 13–14

chilli con carne 154, 155

croque monsieur 33, 34

garlic bread 71, 72

hot chocolate 328, 329

macaroni cheese 247

mulled wine 333–4

panzanella 112, 114

spaghetti alle vongole 237

strawberry jam 10, 11

tomato soup 99

Olney, Richard, gratin dauphinoise 202,
    203

onions
    French onion soup 101–4
    shallots 96–7

oranges: **marmalade 7–9**

Ortega, Simone and Inés, patatas bravas
    78

Ottolenghi, Yotam 218
    hummus 61

ovens xvii–xviii

Oxford Companion to Food, The
    Bakewell tart 318
    Cornish pasties 42
    ginger 304
    porridge 3

pad thai 233–6

paella 224–7

palm sugar 96

Paltrow, Gwyneth, spaghetti alle vongole
    237

pancakes
    American pancakes 20–23
    blinis 56–9

panna cotta 264–6

pantry, well-stocked xxi–xxiii, xxv

panzanella 112–14

Parle, Steve, gratin dauphinoise 202